C0-AWN-176

For Mr. and Mrs. Higginson —
With compliments and
my warmest regards.

Doug

17 Jan 1982

CLEAN SWEET WIND

Clean

Sweet Wind

SAILING
CRAFT
OF THE
LESSER
ANTILLES

Douglas C. Pyle

EASY REACH PRESS

Preston, Md.

Copyright © 1981
by
Easy Reach Corporation

Designed by the Author

Type set by Kent Printing Corporation
Chestertown, MD

Printed by Waverly Press
Easton, MD

Published by Easy Reach Press
Preston, MD

To my Mother
and
To the Memory of my Father

TABLE OF CONTENTS

ACKNOWLEDGEMENTS ix

INTRODUCTION 1

CHAPTER I   In Which I Become a Boat-Measurer 4

CHAPTER II   Boatmeasuring Made Easy 10

CHAPTER III   Passage to Grenada 17

CHAPTER IV   Carriacou You Going 29

CHAPTER V   Bequia Sweet 47

CHAPTER VI   Anguilla Again 63

CHAPTER VII   Make Thee An Ark 84

CHAPTER VIII   Blows!.................................... 114

CHAPTER IX   Homeward *via* Tortola 126

CHAPTER X   St. Martin 136

CHAPTER XI   Saba 143

CHAPTER XII   St. Eustatius.............................. 149

CHAPTER XIII   Nevis and St. Kitts 154

CHAPTER XIV   St. Barts................................. 165

CHAPTER XV   Montserrat 176

CHAPTER XVI   Antigua and Barbuda 178

CHAPTER XVII   Guadeloupe and the Saintes 186

CHAPTER XVIII   Dominica 194

CHAPTER XIX   The Gommiers of Martinique 200

CHAPTER XX   St. Lucia................................. 213

CHAPTER XXI   St. Vincent............................... 222

CHAPTER XXII   Trading with the *Rosarene*.................. 227

CHAPTER XXIII   Trinidad 241

CHAPTER XXIV   Barbados 249

CHAPTER XXV   Culture History of Boatbuilding in the

                                  Lesser Antilles 261

CHAPTER XXVI   The Last Schooner 278

BIBLIOGRAPHY 289

INDEX OF ILLUSTRATIONS................................... 290

SUBJECT INDEX... 291

ACKNOWLEDGEMENTS

There were a great many times — the greater part of the time, if truth be told — between the inception of this project and its realization in a book when there seemed little likelihood of a favorable outcome. That there was any outcome (favorable or not, as you, Gentle Reader, are now in a position to judge) at all is owing to the help and inspiration of many people, key ones of whom are:

The people of the West Indies whose efforts and aspirations form the the subject of this book.

Prof. Edwin M. Doran, Jr. who provided a necessary focus to my previously random efforts and generously made available much original material.

Prof. Arnold R. Highfield who breathed new life into my efforts when they had come to a virtual standstill and then read the manuscript with knowledge and discernment.

Mr. Ames Schuck who patiently and skillfully turned my rough-and-ready lines drawings into illustrations of publishable quality.

Mr. Page Callahan of Waverly Press who initiated me into the arcana of the printer's trade and formed a conduit to the expertise of a high-technology printing plant.

Nancy B. Fowler, my wife, whose eye for a comma, though rusty, is better than mine; who has striven, against increasing odds, to provide me the time and peace to write; and whose faith has never questioned that the task was worth the astonishing amount of trouble it involved.

And finally, I must in no wise neglect to mention those nameless, numberless workers whose loyal labors have helped to pile up this great heap of fact atop which, like a fat, grinning idol, I perch, relieved and triumphant.

Douglas C. Pyle

Preston, Maryland
September, 1981

INTRODUCTION

The quiet magic of early morning wraps the harbor as the little town slumbers away the last cool hour of the night. The heat and bustle of another tropical day await the sun — still hidden behind the high volcanic island. A triangle of weathered canvas glides into the angle between sea horizon and the green mass of the headland. First the jib and then the gaff mains'l of an island sloop ease into view, moved by a breeze too faint to ripple the glassy sea.

I set my coffee on the deck and reach inside the cabin for the camera. As I do, the wedge of faded canvas hesitates, then slowly shrinks into a single vertical slash as the work-scarred sloop swings her bows up into the faint land breeze. The slap of idle canvas and the squeal of wooden sheaves drift across the water. Then the sails fill and take shape again on the opposite tack.

The man at the tiller stands motionless as the vessel drifts across the outer harbor. Then, at his nod, the jib is loosed and comes rattling down the forestay. A black figure moves methodically forward, bunching the sail and stowing it along the rail. In the same unhurried manner the gaff is lowered and the mains'l secured, while momentum carries the cargo-laden vessel the remaining distance. Lines are heaved and the *Delight B* snugs into her berth as the bustle of the day's work begins to stir the port of Kingstown, St. Vincent (fig. P-1).

1

fig. P-1. The port of Kingstown, St. Vincent.
March, 1974.

The whole sequence is so timeless and hypnotic that I might have dreamed it except for the reassuring warmth of the coffee cup. Anachronism it may be, but sailing vessels are still part of daily life in ports from Puerto Rico to Trinidad, enabling West Indians to catch fish, move cargo and transport passengers. On palm shaded beaches caulking mallets still sound their hollow, ringing note as sailing vessels take shape from piles of hand-hewn timbers. The traditions and skills of wooden boatbuilding may still be found in certain island communities.

During the period from 1968 to 1970, while living and teaching in St. Croix, U.S. Virgin Islands, I became convinced that this anachronism represented a unique opportunity — an opportunity to step into the past and record information at first hand about this vanishing way of life. As originally formulated, my plans called for an enjoyable summer project to occupy me until graduate school started in the fall.

As the project progressed, it acquired a life of its own, broadening and deepening until it had gone well beyond the original time allotted.

Five years elapsed before my inquiry finally ran its course and left me with a mass of notes, data sheets and photographic negatives. From the data sheets I made lines drawings of twenty-eight types of sailing craft found between Tortola and Trinidad, which form the core of my results. In addition there were the negatives and my notes — observations, impressions, opinions — to be analyzed, organized and presented.

It was here that the shimmering, mosaic quality of island life got the better of me. Despite repeated and determined efforts, I could not get the information into outline form. And the noisy, exuberant rhythm of West Indian life mocked my stolid attempts to achieve the detached, objective tone of good technical writing.

When I found myself unable to separate the vessels from their builders, the people from their traditions and culture, and my observations from the enjoyment of observing, I was reduced to writing down the information still embedded in the experience of collecting it. In extenuation, it is my hope that not only the watercraft but also the builders, their weaknesses and strengths, and their unique island setting might become part of the record.

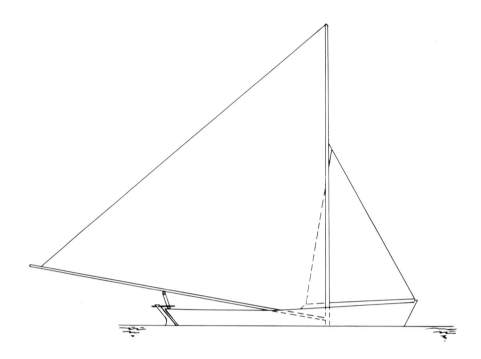

CHAPTER I

IN WHICH I BECOME A BOAT-MEASURER

"Ready?" Bill called as he shipped the tiller into the rudder head. "Let's go on the next good puff."

Picking my way gingerly over the ballast stones, I slid past the thwart where the spindly mast was stepped and handed the mooring line outside the frayed rope shroud. The strain on my arm increased as the jib filled in the light breeze that was riffling the bright blue surface of Christiansted harbor.

"Okay, let go now," Bill said as he handed me the tail of the jibsheet and used his free hand to snag the dancing mainsheet. As he took up the slack, the big mains'l stopped flopping and the little sloop began to gather way.

It was my first sail in the *Flame,* and only the second for Bill Sparks, who had sailed her over from Tortola the week before.

"The old man who built her showed me how to sail her," Bill had assured me earlier as we stepped the mast through a hole in the thwart and swigged tight the forestay to which the jib was sewn. I looked around in dismay at the gray, patched canvas, the frayed rope and the whittled pegs for cleats.

"Pretty rough," I said, feeling a little dubious.

"Yeah, but the old man said she was the fastest of the Tortola sloops," Bill laughed.

4

"For what that's worth," I nearly said — and was later glad I hadn't.

The smooth waters of the harbor gave me an opportunity to look for a comfortable spot on the ballast stones while we learned the drill for tacking: sail full for a monent before putting the helm down, haul the main in tight until the jib backs and pushes the head over, then relead the jib sheet through the thimble on the opposite side. All this had to be done quickly, while sprawled on the stones, out of the way of the boom.

"The old man said to sail her on the leach," Bill said in reply to my skeptical glance at the baggy mains'l, which was backwinded over half its surface, in cheerful defiance of modern sailing theory.

Soon we were through the reef and out of the harbor — sail to the right of us, sail to the left of us, sail all around us — bang in the middle of the Sunday yacht traffic making the five-mile beat out to the beaches on Buck Island. My first reaction was defiant embarassment — something like the emotion one might feel if dropped suddenly into a starting gate at the Kentucky Derby astride a sway-backed plow horse. I kept my head down and tried to pretend that I was busy trimming ballast. Slowly it began to dawn on me that there was nothing to be embarassed about: we weren't pointing as well as some of the better-turned yachts, but we were footing better and clawing up to windward as fast as anyone out that day.

The humble *Flame* — pine planks fastened to hand-hewn frames with rusting nails, frayed lines running through thimbles and rope-stropped blocks, baggy sails of weathered canvas — was sailing as well as yachts — of fibreglass, Dacron and stainless steel — built solely for speed.

The return trip late that afternoon was less of a surprise but no less a thrill. With the long boom eased right out and the jib "goosed" to the opposite side, we cleanly outran all contenders. In the exhilaration and amazement of that afternoon was born my conviction that the sailing craft of the Lesser Antilles represent one of the most notable achievements of the folk culture of the region.

In 1959, when Castro came to power in Cuba, tourism was displaced from that island and began to spread eastward into the Lesser Antilles. At first it seemed that tourism offered an ideal solution to the economic stagnation that had dogged the West Indies more or less constantly since the decline of sugar prosperity in the nineteenth century. But in practice, tourism frequently disrupted the fragile economic relationships of small and unsophisticated communities, offering in exchange chiefly jobs for waiters, chambermaids and taxi-drivers — the attractive and lucrative positions being filled by outsiders with specialized skills.

During the time that I lived and taught in St. Croix, in the U.S. Virgin Islands, I came to feel that West Indians were being undervalued by the tourist industry and, in consequence, by themselves — an even more serious matter in the long run. Perhaps it was for this reason that the *Flame* stirred me so — in her ropey, make-do way, she was pure West Indian — and her sailing ability was the equal of any.

Several weeks after my sail in the *Flame*, I had a week's vacation during which a fortuitous combination of circumstances took me another step down the path to boat-measuring. I had planned to spend my vacation cruising in the British Virgin Islands, forty miles to the north of St. Croix. However, the breeze which carried me out of Christiansted harbor lightened all morning and died completely by noon. After waiting patiently for an hour or so, I concluded that we were in for an Irish hurricane (Cruzan expression for flat calm). So I roused myself from the languor induced by the gently heaving sea and got the engine going, deciding in the process that if I had to motor, then I might just as well motor in an unaccustomed direction.

A direction that I did not ordinarily sail out of Christiansted was east, *i.e.* to windward — not if there was any alternative — and to windward of St. Croix lay Anguilla, a name that had been in the back of my mind for some time. The schooners that called from time to time in Christiansted hailed from Anguilla, and I had heard people say that schooners were formerly built there. More recently the name had been in the news when Anguilla was invaded by British paratroops for some purpose not clear to me and possibly not to them. In the idleness of the Irish hurricane, to know a name was to have a destination; I dropped the jib, sheeted the mains'l flat and began to motor toward Anguilla.

The calm continued all afternoon, until at sunset a very light breeze sprang up in the northwest, just enough to flap the sail and wake me when *Eider* got off course. Later in the night it closed in and began a light drizzle, obscuring the beacon on St. Martin which I had counted on for my landfall. I was beginning to feel a little uneasy when at daybreak the drizzle thinned enough that I could see the high volcanic cone of Saba. I took a bearing, guessed at the distance, found an approximate position and adjusted my course for Anguilla. As the overcast cleared, the Trade Winds resumed, and I was able to finish my trip with a spanking sail up the leeward coast of the island.

The chart showed no off-lying hazards except in the vicinity of Dog Island, so I had ample opportunity for sightseeing, if only there had been some scenery. Anguilla was low, dry, covered with scrub vegetation and showed little sign of human habitation. The shoreline was formed of rocky headlands separated by shallow bays rimmed with gleaming white sand. Road Harbor, when I found it, was just another of these bays — only a little wider and a little deeper.

As I eased the sheets and stood into the bay, it seemed as though I had slipped backward in time. A dozen or so sloops and schooners swung at anchor; about the same number of brightly painted houses were set in the palms that edged the white beach. After letting go the anchor, I stood trying to understand the powerful sensation of well-being that swept over me, for there was in fact very little to see or hear. There were no powerlines, no automobiles, no hotels or billboards; in the stillness of the tropic noon, I heard only the slap

6

of halyards and the nameless creaking of working vessels as they rested from their labors. There was nothing to be seen or heard that would have positively identified the year as 1970 rather than 1870 (fig. I-1).

fig. I-1.   Road Bay, Anguilla. March, 1971.

Ashore in the little yellow-plastered police outpost, I tendered my passport to a tall young man in tropical shorts and the uniform shirt of the London police. He explained that a detachment of bobbies had recently been sent to the island to restore order after Anguilla broke away from St. Kitts (for details see Westlake, 1971). While examining my passport, my informant dispatched another officer toward the dark blue Land Rover with the arms of England painted on the door. Inside, a local woman with a sick child waited to be driven to the infirmary. After giving his instructions, the officer returned his attention to me.

"Schooners, is it? Did you see that one just along there?" He pointed along the shore of Road Bay toward the lonesome jetty. "And then there's Forest Bay. An even bigger one there. I can drive you over tomorrow, if you like. Eight o'clock suit you?"

I accepted gratefully, then set off along the beach, ducking past the palm trunks that leaned over the steep beach until I reached an open area where seagrape branches arched onto the wave-smoothed sand. Just behind the crest of the beach stood the gaunt carcass of a schooner, hauled up to be "stretched" (lengthened) and rebuilt (fig. I-2). My intention had been to watch quietly from the sidelines, but at my approach the workmen rested down their tools and waited expectantly. Under the circumstances it would have been downright unfriendly to remain silent, so I pitched right in: what were they doing? How were they going about it? And without any formal declaration of intention, I found myself conducting an interview.

MacDuff Richardson spoke for the group: it was he who was in charge of stretching the present vessel; it was he who had "set up" the vessel at Forest Bay and, above all, it was he who had been off the island and worked overseas. After answering my questions for a while with patient good humor, Mac asked me one of his own.

"What do you think of the Man in the Moon?" He stabbed his forefinger at me vehemently.

"Well, I don't really know," I replied, uncertain whether to run or stand my ground.

"That right. That right. That what I think, too," Mac exclaimed, seizing me eagerly by the hand and shooting a triumphant glance toward his smirking crew. "There never was a man on the moon and there never will be. It against God. The Bible say..."

fig. I-2. Schooner (later the Miranda Stout) being "stretched" at Sandy Ground, Anguilla. March, 1971.

The exact passage of Scripture escaped me as I groped wildly for understanding. It gradually dawned on me that we were talking about the first successful moon landing, which had occurred the preceding summer. The crew, I now noticed, were openly grinning as they watched the sport; apparently Mac battened onto all newcomers. In addition to sharing his views on the Apollo Mission, Mac told about working in a yacht yard in St. Thomas, about building a schooner in Tortola, about how the dimensions and proportions of a vessel are determined. My first interview was going surprisingly well. Later, when I had time to reflect on it, I realized that Mac's version of the Apollo Project — fooling all of the people all of the time — would be an even greater technological achievement than a moon landing.

The next morning at Forest Bay (not a tree in sight) I found an even larger vessel under construction as well as two smaller vessels intended for lobstering. Here too, the boatbuilders were easy to approach and eager to share their knowledge. To supplement my sentimental interest in West Indian sailing, there now appeared to be concrete information in the form of a fleet of trading vessels, active boatbuilders and two schooners under construction. By accident I had stumbled onto enough material to make at least the begining of a study of working sail. What I needed next were the tools and techniques to make some form of permanent record.

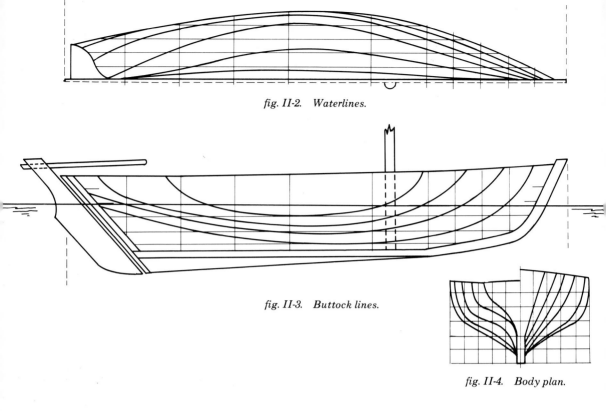

fig. II-2. Waterlines.

fig. II-3. Buttock lines.

fig. II-4. Body plan.

CHAPTER II

BOATMEASURING MADE EASY

Deciding to make a permanent record of island boatbuilding was gratifyingly simple; actually doing it was less so. Representing a complex three-dimensional form — compactly, conveniently and convincingly — on a flat surface is nothing new; one has only to recall perspective drawings, mechanical drawings, architect's plans and the like. And such representations of watercraft hulls also exist, being called lines drawings.

Lines drawings can be more readily explained if one imagines a model of a hull like the one in fig. II-1, which came from Petit Martinique in the Grenadines. Such a model is made by nailing together half-inch slats of wood so as to form a block; then the block is carved into a hull. When the nails are drawn, the block comes apart and the outline of each section may be traced to form a family of nesting curves (fig. II-2) known as waterlines.

Next imagine a similar model, this time sliced lengthwise from deck to keel, the resulting slices being traced to produce buttock lines (fig. II-3). And finally, imagine the model sliced in cross-section like a salami to generate the body plan (fig. II-4) with the front half of the hull to the right and the rear half to the left.

fig. II-1. Lift half-model from Petit Martinique, Grenadines. In the possession of Don Hill, American Museum of Natural History.

"Yes, but so what?" the skeptical reader will surely ask, as did many boatbuilders to whom I showed sets of lines. Well, the answer is that there are several useful things that may be done with and by lines drawings.

There is, first of all, the fact that they may be used to design a hull — to do quickly and accurately in the comfort of a design office a task which is slow and cumbersome to do with a model or a full-scale hull. For this purpose a naval architect seats himself at a drawing board with dimensions and specifications supplied by the owner. From his knowledge and with the tools of his trade, the naval architect produces the three sets of curves which his experience suggests will be best suited to the needs of the owner.

Once drawn, the three sets of curves must be "faired," *i.e.* harmonized by some method so that all three sets reflect the same original hull form. The method by which this is accomplished is called "ticking" and involves superposing a reference grid on each of the sets, then carrying intercepts from one set to another. To make this explanation workable, I suggest that you consult your friendly neighborhood naval architect; I myself consulted Dick Newick, a very successful multi-hull designer (*Cheers* and *Three Cheers*, among others) who was living in St. Croix at that time. No amount of written explanation would have sufficed to teach me what he did with five minutes of demonstration. I therefore unblushingly decline the challenge to attempt an effective written explanation (those interested are hereby referred to a competent naval architect).

When faired, lines drawings may be put to their second use; they may be analyzed to predict to some extent how the hull will move through the water. In particular, the waterlines and buttock lines suggest the flow of water past the hull where abrupt changes of direction and hard curves may disturb laminar flow, creating turbulence and increasing the drag of a hull. Analyzing and altering a set of lines in order to produce an "easy" bottom may not be a substitute for tank-testing but, as remarked before, it is quicker and easier. After analysis any change in one family of curves must be transferred to the other two families by ticking and this process repeated until all sets are again harmonious.

In practice, a designer working on a set of lines may carry out these three distinct operations nearly simultaneously (design work of any kind is rarely done in a perfectly linear sequence — I have presented it that way simply as an aid to understanding). Whatever the sequence, there does arise out of the alchemy of design a set of lines drawings, fair and pleasing by eye and judgement. But again the question is asked, "So what? We still don't have a boat."

The gap between a set of lines on paper and the planks-and-caulking reality of a finished hull is bridged by a process known as "lofting." In this process, the body plan, which played little part in streamlining, now assumes the central role. The reference grid on which the body plan is drawn can be laid out full-scale and the curves of the body plan transferred, point by point, onto the full-scale grid. For a large vessel a large flat floor is needed and a loft is particularly well-suited — hence the term "lofting." From the "lofts" or full-sized curves, "molds" are shaped from rough lumber and used as templates for cutting, bending or shaping the "frames." And the frames are the structural timbers which might be thought of as the "ribs" of the hull mounted along the "backbone" of the keel. Finally then, it is the frames, as will be apparent from a glance at figs. II-5 & 6, which determine the form of the hull — which was the original purpose of this excursion into naval architecture.

From the foregoing it will be evident how easy is the job of a person wishing to make a record of sailing vessels: all that is required is the tact to persuade a builder to permit his lines drawings to be copied in the interests of

fig. II-5. Small vessel being "set up" at Charlestown, Nevis. April, 1974.

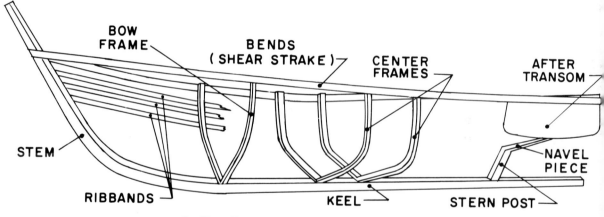

fig. II-6. Key to structural members in fig. II-5.

science and scholarship. The only hitch in this sunny program is that West
Indian builders don't use lines drawings. Their design work is done full-scale
in the process of "setting up" the hull.

In the islands, after the keel has been laid and the stem and sternpost
fitted, the builder sets up his "modeling" frames: bow frames at the forward
end of the keel, main frames at the one-third mark on the keel and the main
transoms at the top of the sternpost (figs. II-5 & 6). Thin strips of wood called
"ribbands" are bent around the modeling frames and nailed bow and stern.
The remaining frames are then fitted into this basketwork shape, the fairing
being done by sighting along the ribbands for bulges and hollows. Design may
be modified by changing the shape of the modeling frames themselves or
by changing their positions slightly when setting up.

Anyone aspiring to make his mark in the world by copying the lines drawings of West Indian builders is thus doomed to disappointment. Fortunately there is another way.

One morning, early in my West Indian sojourn, I found myself in the exuberant midst of the produce market in Grenville, Grenada. Fascinated by the abundance of exotic fruits and vegetables, I asked one of the market ladies about the little heap of round golden fruits she displayed.

"Them's govers, sor," she replied.

After a moment's reflection I decided that govers might be guavas, known to me by name only.

"What do you do with govers?" I asked.

"You makes gover jam, gover jelly and gover cheese," she replied cheerfully.

Jams and jellies seemed pretty obvious, but the notion of cheese made from fruit was definitely intriguing.

"How do you make gover cheese?" I ventured.

"Well, sor, you does buy some of my govers and you takes them to your cook and you says, 'Cook, make me some gover cheese.' "

The above is included so that if you want boat lines, you will know what to say to your friendly local naval architect, thereby transforming him into a boat-measurer whose chief joy and function in life then becomes something called "taking-off lines."

The reader assiduous enough to have read and understood how lines drawings are made, is now in the fortunate position of not having to hear another long-winded explanation; taking-off lines is simply the reverse of lofting. Using measuring tape, spirit level and plumb bob, the eager boat-measurer lays out a reference grid beneath the hull in question, measures from grid to hull according to the scheme depicted in fig. II-7, jots down all data in a neat and orderly manner while maintaining unruffled calm despite blowing sand, biting insects, flapping paper and curious children. Whereupon,

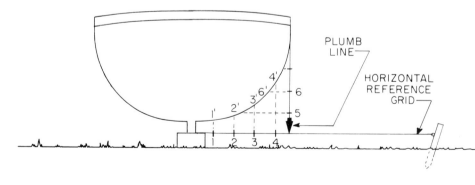

fig. II-7. Basic boat measuring. Distances 1-1',
2-2', etc. are recorded and used to produce
sections to scale.

said boat-measurer retires to the confines of his yacht, shoves aside the accumulated clutter of life under sail, balances his drawing board on his knees while bracing against the roll, pitch, surge, wind gusts or whatever might be the peculiar joy of the night's anchorage, and — still with unruffled calm — turns his data into clear, clean lines drawings. Nothing to it.

In island terminology, *boats* are those watercraft which may be pulled ashore when not in use; *vessels* are watercraft too large for that. Vessels are further divided into *sloops*, which have one mast and are generally under fifty feet in length, and *schooners*, which are generally over fifty feet and generally have two masts.

Taking lines off boats was usually pretty easy since they were, or easily could be, pulled ashore. The reference grid, being smaller, was quicker to stake out and more accurate. Vessels were more of a problem because they were seldom ashore and even then the large size made it difficult to establish the grid. In most cases I was limited to new vessels where construction had reached the stage of planking. In one case (the *Warspite*, Ch. 6) I got desperate and took off lines with the vessel afloat — it worked, but was neither practical nor enjoyable.

My first effort at working up a data sheet into a set of lines was frustrating and discouraging; the data were smudged and often illegible, the reference grid was done in separate sections for bow and stern, and worst of all, I was totally lacking in confidence. Fortunately, there was no choice but to keep plugging until slowly and painfully a set of lines emerged. The second set was just as slow but not quite so frustrating. My confidence was growing until I tried to draw the lines of a sloop that I measured before planking had begun. Somehow the buttock lines in the vicinity of the sternpost would not come fair. On a later visit, I confided my difficulty to the builder and asked permission to measure again and correct my error.

"That no error, man," he chuckled. "When we plank up, we find a little hollow just here (he moved his hand over the area near the sternpost) but we is put a little shim upon the frame and she plank up good."

The shim used was less than an inch thick and yet the unfairness had shown up in a drawing to the scale of ¼" = 1'. After that experience there was no stopping me. The lines I drew are not detailed enough for builder's plans, and are not intended to be. They are, however, an accurate and objective record of the naval architecture of the remaining traditional watercraft of the Lesser Antilles.

At the outset it was my intention to take lines off one or two representative schooners, make a few notes on construction techniques, then submit the information as a brief technical article. However, someone of my acquaintance suggested that photographs ought to be included, and imperceptibly the scope of the project began to widen. It was next pointed out that I ought to develop my own film so as to be able to monitor results.

My photographic activity was pretty perfunctory until I began to realize that photographs also were a unique opportunity. However, I never did become entirely reconciled to the cumbersome clutter of cameras, lenses, tanks, bags and bottles of chemicals. For those who might be interested I will note in passing that for film developer, I used Kodak Microdol-X, diluted 1:3 so that developing time could be extended to around nine minutes, giving better control of negative density at the relatively high temperatures (74-75° F.) at which I worked.

After assembling tape measures, notepads, strings, line levels and camera and learning the rudiments of naval architecture and photography, my metamorphosis into a boat-measurer was complete. When the school term ended in June of 1970, I was ready and eager to set out in pursuit of the elusive island schooner.

CHAPTER III

PASSAGE TO GRENADA

A sailing vessel bound to Grenada from St. Croix has two choices of route: beat ninety miles upwind to Anguilla or St. Martin, then follow the arc of the Lesser Antilles southward to Grenada; or, sail a close reach directly to Grenada and make the return trip by island-hopping. For a variety of reasons the direct route seemed the better choice for me. However, one slight difficulty appeared as I studied the chart — the direct course from St. Croix to Grenada passed very close to Aves Island, an isolated patch of shoals and coral reef capped by a bit of sand bar lying 100 miles southeast of Guadeloupe.

The safest plan, I decided, was to *try* to land on the tiny island, thereby rendering it impossible to find. The morning after leaving St. Croix, I took a sun altitude and got a good line of position; shortly before noon I got a second line and the intercept showed Aves Island five miles dead ahead. A few minutes later a ring of breakers was visible with a sandy islet inside. So much for irony as a technique of navigation.

With the sun high it was fairly simple to enter the small lee behind the curved rim of sand, which was no more than 100 yards from end to end. The holding was good in clean coral sand; but as soon as the mainsail was down, *Eider* began to roll from gunwale to gunwale in the swell which bent around both ends of the island and re-entered the lee in a dizzying criss-cross. Launching the dinghy was clearly impractical, but swimming ahore seemed feasible.

Swimming with mask, fins and spear gun made me feel a little less exposed, but couldn't ward off entirely the loneliness of the spot. As I left the water and stood dripping on the steep beach, clouds of mewing sea birds rose screaming and swirling into the air. In the shallows just behind lay a dozen or so sea turtles waiting for the full moon and spring tide to come ashore and lay eggs. There was no plant life except here and there, a patch of the low-growing succulent called ice plant. A short distance along the beach there was a length of galvanized pipe stuck in the sand with a tattered Venezuelan flag at its top, and at its base a plaque stating that the Radio-Club de Venezuela had visited the island two years previously.

Abruptly I was swept by a sense of futility and desolation which left me acutely uncomfortable. After a scant half hour, my plans for a Robinson Crusoe picnic seemed pointless, and I gladly swam back aboard and got underway again, there being no further obstacles on the course to Grenada.

A landfall, after a four-day passage, is a welcome event; and my first view of the port of St. Georges from seaward was so picturesque that it is still indelibly fixed in my mind. The sun, already dropping into the west, had highlighted the neat brick facades and red-tiled roofs of the little town, transforming the whole scene into the stage set for some impossibly romantic light opera. Behind a steep headland capped by a fort lay the inner harbor — the same brick facades, but here all the hustle and noise of a busy sailing port (fig. III-1).

fig. III-1. Port of St. Georges, Grenada. June, 1970.

18

A few days after getting *Eider* snugged into the yacht anchorage, I began to realize that my timetable — which called for completing my project that summer — was unrealistic. There was, first of all, the period of relaxation justified by an offshore passage: mornings of shopping and reprovisioning, long lunches at the Nutmeg Cafe looking out over the harbor, afternoons of siesta and inspired idleness, evenings of rum punch and conversation, followed by nights of blissful sleep, cradled under the tropic stars by the gently rocking yacht.

Then followed a period of chores and undertakings: a line to be spliced here, a seizing to be redone there, a touch of paint or varnish. Then a round of bigger jobs: rebuilding the dinghy, which was proving too small; replacing a bearing in the gear-box. These items in addition, of course, to the continuing obligations of coffee in the cockpit in the cool of early morning, of visiting with new friends and acquaintances and, now and then, inquiries about boat-building.

With one thing and another, it was late July by the time that I actually set out to stalk my elusive quarry with the aid of that monument to unfettered free enterprise, the Grenada bus system. The buses — unhampered by any consideration other than getting there firstest with the mostest — are individually owned and locally built. Straight-backed wooden benches are set as close together as possible on the back of a flatbed truck, then roofed over from wooden side to wooden side. And, as a final expression of concern for the comfort and convenience of the passenger, there are canvas curtains that roll right down in case there's a change in the weather. Bright paint and an affectionate name are all that are needed to complete the turnout.

Passengers mount a two-step ladder at the rear and shuffle forward to wedge into any empty space to be found. A friend of the driver rides at the back to collect fares, shout directions and act as a living guard-chain when the bus has filled to overflowing. Scheduling and routing are equally straightforward: the bus runs from the home village of the driver to the market square in St. Georges and returns, stopping anywhere and any time along the route. Buses run as often as they get a load and leave when they are filled. As a consequence, the market square is a seething, milling maelstrom of people, parcels and machinery, drowning in the roar of unmuffled exhausts which echoes off the brick facades surrounding the square.

Into this bedlam I wandered, looking for a bus to Grenville. Seeing neither posted destinations nor any other suggestion of a system, I timidly asked a man with a chicken under each arm.

"Grenville?" he screamed. "Is Grenville you want? See over there. Is that one going." He gestured frantically with his head toward a confused tangle of buses and people.

"No, man, no! Over here, over here," a new voice chimed in from the left.

"Try me, man, try me," from still another direction.

The best strategy seemed to be to find a bus nearly full and pile aboard.

And soon we got under way, exhaust roaring, driver honking and screaming for room. By lung power alone we propelled ourselves through the log jam — roaring and jerking up the steep streets and out into the countryside.

The two-lane road which crosses the backbone of the island to Grenville is in constant use: by taxis, trucks and rival buses; by school children in uniform, field workers with their machetes tucked under the left arm and women with improbable loads balanced on their heads; by dogs, donkeys and an assortment of domestic fowl. The rules of the road are simple in the extreme — blare the horn at intersections and blind spots, *i.e.* almost constantly, and forge ahead while traffic scatters into the ditch. Unless, of course, they are bigger and more determined than you are, in which case it is your turn in the ditch.

Our driver, a paragon of dexterity and determination, went unchallenged until he swung out to pass a poky taxi on a winding upgrade — a technique which had doubtless served him faithfully many times before. This time, however, a heavily loaded truck hove into view and it was our turn in the ditch. I use the term ditch, but in reality it was more of a mountainside and we lurched to a stop with the left rear wheels hanging over the void and a tangle of tropical growth holding the weight of the bus. As soon as possible I got out, my movements quickened by visions of the bus tumbling end over end down the mountainside in a cloud of flying splinters. As I stood again on *terra firma*, feeling more than average thankful, my eye lit for the first time on the name our intrepid driver had chosen for his vehicle: *Why Worry?*

When another bus came along I did not linger, as many did, to haggle with the driver over a fare refund; I chalked it up to experience and proceeded to Grenville without further mishap. Once there, it was an easy matter to get directions to a stretch of beach north of the town where a large schooner was being set up. The keel, stem and sternpost were in position, and a few frames had been fastened in place. Two men were at work with adzes shaping additional frames; they worked carefully on the outer face, knocked off the high spots from sides and inner face and called the job done (fig. III-2). The frames, when shaped, were erected in pairs, the lower ends being fastened to the keel, and the upper ends tied together with a wooden stave. The assembled pair was then leveled by sighting across the stave to the sea horizon, thus taking advantage of the world's largest spirit level.

A third man, with tape and chalk, moved between the vessel and a pile of crooked timbers lying nearby, laying out and marking work for the other men. I asked him if there were enough timbers in the pile to finish the framing.

"Oh no," he laughed. "If all be brought at once, then is too discouraging." He went on to explain that when this lot of timbers was exhausted, the crew would spend a week up in the foothills, finding and cutting more crooks. This gave a break in the routine of work and provided an opportunity to look for specific shapes as they were needed.

When I asked how the proportions of the vessel were determined, the builder outlined substantially the same system which I found everywhere in

*fig. III-2.   Frames of schooner under construction
at Grenville, Grenada. June, 1970.*

the Lesser Antilles: with keel, stem and sternpost in position, center frames are shaped so that the center section will have a beam equal to one-fourth of the intended length and a depth in the hold equal to one-half of the beam. On a schooner three sets of frames are made to this mold and set up at about one-third back on the keel. Next, bow frames are shaped and positioned at the forward end of the keel, and transom frames at the head of the sternpost.

Although the method and proportions were substantially the same in all the islands I visited, the shaping and positioning of the modelling frames varied from island to island and builder to builder. In fact, most builders were rather secretive about their own molds, though they spoke openly about general proportions.

Later in the conversation, I asked my informant where he had learned to set up (i.e. design) vessels; he replied that his name was Steill, and he grew up in Harvey's Vale, Carriacou. He made these two statements as if they constituted all the answer required — which they did, as I was subsequently to learn.

Steill's vessel was not far enough along to be measured; not all the frames were in place. However, he told me of another vessel, not visible from the road, being built at Soubise, south of Grenville, by a man he had taught. I was to ask the bus driver to let me down on the low-lying stretch of coast just before the road cut inland and began to climb; I was to ask for the house of George Justlyn.

Justlyn was not at home; but his wife consented to my taking the lines off a medium-sized schooner lying, planked and decked, among the palms behind their house. The lines (fig. III-3) show a hull with strongly marked sheer and very long overhang in the stern. The floors (the lower limbs on the main frame) are moderately sharp and slightly hollow in the mid-section. The stem is long, curved and strongly raked. The waterlines and buttock lines both appear to have good flow characteristics, and my prediction would be that this hull should be fairly easily driven. Unfortunately, there was never any opportunity to verify.

Four years later, when a further concatenation of circumstances brought me back to Grenada, the schooner at Soubise was still unlaunched, unrigged and unnamed. The owners in Trinidad had stopped sending money, and Justlyn had stopped working. The sail plan is hypothetical, therefore — the dimensions and proportions being taken from photographs of similar vessels built in Grenada and Carriacou.

There is a generic resemblance between the vessels of these two islands — as well there might be, since Steill and Justlyn are typical of almost all Grenada builders in having their roots in Carriacou. In most cases the move was made when a Carriacou builder came to Grenada to build a vessel for a Grenada owner or to build near the abundant timber resources of Grenada. Thus it happens that the trading vessels of Grenada are merely built there, whereas in tradition and design they are definitely of the Carriacou model. There are, however, two types of small craft which are unique to Grenada.

North of St. Georges, in the lee of Mt. St. Catherine, lies the village of Gouyave, a straggle of houses and shops between the coast road and the black sand beach. Like most of the coastal towns, Gouyave depends for at least part of its livelihood on fishing, which is done on this stretch of coast in a sailing canoe (fig. III-4). These little craft are canoes both in their fusiform shape and

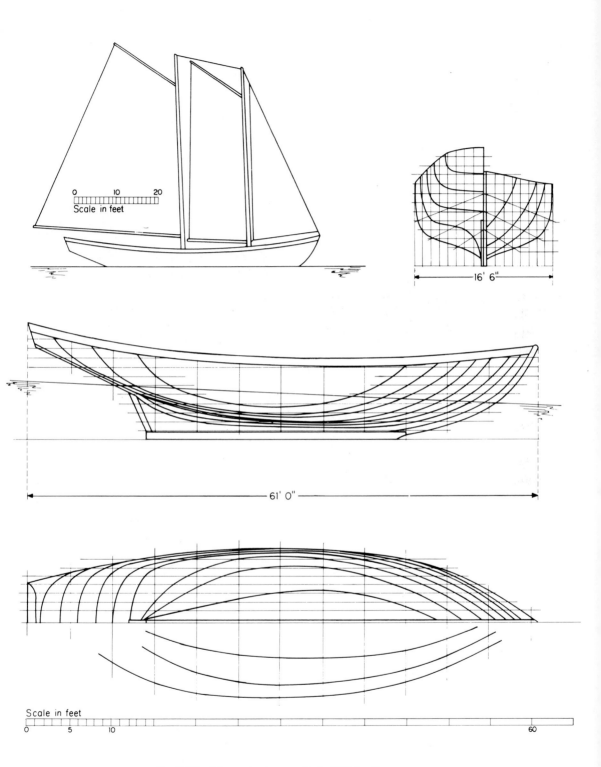

Scale in feet

0   10   20
Scale in feet

16' 6"

61' 0"

Scale in feet

0   5   10   60

fig. III-3.   *Lines of schooner. Built 1970 by George*
Justlyn at Soubise, Grenada. Taken off
at Soubise, June, 1970.

fig. III-4. Sailing canoes at Gouyave, Grenada. March, 1974.

in their construction. They are made from a small hollowed log with three raising strakes (planks) added to form the sides. The strakes are fastened to the log with widely spaced frames, which are fitted after the strakes are already in place (fig. III-5). The lines (fig. III-6) show very clearly that no effort is made to give the hull any shape other than that assumed by a hollowed log which is wedged slightly open in its mid-section.

These canoes are propelled by sailing and rowing simultaneously — a practical mix in the flat water and flukey breezes which prevail in the lee of the high island. They are, however, capable of operating in the open sea, as I was brought to acknowledge when a contingent of eight of these craft turned up in 1970 for a regatta in Carriacou, twenty-five miles to the northeast.

The canoes were easy to follow in the races because they all had dark blue denim sails. Not, I think, that denim makes very good sail cloth — it probably accounted, at least in part, for their notable lack of success against the small double-enders that had come down for the first time from Bequia, to the north — but that denim was simply the cheapest of the available yard goods in the only dry goods shop in the village.

Two years later the Gouyave canoes stopped coming to the regatta — discouraged, I imagine, by their poor showing. In 1975 I returned to Grenada to take lines off one of these canoes and could only find a handful of these craft still in use. Their places on the beach had been taken by roughly-built double-enders of the Bequia model — an interesting example of cultural diffusion.

fig. III-5. Construction detail of sailing canoe,
Gouyave, Grenada. March, 1974.

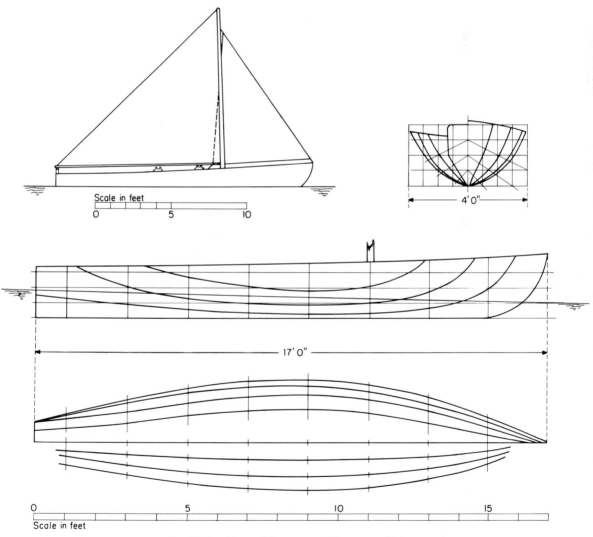

Scale in feet
0   5   10

4' 0"

17' 0"

0   5   10   15
Scale in feet

fig. III-6. Lines of Gouyave sailing canoe. Taken
off March, 1974.

Elsewhere on the island, fishing is carried on in motor launches (fig. III-7 & 8) which, though setting no sails, are so characteristically Grenadian that they seem worth including. At first glance the launch might appear to be a sailing type converted by replacing sails with the single-cylinder Stuart-Turner engine. However, the lines (fig. III-9) show clearly that the hull was designed with an engine in mind. The waterlines are fine forward and maximum beam is abaft the midship, producing a rather sophisticated tear-drop shape.

The double-ended design immediately suggests the Bequia double-enders as an influence, but all the people I asked assured me that the launch had been designed as an "engine boat" and had never had a sailing rig. I finally learned that the design was the work of an English fisheries officer stationed for some years at Grenville, though no one could remember his name. Had the man been a notable drunkard or a woman-chaser, his name would undoubtedly be a household word; but alas, creating something to land fish economically and put food on the table merely entitles the creator to popular anonymity.

fig. III-7. Fishing boat under construction at Soubise, Grenada. June, 1971.

fig. III-8.   Grenada fishing boat, Prickly Bay,
Grenada. March, 1974.

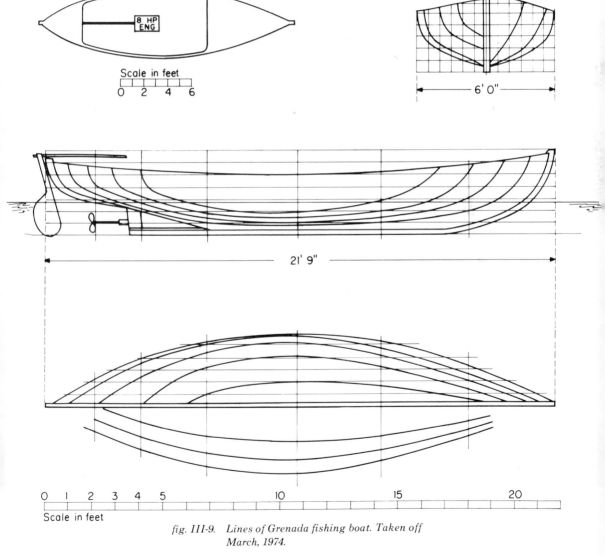

8 HP
ENG

Scale in feet

0   2   4   6

6' 0"

21' 9"

0   1   2   3   4   5   10   15   20

Scale in feet

fig. III-9.   Lines of Grenada fishing boat. Taken off
March, 1974.

Taken overall, there was surprisingly little boatbuilding in Grenada, despite abundant material resources and a need for waterborne commerce. Even in the past, activity was sporadic and mostly done by men from Carriacou. Moreover, nearly all the trading vessels that I saw coming and going in the port of St. Georges were from Carriacou. Grenada, for all its resources, seemed to stand in maritime affairs very much in the shadow of Carriacou - a small, dry island with few inhabitants.

This apparent anomaly was to recur again and again in the course of my study, the pattern so persistent that it gradually became one of my major preoccupations. Meanwhile all sources were agreed, "Is boatbuilding you want, is Carriacou you going."

fig. IV-1. Roadstead at Hillsborough, Carriacou.
August, 1973.

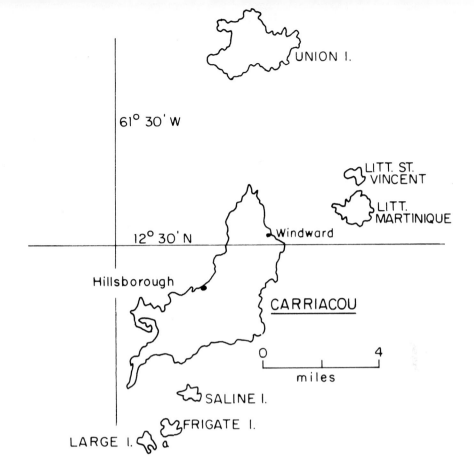

CHAPTER IV

CARRIACOU YOU GOING

It's a stiff sail to Carriacou from Grenada — against wind and tide — but well worth it for anyone interested in working sailcraft. Especially if you can time your arrival for the first weekend of August, when the small island, ordinarily content to doze in the Caribbean sun, comes alive for the annual Carriacou Regatta. Sloops and schooners from up and down the Grenadines gather in the roadstead (fig. IV-1); canoes and fishing boats line the beach. The main street of Hillsborough swirls with people stirred into a West Indian jump-up by bright colors, plentiful refreshments and an exuberant calypso beat. All this in aid and honor of workboats, large and small, which gather every year to race (fig. IV-2) during the August Bank Holiday.

Boatbuilding in Carriacou is an old tradition, whose origins are obscure and surrounded by legend. Interwoven with this older tradition is a more recent thread added by J. Lynton Rigg, an American yachtsman who settled in Carriacou after cruising the islands in 1960 (related in *The Alluring Antilles).* Rigg, who died in the summer of 1976, was the founder of the Regatta and, by his iniative alone, brought about a revival of boatbuilding in Carriacou and the Grenadines.

fig. IV-2. *Large sloops class, Carriacou Regatta.*
August, 1972.

The Mermaid Tavern, located across from the Police Station on Hillsborough's main (and only paved) street, formed the landward cornerstone of Rigg's island domain. There in the cool interior, the jangling cacophony of the street in front was tempered by the gentle slosh of waves at the back door, blending, in the low hum of the overhead fans, into a tranquilizing harmony of the tropics. In the jalousied dimness of the bar, local regulars mingled with passing yachtsmen. Presiding over this gentle anachronism — with his red neckerchief and Panama hat, his fund of stories punctuated by "don't ye knows" — Rigg was the very model of the white man in the Tropics. And nodding gently at anchor on the windward side of the island lay *Mermaid of Carriacou* — the other half of Rigg's domain, and the sloop to beat on race day.

According to Rigg, boatbuilding had all but stopped on the island when he settled there in the early 1960's. He set out to arrest this decline, not from antiquarian sentiment, but from a genuine and realistic concern for the economic well-being of the island and its people. Being small and dry (fig. IV-3) Carriacou offered little opportunity for local enterprise; the usual venture was to open a store and sell things to the neighbors, but that merely recirculated money in the very limited island economy; and eventually someone had to leave and work overseas, away from friends and family, to bring in new money. Building a vessel, on the other hand, takes local skills and some local materials, transforming them into a capital asset which can then generate new money — by freighting between the larger islands in good times, and by going fishing in other times.

fig. IV-3. *Hillside above Tyrrel Bay, Carriacou.*
August, 1973.

For the first phase of his projected revival, Rigg went shares on a sloop being built in the little community of Windward by Zepharin MacLaren. Rigg bought materials and had a suit of sails cut by Ratsey and Lapthorn, while MacLaren did the carpentry. Then, with a pace setter at his disposal, Rigg organized and sponsored a regatta for workboats in six classes: large decked sloops, small decked sloops, open boats in three lengths and a class for canoes. In each class the competitors were to race level, with no handicaps and no rules, points to be awarded for the first four places in each of three heats, and the vessel with the highest total for the series to be awarded first prize of $500 EC, with smaller prizes down to fourth place.

Rigg assumed — shrewdly, as the results testify — that the sporting instinct in humans may well be stronger than the desire for economic independence or even the instinct for survival. Racing for substantial cash prizes certainly produced greater stimulation of boatbuilding activity than any amount of urging or explanation of economic benefits. Once built, Rigg reasoned, the vessels would surely find useful employment, no matter how frivolous the original purpose of building.

Over the years the *Mermaid* (fig. IV-4) proved unbeatable, giving rise to

fig. IV-4. Mermaid of Carriacou *running the line at the start, Carriacou Regatta. August, 1974.*

a legend and, of course, a certain amount of grumbling about Lynton Rigg's "yacht," with her stainless steel rigging and her Dacron sails. Despite the grumbling, no one was fundamentally discouraged, since challenges continued to be made. Many builders were even brought to adopt the amenities of stainless and Dacron — not such a bad influence in the long run. During the four years that I was able to follow the Regatta, six large sloops were built and made their debut racing against *Mermaid*.

The results of this grand plan were all that Rigg could have hoped — by the time of his death a new fleet of sailing vessels had been built in Carriacou, and a new generation of builders had acquired the skills of setting up and building seaworthy sailing craft. One such accomplishment would be a worthy memorial for anyone; Rigg, in fact, had two to his credit. The Out Island Regatta in the Bahamas was also his creation, with similar intent and effect. Both achievements illustrate the decisive role that individual initiative may play, on occasion, within the framework of large and seemingly impersonal economic and geographic forces.

Mermaid's racing record and her unique position among her sisters made me especially eager to have her lines. And here I was definitely in luck because Rigg had a model — not a builder's half-model, because none was used, but a scale model which both Rigg and MacLaren certified as accurate. As a result, I was able for once, to take off a set of lines as it should really be done, *i.e.* seated at a table on the dining terrace of the Tavern, shaded by gently swishing palms, cooled by the balmiest of breezes and watched over by an attentive barman who sent round another cold bottle of Carib whenever it seemed as if the particular muse of boat-measurers had grown fickle.

The resulting lines (fig. IV-5) show a straight-sided vessel with sharp floors, extreme deadrise and a graceful entry. The long, straight run starts at the mid-section and is carried onto the wide counter stern without the cramping of buttock lines which so often occurs in the vicinity of the stern post. However, in exchange, a hard knuckle characteristic of the Carriacou sloops is formed on the transom where the sides join the bottom. It might be expected that such a knuckle would generate undesirable turbulence when the vessel heeled; but when sailing *Mermaid*, beamy by island standards (12'3" beam, 44' length), showed little inclination to heel. As MacLaren told me, "If a vessel build long and narrow, is sailing more on the side. You must give she sufficient beam to sail more up on the keel — so you could walk upon the deck." He made this pronouncement as he counted his share of the previous day's first prize; few who had seen *Mermaid* race would have disputed his judgement.

The *Mermaid* was too large and too busy to sail in circles for me while I collected performance data. However I was able to hitch a ride as she sailed back to Windward after the races, giving me an opportunity to make the following measurements:

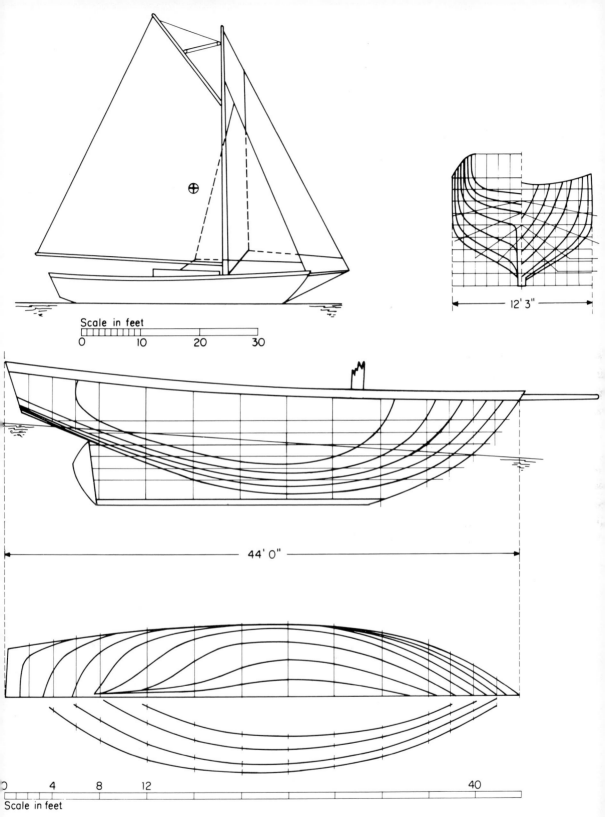

Scale in feet

0   10   20   30

12' 3"

44' 0"

0   4   8   12   40

Scale in feet

fig. IV-5. Lines of Mermaind of Carriacou. *Built 1964 by Zepharin MacLaren at Windward, Carriacou. Taken off August, 1974.*

33

Point of sailing	Angle off the wind	Wind speed in knots	Boat speed in knots	Leeway angle	Boat speed wind speed
Close-hauled	50°	19	6.7	10°	.35
Beam reach	90°	20	7.5	—	.38
Broad reach	135°	20	7.2	—	.36
Running	180°	18	6.8	—	.38

At this point it might be helpful to say something about the speeds attainable by displacement hulls (*i.e.* hulls which must displace water in order to move ahead; catamarans and planing hulls *not* included). As an empirical rule, the maximum speed of a displacement hull is determined by the square root of the length at the waterline (LWL); briefly, the longer the waterline, the higher will be the maximum speed obtainable. This relationship is expressed algebraically by the formula: $SP_{max} = k\sqrt{LWL}$ where k is a constant which depends on the type and the efficiency of the hull; in practice, values of k range from 1.0 for slow, full-carrying hulls to 1.4 for all-out racing types. Assuming that 20 knots of breeze was enough for *Mermaid* to develop her best speed, then she has a measured speed coefficient of 1.25 for her LWL of 36 ft. This value is comparable to that of a fast modern cruising yacht, a remarkable achievement for a working vessel built by eye on traditional lines — restrictions not placed on ordinary sailing yachts.

In competition, *Mermaid* did not always lead on the down-wind leg (fig. IV-6); but once around the leeward mark, she invariably showed her stuff, out-pointing and out-footing all challengers by substantial margins. Her big advantages lay in the deep draft and marked deadrise, which gave very good lateral resistance for windward work, while her beaminess enabled her stand up to her lofty rig. And, inevitably, a well-cut set of Dacron sails gave an edge over the hand-sewn sails of cotton used by her challengers.

fig. IV-6. Downwind leg of large sloops race, Carriacou Regatta. August, 1974.

The advantages of polyester sail cloth soon became apparent to other captains, some of whom set out to neutralize *Mermaid's* edge, with unexpected results. In 1974, during a period of lawlessness in Grenada occasioned by the petition for independence, a night-time raid was made on the yacht anchorage at St. Georges. A considerable amount of boat gear went missing, including a number of sails. Several months later, some of these sails reappeared at the Regatta (fig. IV-7) in a novel configuration (the lighter portion was positively identified at the time as the mizzen sail of Don Street's *Iolaire).* It gives me great satisfaction to report that crime doesn't pay, at least in this case, since the larger challenger was still handily beaten by *Mermaid.*

The little community where *Mermaid* was built lies near the end of a road which winds out of Hillsborough, rises to cross the backbone of the island, then descends again to the shore before turning north to end on a rocky headland facing Union Island. Two small islands, Petit St. Vincent and Petit Martinique, lie to the east, adding to the protection of the coral reef which forms the shallow but well-protected harbor where the vessels of Windward swing at anchor (fig. IV-8).

In August of 1970, I made my way down the road to windward to verify information that a schooner was being built there. Small houses with unglazed windows and wooden shutters fronted the road, their back doors opening onto the sandy foreshore. There, half hidden by the curving palm trunks, I found a large hull, planked and decked, waiting, bows toward the

fig. IV-7. Sloop CCC *with new-fangled mains'l,*
Carriacou Regatta. August, 1974.

35

*fig. IV-8. Anchorage at Windward, Carriacou;
Union Island and Canouan in the
distance. August, 1970.*

sea, to be launched. It was a favorable time for taking off lines, since little work was going on, and the owner/builder, Hobin Roberts, a smiling, soft-spoken man, readily gave his consent ("No objection. Is no objection.").

The resulting lines (fig. IV-9) provide a good example of the larger class of Carriacou-built vessels, the hallmarks being: stem curved and strongly raked, long overhanging stern, strong drag to the keel, moderately sharp floors, and straight sides with no tumblehome. In times gone by, a vessel of this size would undoubtedly have been schooner-rigged. At present, with increasing availability and reliability of marine diesel engines, many owners prefer to save the cost of foremast, sail and rigging and apply it toward an engine (fig. IV-10).

All decked vessels built in the Lesser Antilles have overhanging sterns with the exception of Tortola and Antigua sloops. In Carriacou this overhang is proportionally longer than elsewhere, a fact which deserves some comment. In setting up a vessel, the frames of the "main transom" are butted on the sides of the sternpost at a height which determines the "tuck" (deadrise) of the hull. Next, a thick plank called the "navel piece" is rabbetted onto the after face of the stern post at this same height and supported by shores, thus defining the underline of the counter stern. The frames of the "after transom" are mounted atop this navel piece; when the hull is planked and caulked, the weight of the stern is supported by the planking with some help

36

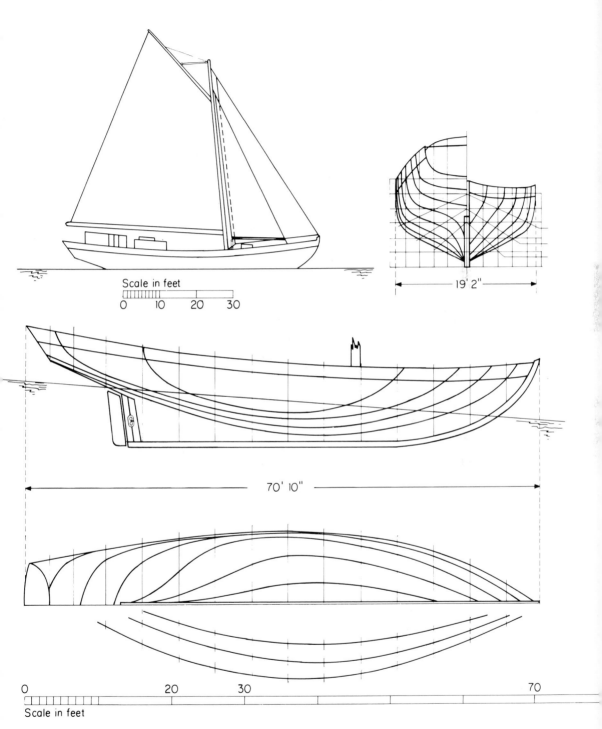

Scale in feet

0   10   20   30

19' 2"

70' 10"

0   20   30   70

Scale in feet

fig. IV-9.   *Lines of sloop* Yankee Girl R. *Built 1970 by Gordon Patrice at Windward, Carriacou. Taken off August, 1970.*

37

fig. IV-10. Sloop Yankee Girl R *anchored at Hillsborough, Carriacou. August, 1974.*

from the beam shelves and the decking. However, as the vessel ages and the hull works, the planking loosens and 'de starn droop" — a common sight among older schooners (fig. IV-11). This tendency has limited the length of the stern in Bequia and Anguilla, but not in Carriacou.

In Carriacou the after transom is supported by heavy timbers called "ledges," which are fastened to the inside of the transom frames and extended forward to be fastened to the sides of the stern post and two or three frames of the tuck. In this way the stern is strongly cantilevered with the stern post as fulcrum. It is interesting that a structurally sound method of supporting the stern should exist in Carriacou and not, for example, in Bequia, which is only 35 miles away.

When I showed Roberts the completed lines of his vessel, he was politely interested and seemed flattered that I would take the time, but it was clear that he did not see the point. However, he was very cordial and reciprocated by asking me to come to the launching, which was planned for October. My plans were already made to go north to Bequia, and a launching in October meant delay and doubling back on my route. Still, it was a unique opportunity, and I was especially interested in view of what I had been told about the last big launching which had occurred in Carriacou.

The *A L Sea Author M*, a large schooner of 76 Reg. Tons, was launched in 1964 at L'Esterre, a boatbuilding community on the leeward side of the island; a Grenadian who was present described the event to me. It began tamely enough with the priest christening the vessel in the accepted manner — then discreetly remembering a pressing engagement elsewhere. Thereupon, the shaman, still a personage of importance in Carriacou, took over for the remaining observances. First, a cock was killed and its blood sprinkled on the deck amidships so that there would always be plenty to eat on board. Next, a ewe lamb was stuck and bled at the stemhead so that the vessel would be docile and go where she was pointed. Finally, a bull calf was sacrificed on the

fig. IV-11. Schooner Lady Angela *of Bequia bound for Trinidad. September, 1970.*

ground near the stern post to give the vessel drive. The entire sequence was so bloody and undertaken with such gusto that several of the white spectators decamped forthwith. It saddens me to relate, however, that despite the elaborate and ecumenical preparations the launching went awry, and the heavy hull was stuck four days in the shallows before it could be floated off on a spring tide.

These lurid details were very much in my mind as the date of the launching approached. Launchings are generally held on Sunday so as to draw a larger crowd, which made Saturday afternoon a logical time to be tacking up the channel between Carriacou and Union Island. When the pass in the reef became visible, I eased sheets and made for it, figuring that if there were enough water for a schooner then there was enough for *Eider*. Once inside, an iron stake with a plastic bleach bottle on top marked the only isolated coral patch, and I took up anchorage without difficulty among the gently nodding schooners.

Ashore, I found Roberts smoking a pipe and working quietly around the vessel — driving tight the water pins in the joint between stem and keel, touching up the paintwork here and there. A ladder stood against the side of the vessel, so I asked if I might look at the deckhouse which had been added since I took off the lines. At the forward end of the deckhouse, on the main hatch cover, a small checked cloth was spread and a simple meal was set out — a plate with several fried cakes, a bottle of Scotch whisky and a glass, a folded napkin and a small vase of plastic flowers. When I asked Roberts about the food, he laughed shyly and replied, "Oh, is an old belief hereabout. Some people does think that jumbies come in the night to take food and you must not disappoint them."

Further to whet my appetite for folklore, there was a young black bull tethered to the smooth gray trunk of a palm tree near the stern of the vessel. Additional questions seemed inappropriate; I simply made it a point to be ashore as early as possible the next morning. Early, but not soon enough — the little bull was nowhere to be seen. Roberts was there by himself, holding in his arms a fine rooster with a glossy tail of green and black plumes. He deftly wrung its neck, then spoke in a low and encouraging voice during its death dance. When the dance ended, he picked up the body and slung blood along the keel. No one else was present, and I remained at a distance. Roberts' demeanor was that of a person who observes the proprieties, as if he were not himself superstitious but had no intention of offending public sensibilities in these matters.

A short distance along the beach in a well-shaded spot, Roberts' wife and her helpers were setting up tables, tending fires and stirring the deep iron pots which are the common cookware of the islands. A big feast was in the making, partly because a launching is a festive occasion, but also because an offering of food and drink is a sure way to draw a crowd. And a crowd is essential at a West Indian launching. Human muscle, known in the islands as

"Norwegian steam," is the cheapest and most portable source of power.

Bottles of Scotch and of "jack iron," a local form of white lightning, were set out on the refreshment table as people began to collect around ten o'clock. Woodsmoke and the aroma of curry mingled with the scent of oakum and pitch. At the far end of the table, a full sheet of plywood was set up facing out over the crowd toward the new vessel. Openings, both round and rectangular, had been cut in the plywood, giving it the appearance of an enormous primitive face. Ever alert to the ritual aspects of the occasion, I took opportunity to ask Roberts what it was.

"Oh," he replied cheerfully, "it have a fella over Bogley have a very good hi-fi he does bring to all fete and thing. It having a very good bass. You wait and hear."

So much for folklore.

Shortly after eleven o'clock, when Mass was over, the village priest arrived with a flock of his parishioners. The plywood jaws of Big Brother obligingly ceased to proclaim the calypso Gospel, and the secular crowd detached itself from the refreshment counter and reformed near the waiting vessel. The priest and his acolytes carefully climbed a ladder set against the vessel's side, followed by the vessel's godparents — a little boy and little girl, shy and awkward in stiffly starched Sunday clothes. The rite of baptism was read at the forward end of the deck and the name of the vessel revealed by unfurling the name banner from its staff — white letters on a red banner, *Yankee Girl R*. A murmur of speculation and appreciation ran through the crowd because the name was known only to the owner until this moment.

When the priest and his party had backed carefully down the ladder, the little godmother in her bright yellow dress skipped happily around to the stern of the vessel. She handed her purse to Roberts and stepped back while he tied it to the sternpost, then again stepped forward and stuffed a folded banknote into the shiny plastic bag. This was a signal for others to come shuffling forward with good will offerings — more token than real, I assumed, since a person capable of offering an open bar to a crowd made thirsty by the tropic sun surely doesn't lack financial reserves.

While these formalities were taking place, a small group of men was working quietly at making final adjustments to the launching tackle (pronounced TAY-kel) with the slightly aggrieved air always assumed by ants in the immediate vicinity of grasshoppers. They had fastened a two-inch diameter hemp cable to the sternpost, led it forward to the bows and were now using a lacing of lighter line to position the cable along the sides of the vessel. At the bows this heavy strop was made up to the near end of a six-part tackle whose far end lay on a little raft in the bay, held in its turn by a heavy kedge anchor.

As with all vessels built in the islands, the *Yankee Girl R* had been braced upright by shores placed along the sides as the vessel was built. In consequence, the first step toward launching had to be the removal of the shores

41

along one side so that the hull could be laid over onto the waiting rollers; these, in turn, would become the eventual means of moving the heavy hull across the beach to the water's edge. In the islands this first step is known as "cutting down" because the shores are literally cut away at the base, all being shortened slowly and simultaneously until the hull comes to rest gently on the rollers.

It was obvious to me that this was going to be a very delicate operation because if the cutting down were not carefully coordinated, too much weight would be thrown onto too few shores; and once breaking began, it would accelerate and bring the vessel smashing down onto the turn of the bilge — not a strong point since the frames are lapped there. To perform this delicate operation, I had imagined a team of the oldest and most trusted men of the community swinging in stately unison their razor-sharp machetes — perhaps to the measured rhythm of some old chantey.

In fact, there was no chantey and no unison. In their stead there was boundless enthusiasm (directly proportional, I suspect, to the number of pulls at the jack iron jug) and an apparent belief that speed was of the essence. Some chopped high, some chopped low and all chopped rapidly (fig. IV-12); the crowd cheered, and I held my breath. Fortunately, the sharpened ends sank into the soft sand, which acted to moderate and integrate individual

fig. IV-12. Cutting down the Yankee Girl R *at Windward, Carriacou. October, 1970.*

fig. IV-13. *Launching the* Yankee Girl R *at Wind-ward, Carriacou. October, 1970.*

effort. And in a surprisingly short time, the vessel was lying on the rollers, her weight divided between the keel and a strip of planks nailed along the bilge to protect the new paint.

After the cutting down there was a brief intermission while another round of jack iron was prescribed. Then eager hands were laid on the tackle, and the sheaves began to squeal in the heavy wooden blocks. A current of excitement ran through the onlookers as the heavy rope rose dripping out of the water and began to shudder under the load. But the fifty-ton hull didn't budge, and the eager haulers stumbled to a halt. Another excited rush was made, and again the rope stretched its limit before recoiling and pulling the crowd with it. After several of these fruitless rushes, an old woman, wizened and brown as mahogany, her braids done up in the bandana of a field worker, reached into her past and began to chant:

> Long TIME on the labor GANG
> YO, heave HO
> Had a good TIME on the labor GANG
> YO, heave HO

Up and down the line, older people began to take up the heavy beat of the chant. Slowly, the confused and ineffectual heaving of the crowd subsided as the rhythm of the chantey became established and made itself felt. Now, the stretch was taken out with slow steps taken in time to the plodding beat. Now, when the strain came on the heavy hull, there was no recoil, and the vessel began to move (fig. IV-13).

43

Once started, the *Yankee Girl* moved readily enough, and excitement mounted as she crossed the flat foreshore and approached the last gentle slope down to the water's edge. Then, without warning, an old man at the stern wrapped the end of his checkline around a palm trunk and held hard. The crowd groaned as the life went out of the rope and the vessel stopped. There were angry shouts, but the old man paid no heed, quietly directing his helpers to bring four rollers already left astern down to the water's edge ready to receive the weight of the bows. It was failure to do this that had caused the *Sea Author* to stick in the shallows for four days.

This time the vessel was easy to start, and the heaving became a walk and then a run up the beach. People stumbled backward, laughing and falling as the rope went slack and the vessel began to move under her own weight. With a rush and a cheer, the *Yankee Girl* slid into the water and floated free of the rollers (fig. IV-14). A swarm of boys swam out, clambering aboard and wrestling in an island version of king-on-th-mountain. Ashore, the festivities, congratulations and glow of accomplishment continued until the soft hour of island twilight had settled onto the crowd.

Rigging and fitting out of the *Yankee Girl* took another year because Roberts worked carefully and to a high standard. The following summer he sailed the vessel down to St. Georges and installed the engine. Another year went by before I ran into Roberts one morning in St. Georges and asked how he was doing with the vessel. He smiled his cautious smile and replied that he was just on his way to close a deal with a young American who wanted the *Yankee Girl* to haul fruit from the Dominican Republic to the Virgin Islands. Roberts volunteered that he had been offered $70,000 EC (about $35,000 US, at that time) and was well pleased at the offer. The deal fell through when

fig. IV-14. The Yankee Girl R *afloat for the first time. Windward, Carriacou. October, 1970.*

44

fig. IV-15. Small Carriacou sloop hard on the wind during the Carriacou Regatta. August, 1973.

the buyer was unable to raise the money, but it did give me some idea of the value that an owner placed on such a vessel.

The last time that I saw the *Yankee Girl,* Roberts was freighting biscuits and soap powder from Trinidad to St. Lucia under contract to Lever Brothers Mfg. (Trinidad). The contract was especially favorable since the cargo was light and easy on the vessel and the trips were scheduled, thus avoiding both agent's commissions and long waits in the hot inner harbor at Port-of-Spain. Most vessels spend two and three weeks locating a cargo, finding space at the dock and loading — just to make a single two-day trip with no assurance of cargo for the return.

Carriacou builds sloops in abundance, schooners in fair numbers, but no characteristic small craft for fishing. For this purpose a decked vessel is used which is simply a smaller version of the large sloops (fig. IV-15). When I found one of these small sloops under construction on the shores of Tyrrel Bay (fig. IV-16), I asked in the local grog shop for the builder.

"Him?" replied the young man behind the counter. "He's probably the worst builder on this island. You're wasting your time and his."

A glance at the vessel convinced me that the young man was right; all I was going to get for my trouble was a smaller version of the lines of *Mermaid.* Besides, with the launching of the *Yankee Girl,* my principal aims in Carriacou were accomplished and it was time to move on to Bequia, another small island with a widespread reputation for boatbuilding. However, the attractions of Carriacou remained, and I managed to get there annually for the Regatta as long as I remained in the islands.

fig. IV-16. Small sloop abuilding at Tyrrel Bay, Carriacou. August, 1974.

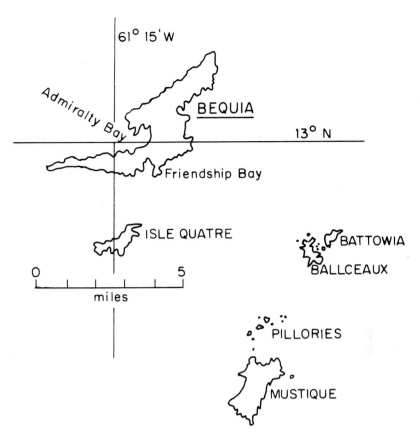

61° 15' W

Admiralty Bay

BEQUIA

13° N

Friendship Bay

ISLE QUATRE

BATTOWIA

BALLCEAUX

0   5

miles

PILLORIES

MUSTIQUE

CHAPTER V

BEQUIA SWEET

The Trade Winds dropped to nothing as the sultry afternoon wore on. A dark cloud appeared to windward and came drifting slowly down as *Eider* approached the two rocky cays which lie just off the southwestern tip of Bequia. The squall hit just as we brought the cays abeam, and for a few moments I was fully occupied hauling in the mainsheet. When I looked up to get my bearings, a small open boat had cut through a narrow pass between the two cays and taken up a windward course just ahead of us.

The wind was strong, but in the lee of the island there was only a small chop — ideal conditions for a brisk sail and an upbeat finish to what had been a dull day. The prospect of a brush with another boat added the frosting, and I leaned eagerly into the tiller. When we did not gain an inch in the course of ten minutes, I concluded that *Eider* was carrying too much sail, heeling out of her waterlines and generating too much turbulence. Ordinarily, I would not have taken the trouble to reef so close to port, with no danger to the yacht or her gear, but it vexed me not to go powering past that bobbing little boat. I went forward and rolled down the mainsail until the helm was balanced again.

"Now we will see the benefits of well-cut sails and a longer waterline," I told myself, smiling as I settled again at the tiller. But the little blue boat

47

fig. V-1. *Two-bow boats drawn ashore at Friend-ship Bay, Bequia. October, 1970.*

continued to dance provocatively ahead, the helmsman flinging water over his shoulder with the baling gourd while his companion, standing on the weather gunwale to stay the mast, appeared to leap with joy in the gusts.

I bore down grimly now, concentrating all my attention on overtaking the upstart. At last I sensed rather than saw a slight weakening, a sag to leeward not fully recovered.

"Well," thought I, "if I can't outfoot him, at least I can outpoint him — a taller rig and better cut sails are bound to tell." Soon the angle was wider and we were standing well over the little boat. Then suddenly, the helmsman eased sheets and bore away two points. It took a couple of seconds for me to register that the little boat was not bound to Port Elizabeth at the head of the bay as I was — he was off across the channel to St. Vincent, nine miles of open water with a strong tide running against the winds of the squall.

Any chagrin I may have felt was swept away in my admiration of the performance of the little boat; a closer look at these unique double-enders was well worth the trip to Bequia, even if nothing else was going on. Riding the wave of my enthusiasm, I set out the next day to do some measuring. This being Sunday, there was a good selection of fishing boats pulled ashore at Friendship Bay (fig. V-1).

One of these stood out in being especially well-maintained and having an unusual flared bow. Choosing *Country Girl* to measure turned out to be a particularly happy inspiration, as I later discovered, since she had won the medium-sized open boat class for the last three years at the Carriacou Regatta. As a result, a new generation of double-enders had been built to her lines.

48

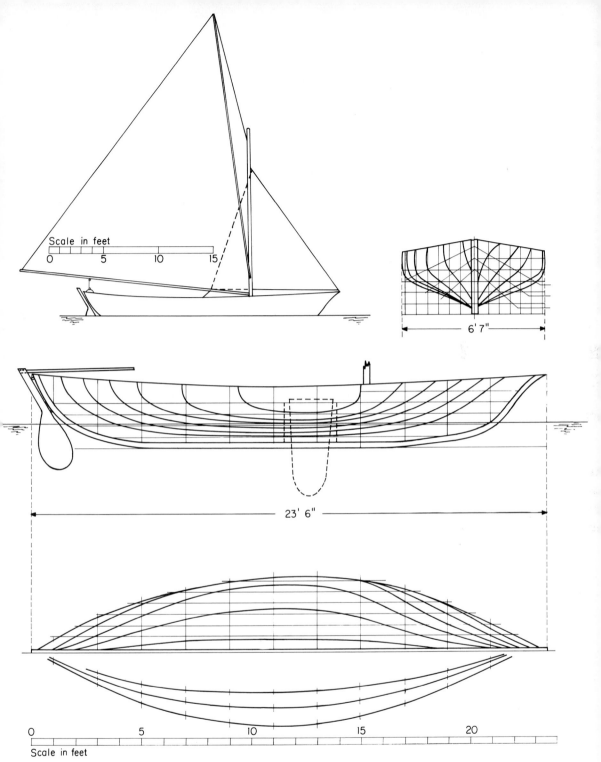

fig. V-2. Lines of Country Girl. *Built 1963 by Lennox Taylor. Taken off October, 1970.*

The lines of *Country Girl* (fig. V-2) reveal at a glance her aptitude for speed: extremely fine entry, sharp floors in the mid-section and fine run aft made possible by the double-ended design. As a matter of fact, the lines are so fine that one might well wonder if they are exaggerated. However, a glance at

fig. V-3. Bequia fishing boat Leopard *at the Whitsun Regatta. Admiralty Bay, Bequia. Photo by Ian Child.*

Ian Child's photo of *Leopard* (fig. V-3), built to the same lines as *Country Girl*, dispels all doubt — the lines are, in fact, extremely fine.

Two other features of these craft deserve comment since they are characteristic of the two-bow boats, as they are called in Bequia: the dagger board and the spritsail rig. The dagger board is, of course, a big factor in the weatherly ability of these boats — an ability of great importance since the better fishing grounds lie to windward of Bequia. The spritsail rig, in its turn, seems to be a handy means of increasing the height of the sail set without either a taller mast or an awkward gaff.

Just as I finished measuring, a pedestrian halted his somewhat erratic progress along the beach, stared for a moment, then sidled over.

"You must pay to take the model," he announced in a no-nonsense tone of voice.

"Are you the owner then?" I asked, playing a hunch.

"I is know him. You pay me and I giving to him." Bloodshot eyes measured me from the seamed black face.

I stalled a little longer by explaining what I was doing and why I wanted the lines. It seemed best to lay it on pretty thick, and the light of inspiration went on as I related the preceding day's impromptu race to explain my admiration.

50

"Oh, is you in the little yacht, then," interrupted my new friend, who had been, it developed, at the helm of the little boat bound for St. Vincent in the squall. Waving aside my continuing apologies, he proceeded with great gusto to tell me of his trip.

"After the fish done sell, we having a Good Time. Having a Good Time with the Boys. Having a Good Time with the Girls. Having a general, all around Good Time."

And still having one, by the look of it.

Later, after spending more time in Bequia, I learned that what my new-found friend was so exuberantly relating was, in fact, the downhill portion of a typical day for the Bequia fishermen: they leave the beach at 4 a.m. for the nine-mile beat out to the fishing grounds northeast of Mustique, trolling on the way out and hand-lining on the grounds. If the catch is good, they set sail shortly after noon for St. Vincent, a distance of about 15 miles. After the fish are sold, they sail home, again about 15 miles. In round numbers this makes a daily outing of some 40 miles plus fishing — all of it in an open boat, and most of it in the open sea.

Little more need be said about the seaworthiness and sailing ability of these small boats. However, at a later stage in my understanding of these matters, I decided that it would be better to have some hard data on performance. *Country Girl* had been sold to someone in St. Vincent, so I arranged a sailing trial with *Big Stuff,* another of the boats built to *Country Girl's* lines and that year's winner at Carriacou:

Point of sailing	Angle off the wind	Wind speed in knots	Boat speed in knots	Leeway angle	Boat speed - wind speed
Close-hauled	45°	12	5.4	10°	.45
	50°	16	6.1	6°	.38
Beam reach	90°	10	5.8	5°	.58
	100°	9	6.5	3°	.72
Broad read	135°	4.5	4.7	2°	—
Running	180°	4.5	4.8	0°	—

In Bequia there are several different classes of open boats, all of which are double-ended, spritsail rigged and equipped with some form of centerboard. The parent type is unquestionably the whaleboat — as any one on the island will tell you at the drop of a hat, "In Bequia, it having aplenty whalerman." In fact, whaling was such a focal point of island life that it seemed to merit a chapter of its own (Chapter VIII).

The lines of the *Dart* (fig. V-4), one of the two whaleboats still in service, are very similar to those of the Nantucket and New Bedford whaleboats (from which they are undoubtedly derived, cf. Chapter VIII), though perhaps just a little higher at the turn of the bilge. Also, the after sections are fuller than the forward sections, showing a greater assymetry in this respect than the lines of

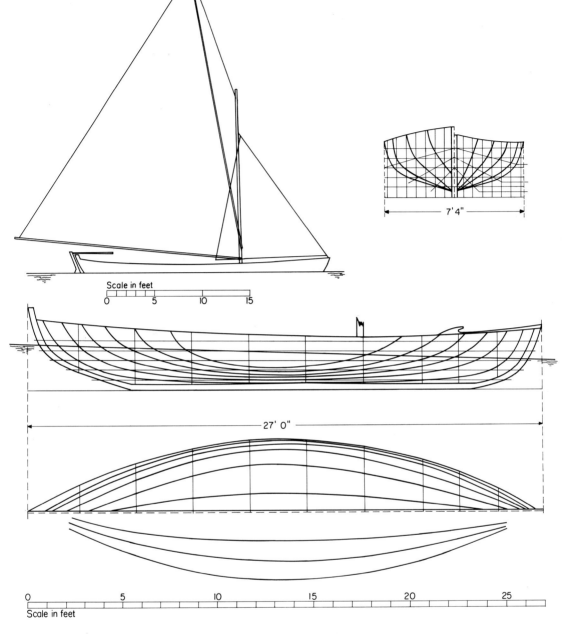

Scale in feet
0   5   10   15

7' 4"

27' 0"

0   5   10   15   20   25

Scale in feet

fig. V-4.   Lines of the whaleboat Dart. *Built 1955 by Athneal Olliverre. Taken off August, 1973.*

the Beetle whaleboat which I used for comparison. This difference is probably the result of recent and individual innovation; Athneal Olliverre, the builder and head harpooner, told me that he had made the *Dart* fuller aft so that she would not "squat" when being towed by a harpooned whale.

Along the south side of the island, I found several seine boats (fig. V-5) with lines and dimensions so similar to the whaleboats that I did not make a separate set of lines. These boats set sail with a large seine entirely filling the midships and patrol back and forth across the Grenadines Bank until they

fig. V-5. Seine boat being hauled ashore at Pagett
Farm, Bequia. December, 1971.

locate a school of the small, pelagic carangids locally known as "robin" (probably *Decapterus punctatus*). The seine is paid out as the boat circles, until the school is penned. Then the fish are dipped up in hand nets from the edges of the pen. Sometimes, by careful management, a single school can be worked by several boats for two or three days. During this time the boats shuttle to Bequia or St. Vincent as quickly as they are filled, which is why fast sailing is such an important characteristic of this type.

The commonest of the Bequia two-bow boats are the 16-18 footers (fig. V-6) which abound on all the beaches of the island. *Cedar Blossom* (fig. V-7) is typical of these hardy craft in which Bequians travel, fish, race, and voyage as far as Grenada. The lines show the expected similarity to the Nantucket whaleboat, with, however, proportionally higher sides than the larger classes, producing the same actual free board required for seaworthiness. In recent years, as small outboard motors have become available in the islands, many of these 18 footers have begun to carry a 7½ HP motor on an offset bracket fastened to the port side in the stern. When the outboard is in use, the rudder is unshipped; when sailing, the outboard is cocked up and lashed.

fig. V-6. Downwind leg of the Whitsun Regatta in
Admiralty Bay. Photo by Ian Child.

53

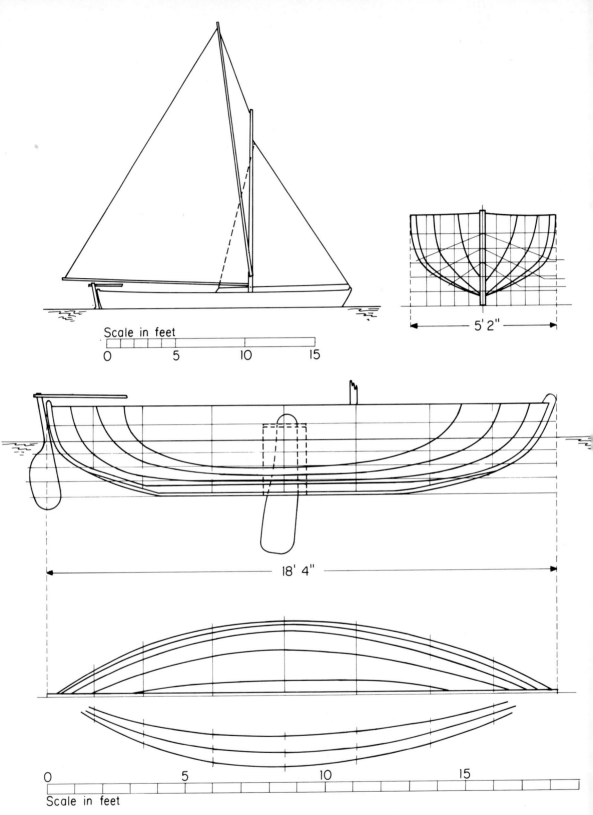

Scale in feet

0   5   10   15

5' 2"

18' 4"

0   5   10   15

Scale in feet

fig. V-7. Lines of fishing boat Cedar Blossom.
*Built 1968 by Haakon Mitchell. Taken
off May, 1971.*

54

fig. V-8. View of the harbor at Port Elizabeth, Bequia. October, 1970.

Port Elizabeth, at the head of Admiralty Bay, was still an active schooner port (fig. V-8) in 1972, though there no longer appeared to be any active building of large vessels. The "old heads" who foregather in the shade of the almond tree to discuss and decide these matters were all in agreement: the *Friendship Rose* (fig. V-9), launched in 1969, was undoubtedly the last of the

fig. V-9. Schooner Friendship Rose *beating up Admiralty Bay on a failing breeze. March, 1971.*

fig. V-10. Friendship Rose *careened in Admiralty Bay, Bequia. May, 1971.*

Bequia schooners. This being the case, I made the most of the opportunity offered when the *Rose* was careened (fig. V-10 & 11). Though insufficient for drawings, the photos give a fairly good idea of her lines.

fig. V-11. Friendship Rose *hauled down for painting in Admiralty Bay. May, 1971.*

fig. V-12. Launching the tern schooner Gloria
Colita, Admiralty Bay, Bequia. February,
1939.

In the course of my researches under the almond tree, repeated mention
was made of Reg Mitchell, a schooner-owner and captain of former times.
Though he was lost at sea only some 30 years earlier, Mitchell was already
legendary: he was seven feet tall; he was the only West Indian who ever
learned celestial navigation; and he went missing under circumstances absolutely guaranteed to endow a considerable body of folklore. Further information, first-hand and factual, was readily available — just down the beach at
the Frangipani Hotel, owned by the Hon. J. F. Mitchell, son of Reg. and M.P.
in St. Vincent for the Grenadines Constituency. "Son" Mitchell talked interestingly and well, about his father and his father's last vessel, the *Gloria
Colita*, reputedly the largest schooner ever built in the Lesser Antilles.

He brought out a snapshot of the 1939 launching of the *Gloria Colita*
(fig. V-12), and noting my interest, asked if I would like to see a model of the
schooner. To my delight and astonishment he brought out, not a painted toy
to be admired politely and put aside, but in fact the actual builder's half-
model from which the vessel was lofted (fig. V-13).

fig. V-13. Builder's half model of the schooner
Gloria Colita. Owned by Hon. J. F.
Mitchell.

The lines of the model might have been taken by unpinning the lifts and measuring them as was originally done — the ends of the pencils marks were still visible at each station. However, I hesitated to take such liberty with an object of obvious sentimental value, and was able to devise another method. The model was 55 inches long, which made it convenient to designate stations at 5 inch intervals. At each station I pressed a short length of copper wire against the model and then traced the curve so formed onto graph paper, thus forming the body plan of the hull. The buttocks and waterlines could then be developed from the body plan (fig. V-14).

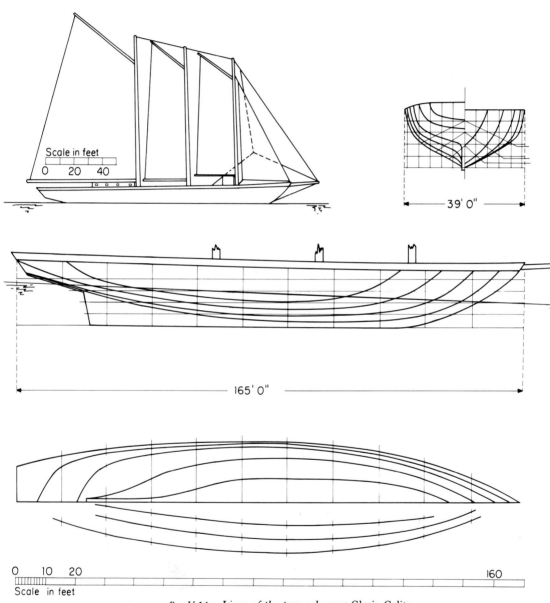

Scale in feet
0   20   40

39' 0"

165' 0"

0   10   20   160
Scale   in feet

fig. V-14.   *Lines of the tern schooner* Gloria Colita. *Built 1939 by Reginald Mitchell, Admiralty Bay, Bequia. Taken off, March, 1974.*

The *Gloria Colita* is interesting not only for her size (165 feet, 178 tons; largest vessel for which I found records in the Lesser Antilles), but also for her sharp bottom, extreme deadrise and three-masted rig. Sharp floors and marked deadrise are generally recognized as important characteristics of a fast-sailing hull. There is also the fact that the vee-bottom formed by sharply rising floors would have much greater longitudinal strength, an important consideration in such a long vessel.

Having gotten the lines of the hull from the builder's half model, I continued in luck and was able to make a sail plan by using the recorded length of the vessel and another photo which Son Mitchell had.

Even after allowing for the well-known inflationary tendencies of folklore, the builder of the *Gloria Colita* must have been an man of unusual abilities. Himself the son of a schooner builder, Mitchell owned two schooners before building the *Gloria Colita*. His first was the *Water Pearl* (94 feet, 68 tons), built in partnership with his father and launched in 1932. Two years later the schooner failed to come about when tacking over Bequia Head and was blown ashore. Next came the *Juliana*, a Nassau-built schooner, larger than the *Water Pearl*, though the size is not recorded in St. Vincent. With her, Mitchell freighted between British Guyana and Cuba and on one occasion set out to New York until turned back by heavy weather off Cape Hatteras.

Mitchell's widow, who now lives in St. Lucia, told me these and many other details of trips she made sailing and trading with her husband. She told of loading rice in BeeGee for Cuba, there loading sugar for Mobile, Alabama and finally returning to Cuba with lumber. She had particularly fond memories of Batista's Cuba — everything very cheap, and customs officers who brought fruit and flowers to the schooner as she lay at dock. She recalled holding the deck watch when Reg made his sights at noon and 4 p.m. (thus confirming one of the legendary attributes without my asking). She spoke fondly of the luxurious master's accommodations aboard the *Gloria Colita*, and less fondly about her responsibility for turfing out the crew's quarters when the vessel came to Bequia for a refit.

On his last voyage, Mitchell again loaded rice in BeeGee for Havana, and then loaded sugar for Venezuela. There he discharged his Bequia crew without explanation and sent them home. He shipped a Spanish-speaking crew and returned to Mobile, where he loaded lumber and cleared for Havana. No overdue report was ever made. The *Gloria Colita* was simply found abandoned and awash in the Gulf Stream by a U.S. Coast Guard patrol plane, which photographed her as she was found (fig. V-15). No report was ever had of Mitchell or the crew. The schooner was towed into Mobile and sold to one Hans Kulsen, U.S. citizen. This much is a matter of record, but the popular imagination of Bequia ranges well beyond the merely factual.

It is told in cryptic tones that there was food on the table in the captain's quarters, that no personal gear was found in the crew's quarters, that the

fig. V-15. Schooner Gloria Colita *awash and abandoned in the Gulf Stream. May, 1941. U. S. Coast Guard photo.*

ship's boat was gone, that the ship's dog was aboard and alive. In the photograph the foresail is still standing, which suggests that it was not storm or high winds that disabled the schooner. The version chiefly favored by the old heads is that the Spanish crew mutinied and abandoned ship after murdering Reg ("You can't trust a Spaniard. Never can. Ask anybody."). The heroic theory — chiefly favored by the younger set — is that Reg was kidnapped by a U-boat and pressed into service as a pilot, since it was surely known to the German High Command that "it only in Bequia you could get real true navigators." In support it is claimed that on several occasions when schooners were being sunk by the deck gun of a surfaced U-boat (as was frequently done), a tall dark man without uniform was seen on the bridge.

The most plausible suggestion I heard — too hardheaded and unromantic to find a place in the folklore — came from Emil Gumbs, a schooner owner and former captain from Anguilla who saw the *Gloria Colita* when she was being built, and noticed at the time that the planks were being butted on the frames. This is standard practice in vessels of moderate tonnage where the planking lumber is not long enough to stretch "from stem to stern." For a vessel as long as the *Gloria Colita*, Gumbs felt that the planks should have been butted between frames and through-bolted onto butt plates to compensate for the loss in strength at the butt joint. His theory was that the *Gloria Colita* ran into rough seas but little wind (not unusual in the vicinity of the Gulf Stream) which caused her to start some seams and make more water than the pumps could handle. The crew panicked and abandoned ship, perhaps in defiance of the captain's orders (with the possibility of bloodshed). And, as frequently happens in these cases, the boat and crew were lost while the schooner, loaded with lumber and unballasted, remained awash. Plausible it may be, but no account of loss at sea can ever answer all questions and conjectures. I'm sure that Gumbs' version will dampen no spirits in Bequia.

Although there was much of interest in Bequia, there appeared to be no further building of larger vessels. It saddened me that an island where seafaring was so much a part of an independent and enviable way of life should build no more schooners. But everywhere I inquired, the answer was the same: "No more vessel is building in these times." So Monday, November 2 was set for departure, and on Saturday afternoon I took my last stroll around an island that I had come to admire.

I climbed the steep, winding road which leads upward from the harbor to the top of a ridge, then drops down again to Friendship Bay and the communities along the South Side. At the top, I left the paved road and took an unpaved fork that dropped down to the bay at a new point. There, across the bay on a low bank above a small peeble beach, stood the gaunt carcass of a vessel in frames. Everyone had been so definite about no vessels being built that at first I doubted my eyes. But the long rays of the afternoon sun highlighted the far shore so that there was no possibility of question.

As I walked along the shore toward the vessel, the sand beach narrowed until I was forced to scramble up a steep bank and make my way along a footpath through the dry, thorny scrub. When the path emerged from the scrub, I was looking across a cleared and cultivated hillside at a small wooden house painted blue. An old white woman sat at the front window, her arms folded on the sill and her chin resting on her arms. As I approached, a small girl looked up, then scampered up the steps and disapeared.

"How do, sor," the old woman called.

Inside the urgent voice of the little girl was saying, "Mama, Mama. White man coming."

A slender, brown-skinned woman came to the half-door, wiping her hands on her apron and repeating the old woman's greeting.

When I asked who was building the vessel I had seen, she answered obliquely, "Yes, sor. Is he down by the bayside now."

She stood quietly with the little girl clinging to her skirts as I made my way past the house, over a low stone wall and down another footpath to the bay. There I found a man sitting on his heels among the shavings and wood chips, staring up at the frames of a small vessel. He was wearing faded shorts, a short-sleeved white shirt and a billed cap, homemade by the look of it. I greeted him and asked if he was building the vessel.

"Yes, sir," he replied, "The keel laid in August month."

"You're moving along very well, then."

"Well, is very hard these days, you know. Materials is very dear and no one want to work at all."

The remarks were pessimistic, and yet I sensed determination, too. He was lean, of medium build and deeply tanned, with a reserved and diffident manner. As he turned to speak to me, I noticed that his left hand was gone at the wrist and he had a long scar on his left thigh.

As we talked, he dropped the "sir" and began to speak more animatedly. Although he had never been to the Carriacou Regatta, he knew *Mermaid* and was planning to challenge her. He told of trips he had made as a boy to Barbados in his father's schooner, of the Nova Scotia-built vessels he had seen there. He told about the stockpile of suitably curved timbers under his house which he had been gathering for six years, and which he and two teen-aged boys hoped to turn into a vessel.

We talked until the sun was behind the island and it was time to start back to the harbor. Our conversation had produced much useful information about methods and possible design influences. Moreover, I felt a strong sympathy for the man's aspirations — he was building more than a vessel: he was trying to provide growing room for his family, which otherwise had two acres of rocky hillside as the limits of their world. A delay of a day or two to take off the lines would not have mattered; but nothing could be done before the hull was planked, and that was still a long way off. With regret, I wished the man well and went ahead as planned.

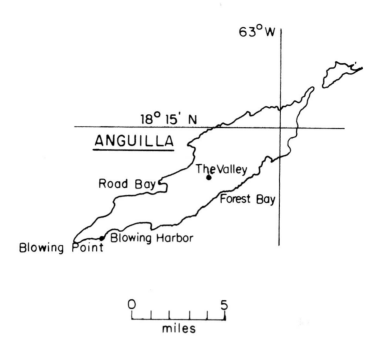

63°W

18° 15' N

ANGUILLA

The Valley

Road Bay

Forest Bay

Blowing Harbor

Blowing Point

0   5

miles

CHAPTER VI

ANGUILLA AGAIN

As I made my way north from Bequia, island-hopping and looking for schooner construction, it began to seem as if my project were in the home stretch. The end of the island chain was already in sight, and it had gotten noticeably easier, with practice, to take off lines.

Anguilla, as I knew from my earlier visit, was still an active boatbuilding center and had a sizable schooner fleet. These two facts, however encouraging for a boatmeasurer, constituted a somewhat startling defiance of certain geographical and meteorological realities. Anguilla, being low and flat, does not force the moisture-laden Trade Winds to rise and cool; consequently there is little rainfall. Moreover, the scant rain hardly even slows down as it soaks into the loose, limestone rubble of which the island is composed. Under these circumstances, there are no timber resources at all on the island, and I question whether there ever were.

Another problem is apparent from the geography of the coastline; Anguilla has many shallow bays, but not a single all-weather, hurricane-safe harbor. The upshot of these two unpleasant realities is that Anguilla has a boatbuilding industry without timber and a schooner fleet which is annually in jeopardy during the hurricane months of August and September. And these were not the only surprises, as I soon discovered.

One sun-baked afternoon while walking the dusty road from Sandy Ground to wherever else you want to go in Anguilla, I pondered the desolate and unproductive landscape dotted, this time in defiance of economic reality, with houses. Not just any houses, mind you, but solid houses, built of cement blocks, brightly painted and each showing, by many small signs, the pride of ownership. The Rev. Carty stopped to offer me a ride and explained as he drove.

"Anguilla is a remittance society; money is sent back to the island by Anguillans overseas. Husbands, sons, boyfriends — they work overseas and send back money so that a house is ready when they return. Why, do you know that there are more Anguillans in Perth Amboy than in Anguilla?"

I had not known, but could see the point. There was very little to do in Anguilla. In the past, sea island cotton was grown, and seed from Anguilla was in demand as far away as Louisiana since a small, dry island is ideal for maintaining the genetic purity of the longstaple varieties of cotton. However, synthetic fibers put an end to all that.

There is a small salt works operating at Sandy Ground; for this, at least, the climate of Anguilla is ideally suited. The large shallow lagoon lying behind the beach is flooded with sea water in late December, at the beginning of the dry season (i.e. when it is even drier than usual). By March, sufficient water has evaporated so that large crystals of nearly pure sodium chloride begin to form and settle to the bottom. Then the harvest begins. Workers, pushing small flat boats, wade the lagoon, scooping up the wet crystals, which are dumped on the beach to dry. Gradually a gleaming white mountain grows as the crystals dry before being ground and bagged. Much of this salt is sold to Trinidad, where it is used in the oil fields.

Apart from salt, Anguilla produces little except Anguillans. In most cases they must leave the island to find work, but for those with the necessary skills, boatbuilding becomes an alternative to exporting manpower. In boatbuilding, materials acquired elsewhere are brought to the island, there to be assembled into an asset which can return to the outside to earn.

Boatbuilding, Anguilla-style, is carried on in an informal manner ideally suited to the rhythm of island life. It all begins when someone gets together a little money and contacts MacDuff Richardson or Egbert Connor. Whichever man is available finds additional carpenters and arranges to use a section of beach. The keel is brought from Guyana by schooner, and the framing timbers are cut on St. Martin or St. Eustatius. The materials are dumped on the beach, and work begins, continuing as long as money and materials last. When either runs short, the carpenters return to fishing and subsistence agriculture until work on the vessel resumes. No rent is paid for the building site, there are no formal contracts with delivery dates and penalty clauses, no minimum wage, no witholding tax and no bookkeeping chores. In short, there is very little overhead and no reason at all to make haste and fly in the face of circumstance — that only get folks vexed and creates additional delays.

fig. VI-1. Schooner New London *under construction at Forest Bay, Anguilla.* March, 1970.

This was definitely the timetable followed in the construction of the first vessel that I measured in Anguilla — and incidentally, the largest I saw being built anywhere in the islands. The *New London,* set up by MacDuff Richardson, had been three years under construction when I measured her in 1971 (fig. VI-1) and was not launched until two years later. At the time I took off the lines, Egbert Connor (fig. VI-2) had taken over as master carpenter and was working with two helpers and a caulker (fig. VI-3).

The large size of the *New London* made her something of a chore to measure, but on the other hand, the flat floors and full bow sections made it easy to draw and fair the lines (fig. VI-4). The result is a very full-carrying hull which was said to carry as much as 140 tons of cargo for her owner, Albert Lake (fig. VI-5, at left). Although decidedly unglamorous in other respects, it is interesting to note that the run of the *New London* is smooth and well formed. The broad, flat transom would immediately mark her as Anguilla-built in any port in the Lesser Antilles.

In her rig the *New London* goes one step beyond the *Yankee Girl* in yielding to the attractions of diesel power. The *Yankee Girl,* though rigged with only a single mast, was proportioned for a full sailing rig, whereas the *New London* is rigged as a schooner without a mainmast (fig. VI-6). There is a logic to this, since the *New London* was built to trade primarily between

fig. VI-2. *Egbert Connor at work on the* New London, *Forest Bay, Anguilla. March, 1970.*

fig. VI-3. *Rueben Richardson caulking on the* New London, *Forest Bay. March, 1970.*

Anguilla and Puerto Rico with stops in the Virgin Islands. On this route the wind is either dead ahead or dead astern, and the schooner rig is not well suited to either point of sailing.

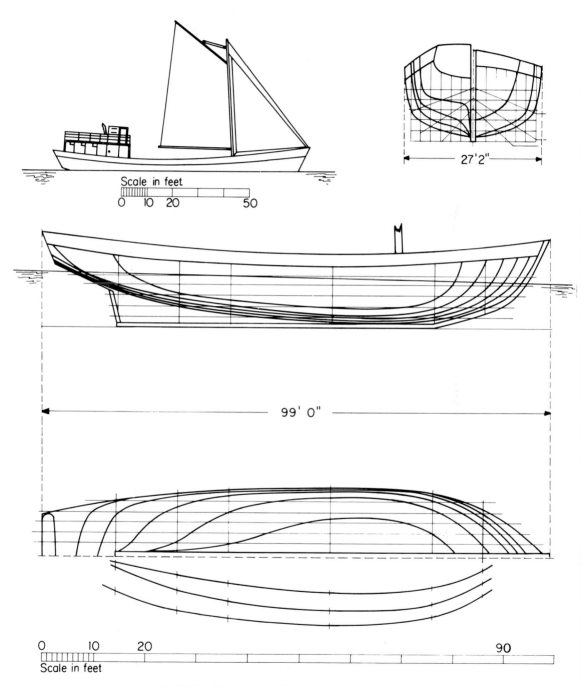

Scale in feet
0   10   20   50

27'2"

99' 0"

0   10   20   90
Scale in feet

fig. VI-4. Lines of the New London. Built 1972
MacDuff Richardson and Egbert Connor
at Forest Bay, Anguilla. Taken off,
January, 1971.

*fig. VI-5.   Owner Albert Lake (left) and the builders
of* New London, *Forest Bay, Anguilla.
January, 1971.*

fig. VI-6.   The New London *waiting for dock space,
Port-of-Spain, Trinidad. February, 1975.*

fig. VI-7. *Mack Connor (right), owner of the* Lady
Mack *(background) at Blowing Point,
Anguilla. January, 1971.*

At Blowing Point, a reef harbor near the southwest tip of the island, the
Lady Mack was hauled ashore for repairs (fig. VI-7), giving me an unusual opportunity to take the lines of an older vessel. Although the *Lady Mack* was
built as recently as 1966 and fitted with an engine at launching, she had the

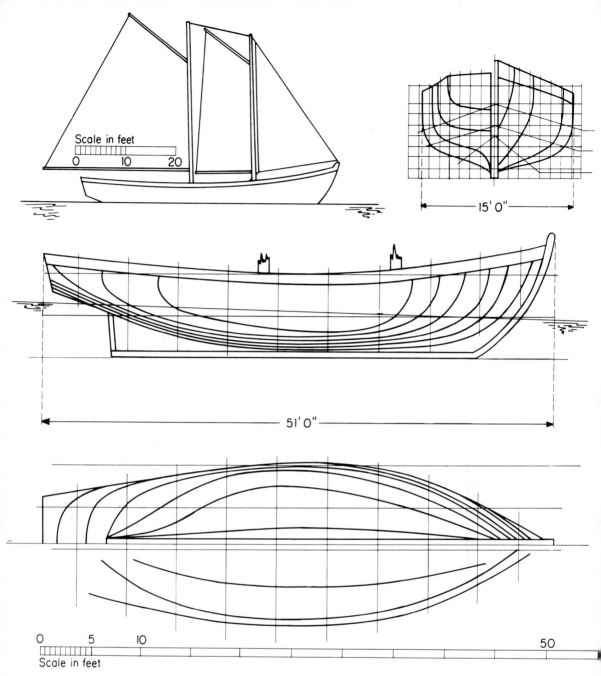

Scale in feet
0   10   20

15' 0"

51' 0"

0   5   10   50
Scale in feet

fig. VI-8.   Lines of schooner Lady Mack. Built 1966
by Mack Connor at Blowing Point,
Anguilla. Taken off, January, 1971.

unmodified lines of a traditional all-sail schooner (fig. VI-8). The marked sheer
of the deck provides generous freeboard despite relatively little drag to the
keel. The stem, less raking and curved than the New London, gives the Lady
Mack the correspondingly finer entry which might be expected of an all-sail
vessel. The floors of the mid-section are a compromise between the flat floors
of a full-carrying hull and the sharp floors of a fast sailer. The run aft is well-
formed and has a hard knuckle on the transom, as can be seen in the photo.

The *Lady Mack* was the third schooner built, owned and captained by Mack Connor (fig. VI-7, on the right). His earlier vessels were lost in the hurricanes of 1950 and 1960 (underscoring the hazards of not having a hurricane hole). In setting up his vessel, Conor used the general rule of thumb — a beam-to-length ratio of 1:4 — with, however, an individual variation.

Speaking of his first schooner, the *Baby Mack*, which had a long overhanging stern, Connor said, "When she load heavy, the stern steer the boat." After a couple of near disasters when the vessel was hard to bring about, Connor concluded, "If is a longer vessel you want, then put a longer keel." And in fact, the *Lady Mack* is noticeably short-ended, being some 9 feet shorter than a strict 1:4 ratio.

fig. VI-9. *Anguilla fishing boats, Sandy Ground,
Anguilla. January, 1971.*

Fishing and fishing boats are an integral part of the subsistence livelihood pattern in all the islands, including Anguilla (fig. VI-9). In addition to everyday practical employment, these boats are spruced up and raced on New Year's Day, Whitsun, the August Bank Holiday, and on Bastille Day in nearby St. Martin.

fig. VI-10. Egbert Connor's fishing boat, Bluebird. *Sandy Ground, Anguilla.
January, 1971.*

Egbert Connor's boat, *Bluebird* (fig. VI-10) — an obvious choice since I
already knew the owner — yielded the set of lines shown in fig. VI-11. The
upright stem and straight bow frames produce a very fine entry, so fine that
the waterlines forward appear to be hollow, though they are not. Sharp floors
and a very high "tuck" result in a smooth run and a very easy bottom. Much
time and thought have been given to modifying these boats for racing (fig. VI-
12), with the result that they have acquired some impractical traits: the sharp
bottom makes them a little "cranky" (unsteady), and the deep draft makes
them difficult to haul shore. In compensation, they are very graceful and fast,
though I am not sure just how fast since I never had the opportunity to get
sailing data (I did get data for a similar type in St. Martin, cf. Chapter XII).

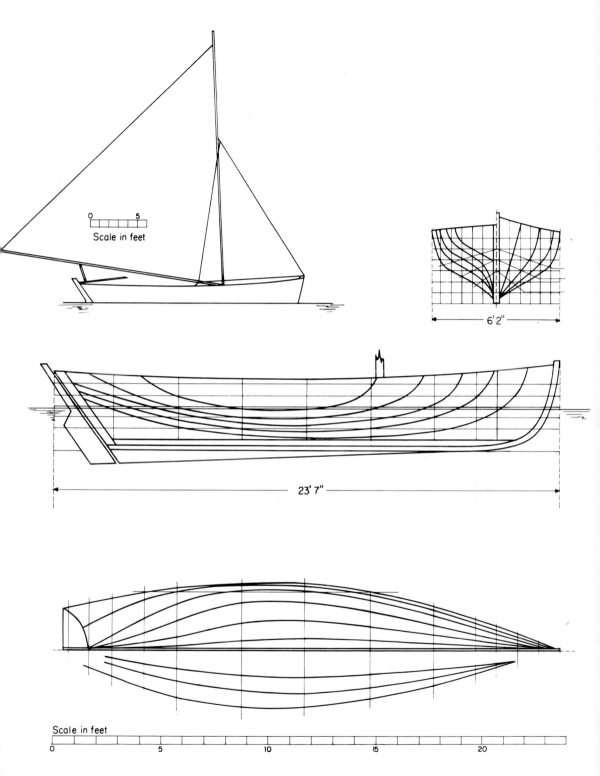

Scale in feet

6' 2"

23' 7"

Scale in feet

fig. VI-11. Lines of Bluebird. *Built 1960 by Egbert Connor, Sandy Ground, Anguilla. Taken off January, 1971.*

fig. VI-12. Anguilla fishing boat racing on Bastille Day at Marigot Bay, St. Martin. July, 1974.

On my second trip to Anguilla I stayed longer, became better acquainted, and as a result got a chance to sail aboard the *Warspite* (fig. VI-13), grand old lady of the Anguilla fleet. In addition to her monthly trips carrying salt to Trinidad, the *Warspite* had a contract to carry supplies and relief crew twice a month to the lighthouse on Sombrero Island, 40 miles northwest of Anguilla. In January of 1971, Emil Gumbs, owner of the *Warspite*, suggested that I go along to get the feel of a schooner at sea.

Departure time was 4:00 A.M., but I was awake by 2:30, too excited to stay in my bunk any longer. The moon was down, and *Eider* rocked gently in the soft, inky darkness. After a time, sounds began to reach me from the shore — the murmur of voices, the hollow grating of a boat dragged across the beach, the thud and splash of oars being shipped. I hailed softly and went aboard with the crew, who began to clear off gear while the boat returned to the beach for passengers and supplies.

Four men moved forward in the darkness and set about shackling the two-part jib halyard to the heavy anchor chain. Three men tailed the halyard and began to take out the slack while the fourth cast off the chain from the samson post. Then all four began to heave, transmitting the rhythm of the work with body and breath, until all had settled smoothly into the load. At each heave, the rattling chain rose dripping from the water, sinking again as its weight pulled the schooner forward. When the jib halyard was two-blocked, one man stopped the chain at the hawse pipe while the halyard was let run, dropping

fig. VI-13. Schooner Warspite *bound for Sombrero*
Island. January, 1971.

the chain along the deck. The block was unshackled and taken forward so that
the sequence could be repeated. In this leisurely manner, it took a little over a
half hour to bring the *Warspite* short on her anchor.

When the lighthouse crew and supplies were aboard, the boat was hauled
up on the throat and peak halyards of the foresail and secured on deck. As each
job was finished the crew moved without instruction to the next. Soon the big
mains'l was peaked up and flopping idly in the faint breeze, a pre-dawn har-
binger of the Trade Winds. Abruptly, the engine roared into life, and we
powered forward over the anchor until it broke out and we had room to swing

the head of the vessel around. As the mains'l caught the breeze and filled, it dragged the sheet squealing through the blocks, to slap tight against the stern rail. Two men forward worked to get the heavy anchor catted. Another group hoisted the jib, and then the stem staysail.

Once clear of the bay, the *Warspite* took the freshening breeze on her starboard quarter and began to quicken to her sails. The helmsman leaned forward, peering into the dark as he piloted the schooner past the shoal patches which lie to the south and the west of Dog Island. After half an hour, he relaxed visibly and lit a dim light inside the cabin, slid aside a small wooden panel and exposed the compass which was mounted on the cabin trunk. He glanced up and motioned me to a seat beside him on the wheel box. I slid into place and gingerly grasped the iron spokes of the wheel, while the helmsman stepped back to the big cleat where the mainsheet was secured.

"Shake her, boy," he called abruptly, "Shake her."

The command came as a complete surprise to me, but the expression was so apt that it took only a second to grasp what was wanted. I spun the wheel and luffed while he overhauled the mainsheet.

"Again," he urged, then stood for the space of a minute looking at the mains'l, stretched in a taut curve upward to the gaff. Apparently satisfied, he made up the sheet on the heavy cleat and returned to the wheel box. I started to yield my place, but he motioned me to stay.

We were going at a good clip, and the schooner held her course with little help from me. As the overtaking waves rose under the starboard quarter and gurgled forward along the keel, the *Warspite* first lifted, then surged diagonally across the face of the wave to settle softly into the trough as the next wave gathered. Out away from the island, where the Trade Wind was well-established, I waited expectantly for the engine to be shut off, now that its work was done. I wanted my night passage on a windjammer pure and undefiled by the whine of a GMC diesel.

The engine droned on, however, oblivious to the delicacy of my sentiments. As it became obvious that it was going to be with us for the duration, I gave the matter a little further thought. However romantic it might be for me, this was not, for the captain and crew, a nostalgic journey to recapture the sensations of the age of sail. For them, it was simply another day's work and not an especially easy one at that. An engine makes the work quicker, easier and safer; for these benefits, a little unromantic noise is not too high a price. Besides, the worst thing in the world for a marine engine is to be used briefly, then shut down to sit in the salt-saturated damp of the bilge until needed again.

So we continued, the whine of the engine punctuated by the squeal of the gaff as it swayed with the lift and roll of the swells that sweep through the Anegada Passage into the Caribbean Sea. The sun rose behind us, slowly warming into activity the passengers and crew, drawing them out of the corners where they had been sheltering from the night's chill (fig. VI-14). Soon the cook, muttering and grumbling to himself, began to serve tin cups of hot,

fig. VI-14. Sunrise aboard the Warspite *en route
to Sombrero Island, January, 1971.*

sweet tea along with a thick slice of bread and a cold piece of fried barracuda.

Two hours after we set sail, the loom of Sombrero Light became visible; by nine o'clock we were lying-to in the lee of the island, a high-sided disk of pitted limestone punched up from the ocean floor to stand as a sentinel in the middle of the Anegada Passage. There was, in the lee, a three-fathom bottom over a rocky shelf, but holding was poor and the chance of fouling too great to anchor. In consequence, the *Warspite* lay-to with mains'l sheeted close and the helm lashed hard over (fig. VI-15).

The boat was gotten over the side, and the first load of passengers started ashore as the schooner slowly side-slipped downwind. When the boat was ready to return for another load, the mate put the engine in gear and edged in toward the cliffs. All of the crew not otherwise occupied got fishing lines over the side and were soon hauling in snapper and grouper in profusion.

I went ashore in the second boatload to see what there was to see: the concrete tower which housed the light, concrete living quarters for the crew — and the twisted and rusting girders of the former light tower which was destroyed when waves swept the island during the hurricane of 1950. The base of the old tower was located at least fifty feet above the surface of the sea, and the rusted girders had been structural grade steel — the storm that destroyed these must have been awesome indeed.

The relieved crew was aboard by noon, and the boat was again stowed on deck. The return trip was sailed on a close reach, bringing us to Anguilla at 4:00 P.M., 40 miles in 4 hours exactly, an average of 10 knots. Later, I asked

fig. VI-15. Schooner Warspite *lying-to in the lee of*
Sombrero Island. January, 1971.

the *Warspite's* captain, Arthur Connor (fig. VI-16), about some of the schooners passage time. He replied eagerly, with obvious pride in the *Warspite's* reputation:

Anguilla to Sombrero, 40 miles in 3½ hours. 11.5 knots, light.

Anguilla to Guadeloupe, 195 miles in 26 hours. 7.5 knots, loaded.

Anguilla to San Juan, 170 miles downwind in 22 hours. 7.7 knots, light.

And then he told again, in loving detail, the story of the *Warpite's* most famous passage, though it had occurred when he was no more than a boy. In the 1920's workers went every year from Anguilla to the Dominican Republic to work in the sugar cane harvest. On these trips the *Warspite* carried as many as three hundred cane cutters; she and the other schooners making the trip had to clear from St. Martin since British regulations did not permit such loading. On the return trip in 1929, the *Warspite*, the *Eagle*, the *Betsy*, the *Ismay*, the *Gladys*, and the *Industry* cleared together from La Romana in the Dominican Republic.

The rest of the schooners began the long beat home in the usual way — tacking off and on, under the southern coasts of the Dominican Republic and Puerto Rico, hoping for relief from head winds and currents by hugging the shore. The *Warspite* took a chance and held on the port tack, taking a long board to the south until even the heights of Puerto Rico were lost to view. On

fig. VI-16. Arthur Connor, captain of the Warspite.
Road Harbor, Anguilla. May, 1975.

the second day out, the Trade Winds backed well into the north, bringing the *Warspite* home in 3½ days, still on the port tack.

The straight line distance for this passage is 360 miles but a vessel going to windward sails a distance roughly twice the chart distance. In addition, I figured 84 miles (84 hours x 1 knot equatorial drift current) of leeway and computed the average speed for the passage to be 9.8 knots — on the wind and without an engine! Using 11.5 knots and 9.8 knots, I calculated speed/length ratios of 1.44 and 1.22 respectively. In *The Search For Speed Under Sail*, Howard Chapelle, who devoted much of his life to these matters, remarks, "Long and intensive observation shows that the highest service speed usually recorded in a seagoing sailing vessel of good design, with an efficient rig, is in the neighborhood of a speed/length ratio of 1.25 - 1.35."

From the foregoing it is clear that the *Warspite* is a fast sailer by worldly standards as well as by local tradition. And, in addition to being a fast sailer, she was also the oldest vessel that I found in active service.

The *Warspite* was built in 1918 by J.T. Hughes to the design of her original owner, A.R. Carty. Materials were so scarce (then as now) that timbers were used from an abandoned sloop, the *Gazelle*. Originally the *Warspite* was 62 feet long, 18.3 feet in beam, 7.6 feet in the hold and 37 registered tons. Later, in 1928, she was "stretched" — meaning in local parlance that she was cut in two, a fourteen-foot piece was scarfed into her keel, frames were added and the vessel rebuilt to her present dimensions of 78 feet in length, 20 feet on the beam, 9.6 feet in the hold and 72 registered tons.

The details of the *Warspite's* colorful career seem worth recording, not only because they form an important part of the folklore of Anguilla, but also for the clues given about her long and profitable life. In this, I was fortunate because Emil Gumbs, the *Warspite's* present owner and the nephew of her original owner, lived at Sandy Ground and was exceptionally well-informed about his venerable schooner.

Gumbs laughingly said that the schooner had been repaired and rebuilt so extensively over the years that she contained none of her original wood. She has twice sunk at her moorings and once been abandoned at sea. But always she has returned to service — largely, I conclude, from the persistence and ingenuity of Gumbs.

In 1954 on a return trip from Trinidad, the schooner was sailing to leeward of the Grenadines when water was found in the hold. Pumping did not reduce the level and the crew put the boat over the side. The captain refused to leave the vessel and shamed the crew into returning aboard. Between them, they managed to get into Admiralty Bay and beach the schooner. Gumbs then went to Bequia and stayed for several months, supervising the replacement of the keel — with the vessel careened!

On another occasion Gumbs himself was captaining the *Warspite* on a return trip from Trinidad with a load of cement. They passed the heavily-trafficked Bocas (at the mouth of the Gulf of Paria) at sunset and Gumbs took the wheel through the night. Toward dawn, he raised the light at Pt. Salines, Grenada and, calling the mate to relieve him, went below to sleep. In midmorning he waked with the sensation that something was wrong. Scrambling on deck, he found that the schooner had fallen into the morning calm that prevails behind Grenada and drifted gently onto a coral patch that lies off Long Point. The sea was flat and the day fair, so the mate was admiring the green splendors of Grenada's heights and waiting for the tide to float the vessel off.

Without hesitation, Gumbs roused the crew, got the hatch cover off and began to throw sacks of cement into the sea until the schooner had been lightened enough to kedge off the coral. He judged it the height of folly to sit idle while the vessel was in danger, however remote the danger might seem.

Such a response is unusual in the islands, where sailing conditions are so nearly ideal that it is easy to become careless. Few captains have formal training, navigational aids are scarce and unreliable, but above all it is simply hard to believe that danger can exist in such a warm and wonderful world. In fact, there is on occasion a strong surge that sets onto the leeward coast of Grenada out of a clear sky and sends breakers smoking across the shoal where the schooner was stranded.

Gumb's response, to my mind, represents the very highest calibre of seamanship. Many people are capable of prudence when facing a clear and present danger, but it is much rarer to find someone able to anticipate hazards while the sea is calm, and who, moreover, does not hesitate to take measures that may appear unnecessary, even faint-hearted and foolish. In the long run such prudence pays off, as I believe the age of the *Warspite* admirably demonstrates.

There were many excellent reasons for taking off the lines of the *Warspite*, but it meant catching her when she went up on the marine railway in St. Lucia, which I never managed to do. On my final trip to Anguilla it occurred to me, *in extremis*, that the job might somehow be done with the vessel in the water. The method I adopted was simple enough in conception: I marked stations on the rail where convenient, measured the beam at each station and hung over the side a string, weighted and knotted at one-foot intervals. With diving mask, snorkel and a waterproof carpenter's rule, I dived into the water to measure the horizontal distance from the knots on the string to the hull, calling out the measurements to a helper on deck. It was all pretty straightforward except for the communications link. For each measurement — and there were a lot of them at each station and ten stations in all — I had to surface, remove the snorkel from my mouth, spit out my ration of sea water and call out the numbers loud enough that they could be heard over the slap and creak of the schooner.

The method, however cumbersome, did work, and I got my measurements. But by the time the job was done, I was so cold, hoarse and waterlogged that it was a distinct relief that the method had not occurred to me earlier.

The lines of the *Warspite* (fig. VI-17) are an excellent example of the principle characteristics of a fast-sailing hull: sharp floors in the mid-section with a high easy turn of the bilge; a fine entrance with slight hollow in the lower waterlines; and a long easy run begun well forward and carried smoothly past the stern post and onto the transom.

The rigging plan shown is much shorter than the original; the masts have twice been cut down — first when an engine was fitted and later, when a larger engine was installed. Once, during World War II when materials were scarce, the mainmast broke and the mains'l was set on the foremast. With that rig, she sailed even faster than before, Gumbs told me with a chuckle. At the time I made my measurements, the foremast was out and Gumbs was considering rigging her again with topmasts. He had an eye on the day-charter business in

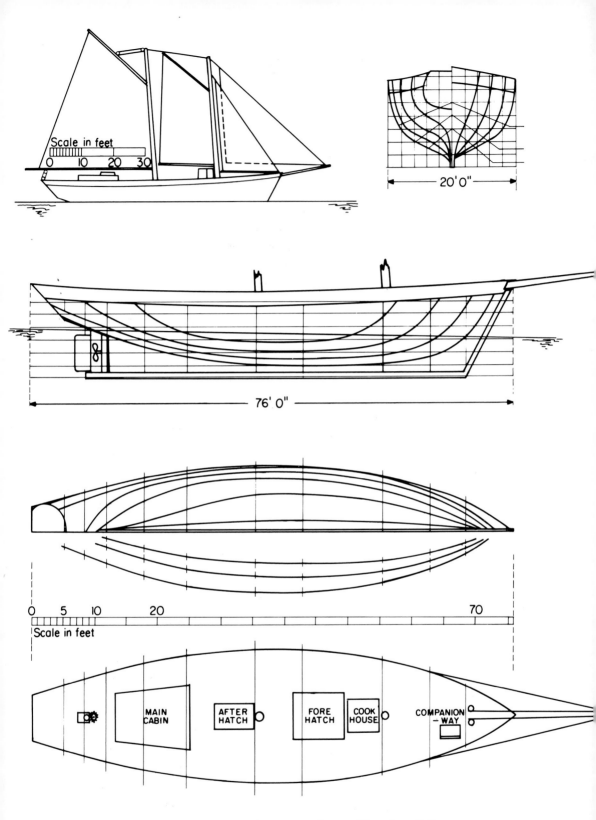

Scale in feet
0   10   20   30

20' 0"

76' 0"

0   5   10   20   70
Scale in feet

MAIN
CABIN

AFTER
HATCH

FORE
HATCH

COOK
HOUSE

COMPANION
— WAY

fig. VI-17. Lines of schooner Warspite. *Built
1918 by J. T. Hughes at Sandy Ground,
Anguilla. Taken off May, 1975.*

82

nearby, tourist-booming St. Martin. I wished him well with the project for it would be a grand thing to see once again a schooner with top hamper standing into Road Bay.

In a conversation with Arthur Connor, the *Warspite's* captain, the following interesting fact came to light:

"In Anguilla we does sail on the shares. Can't get people to sail on the month, only on shares. Been so since ancient time. If the owner is buy a car, we is buy a chair."

He was referring to the fact that in Anguilla, alone among the islands I visited, trading vessels operate on a share plan similar to that used by fishermen the world over: from the gross earnings of the vessel, running expenses (fuel, food, harbor dues, commissions, etc.) are deducted. Of net earnings, the owner takes one-third, and the crew share equally in the remaining two-thirds. Then the captain is paid an additional half-share from the owner's portion.

The advantage to the owner is obvious — when the vessel is not earning, there is no labor cost. But the advantage to the crew is less obvious. It would appear that it suits the crew to work intermittently and to know that they have an assured share of a profitable venture. It was a little startling that all members of the crew share equally from captain to cabin boy, but Connor was very definite on that point. It was another one of those surprising discoveries which, taken altogether, constitute the uniqueness of Anguilla.

The skills and traditions of boatbuilding were already well-established in Anguilla when official records were begun in the 1840's, even though the island lacks those natural features favorable to sea-faring. There are, as remarked earlier, no timber resources on the island and probably never were. Of the island's four anchorages, three are reef-struck and difficult of access and the fourth is shallow and subject to rollers from the north in the winter months. None provides a secure, all-weather moorage.

By contrast, the nearby islands of St. Martin, St. Barts, and St. Eustatius have better resources — timber or harbors or both — and appear to have similar ethnic and cultural backgrounds. Yet these islands have seen only sporadic maritime activity, whereas Anguilla has had a well-founded and continuous industry from early times.

My best explanation for this enigma is that the difference is to be found in the Anguillans themselves. Though they come in all shades from black to white, they seem to have the cohesion and the shared attitudes which may be an outgrowth of their common poverty. In conventional terms, Anguilla is poor and unproductive and probably always was. However, it is my observation that to be barren and unproductive in the Caribbean is frequently a blessing in disguise: there is little to attract the exploiters who come in the first wave, and therefore, little to do for the reformers who come when times change. This is certainly the case in Anguilla where Anguillans have been left almost entirely alone to make their own way in a harsh environment, developing in the process a sense of purpose and independence which is their heritage and principle natural resource.

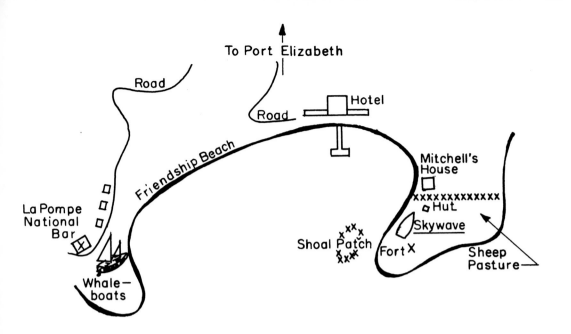

CHAPTER VII

MAKE THEE AN ARK

The big tamarind tree cast a welcome shadow in the glare of the afternoon sun, strong even in January, and I was glad to stop. The road that wound upward from the harbor was steep, and the view from the top was spectacular. I rested and drank in the always-new panorama of sea and islands, while my eagerness struggled with a nagging uncertainty. While still in Anguilla, it had seemed a fine and workable plan to return to Bequia and help with the building of the little sloop that I had seen on the shore at Friendship Bay. This plan, already stirring the first time I talked with the builder, had teased at the back of my mind for three months. Now, with new arrangements and a more flexible schedule, I was back for as long as it took, and feeling more than a little sheepish.

How much help was I really going to be? I had some tool-handling ability, but certainly not the skills of a ship's carpenter. How would the solitary builder on Pt. Hilary regard my offer of help? I felt entirely incapable of walking up and announcing the simple truth: that I was deeply moved by the dreams and plans of a poor and simple man to provide for his family and himself by building a vessel; that I wanted to watch and help and learn from him. Such an announcement, no matter how sincere, would surely convince the man that I was eccentric if not actually dangerous. I felt more ill at ease with each passing moment.

From the branches above my head, a white-eyed grackle called, "Bek-wee, bek-wee. Tsweet, tsweet." (The grackles in Bequia really say this and say it clearly. Elsewhere, even only nine miles away in St. Vincent, this species, *Quiscalus lugubris*, sings a different tune.) Having stated his opinion, the glossy black bird edged a little closer, rolled his pearly eye at me, then retreated to a higher branch. Taking this as a good omen, I allowed eagerness to prevail over uncertainty and resumed my trek, downhill now, on the narrow road leading to the bay.

When I reached the little blue house, the old lady was seated at the same window in the same attitude, and the builder was sitting on a plank nailed between the two palm trees that grew in front of the house. Their greeting was warm and natural. My uncertainty vanished; these were unaffected people, glad to welcome a face that a single visit had made familiar. I asked how they were and how the vessel was progressing. No other explanation of my presence was necessary.

Down by the bayside the vessel stood (fig. VII-1), all the frames now in place and secured by the "bends" (sheer planks). The builder and I squatted on the wood chips in the shade and talked. We talked of high prices and the

fig. VIII-1. *Mitchell's vessel in frames. Friendship Bay, Bequia. January, 1971.*

85

difficulties of getting materials. We talked of what it cost to build a vessel and what one might earn. We talked of *Mermaid* and what it would take to beat her. We talked ourselves onto familiar ground and then onto personal ground.

The builder's name was Haakon Mitchell, he was born in 1928 and he rented from the government the 13 acres that formed Pt. Hilary. In addition he owned 2 adjacent acres where his house stood, where he planted his crops and raised his family of seven. On the rented land he grazed sheep, which had been his principle source of income since losing his left hand in a fishing accident five years earlier.

Sensing my interest, Mitchell began to explain in greater detail what had gone into the vessel thus far. He had begun to put aside money and materials five years earlier, soon after he returned from the hospital, knowing that his days as a fishermen were over when he lost his hand. Under the little house an assortment began to grow of bits and pieces that might someday be woven into the fabric of a vessel: pieces of timber with a useful curve, lengths of rope, odd blocks, pieces of iron rod. An odd collection it seemed to me until I knew more about the difficulties of supply in the islands. All manufactured goods are imported and frequently scarce even on the larger islands; items as common as nails are sometimes unavailable for extended periods. It is a good rule, I learned, never to pass up anything that might eventually be useful.

After five years, when everything seemed right, Mitchell sent to Guyana for the keel, relying for transport on the good offices of his half-brother, mate on the *Lady Angela.* In August of 1970 the keel was laid on a low bank above the pebble beach below the Mitchells' house. The sternpost was mortised into the keel 18 inches ahead of the butt and raked to a degree that "seemed right." Next the stem, a single curved timber, was butted onto the forward end of the keel, with a small shoulder left on the upper surface of the stem to support it where it joined the keel. Both stem and sternpost were supported with a miscellany of posts and props.

Two pairs of center frames were set up at the mid-point of the keel. These "modeling" frames were shaped, before erecting, to a mold nailed up from rough lumber (Mitchell was somewhat secretive about his molds and did not show them to me until much later). After the centers were in place, a pair of bow frames were set up at the forward end of the keel, and finally the main transom frames were butted onto the sides of the sternpost at the top of the "tuck" (the tuck, also called deadrise, is the vertical area from the keel up to the point where the run passes the sternpost and opens onto the transom; the height of the tuck is a major factor in lateral resistance and the windward ability of a hull. It also contributes materially to the difficulties of planking).

With these key elements in place, long strips of wood called "ribbands" were nailed to the stem and bent around the modelling frames to form a shell into which the intermediate frames were fitted one by one. This was a slow process: scraps of sawn lumber were nailed together and cut to approximately the shape required. This shape was then scribed onto a naturally curved timber, which was then shaped with saw, axe and adze. After roughing to the scribed line, the timber was lifted into place and the high spots marked, before being returned to the ground for more shaping. When the frame fitted into the ribbands without producing any "unfairness," the lower end was spiked to the keel and the upper end braced across to the top of the opposite member of each pair. Shores were also placed as needed (fig. VII-1).

All the structural timbers of a West Indian vessel (excepting only the keel) are shaped by hand as needed from West Indian white cedar *(Tabebuia heterophylla)*. This wood is so important in the islands that it deserves additional comment, the first being that it is not really a cedar at all. In fact, it is a deciduous tree with glossy, dark green leaves and pale purple, trumpet-shaped flowers; except for the flowers, it might better be called West Indian oak. Like oak, the wood is light in color, tough, rot-resistant, and holds fastenings extremely well.

In habitats with abundant rainfall, this species forms a tall, straight tree; on the arid, salt-sprayed windward coasts, the tree grows tougher and denser, forming the curved and twisted shapes that are ideally suited to boat-building. Mitchell, in common with many other builders, preferred to cut his timbers during the waning of the moon, a time when, it is believed, the sap is out of the wood, allowing better curing and greater rot-resistance. When possible the timbers were worked while still green and relatively easy to shape.

One afternoon, during the "observer" phase of my stay in Bequia, I walked to Pt. Hilary to see if anything new had taken place with the vessel. Mitchell's wife, Winnie, came out as I approached the house.

"No one down by the bayside, sir," she said. "Gone to Ravine to cut a timber."

She indicated a direction up and over the ridge that lay behind the little house. After a steep climb and a scrambling descent, I came to a tiny bay where a dry water-course (called a gut in the islands) entered the sea. I followed the sound of an axe, climbing the steep-sided gut until I found Mitchell and the second oldest boy, Earlin, felling a white cedar. When trimmed, it made an eight-foot log, which was about as much as two men could carry. It had never occurred to me until this writing to wonder how Mitchell intended to move this log: it was too heavy for a man and a twelve-year old, and my visits at that early stage were too irregular to be counted on.

In any case, Mitchell gladly accepted my offer of help, and we set out along the rocky trail that angled upward to the ridge. I took off my cap to make a cushion where the log rested on my shoulder. It took all my strength and balance to follow the bare-footed, bare-legged man ahead. He walked with his knees bent, in an easy, gliding gait which I later learned to imitate — by walking bare-footed on stony ground. We had traversed about half the hill and my teeth were clenched with the effort when Mitchell grunted and signaled a halt.

"I didn't think I could keep it up," I gasped.

"I was testing you, Douggie," Haakon laughed. "Ravine plenty steep, man."

It was the first time he had addressed me by name and he had used a diminutive into the bargain; I felt a measure of acceptance. By the time we reached the top of the ridge and stood looking down into Friendship Bay, I was past caring about acceptance or anything other than my trembling, aching legs.

We rested for a long, leg-gladdening time, looking out over the Grenadines. With the air of a bright child making a recitation, Earlin called out the names of the islands: to windward, Baliceau, Battowia and Mustique; near at hand below us, Semple's Cay, Petit Nevis and Isle du Quatre (pronounced Oily Cot); farther away, Canouan, Mayero and the Tobago Cays; and finally because it was a clear day, Union and Palm Islands. Haakon stood silently until the recital was finished and then asked,

"You ain think that beautiful, Douggie?"

I murmured my agreement, but was thinking more about the heavy log and the distance yet to go. Fortunately Earlin had another plan; he uncoiled a length of rope from his waist and made a timber hitch around the small end of the log. The three of us began to drag the log, which was much easier than carrying even on the level at the top. Soon we were moving at a trot and then a wild run, whooping and dodging as the log bounced behind us.

Down at the bayside work started immediately to turn the log into a 4x4 inch "scarlin" — a fore and aft member running between two deck beams to frame a hatch or other opening in the deck. While I was still wondering how the job was to be done, Earlin had grabbed a straight-handled hatchet and set to work. He stood atop the log and worked within inches of his bare toes, chopping first a series of cuts at 45° to the axis, then making a quick swipe to shear away the chips and leave a surprisingly (to me) smooth surface. The hatchet was sharpened at frequent intervals on an oil stone, and one face of the log was quickly flattened — as I watched in fascinated horror.

When this was finished, we laid the flattened log on a pair of sawhorses and Haakon scribed a straight line on the flattened surface. Orbin, older of the two teenaged boys, had come in from fishing and now began to help with the sawing. He stood facing the work, the saw held in both hands with blade down and the teeth away from him. Keeping his legs straight, he sawed using the strength of both arms while the other boy steadied the log. The saw was sharp and cut evenly; nevertheless it was tiring work, and we had all taken a turn before the long cut was done. The two remaining faces of the timber were then quickly dressed with the hatchet, leaving me puzzled why we had bothered with the laborious sawing. Haakon explained that a hatch coaming was to be fitted against the sawn face, which had to be absolutely straight so that a tight seam could be fitted.

After we had spent the entire afternoon on that single timber, I looked up at the skeleton of the little sloop in despair. What sort of foolishness had I let myself in for? How many more timbers were needed? With only a hatchet and a hand saw to cut them? Haakon, on the other hand, seemed well-pleased with the afternoon's work and thanked me politely for my assistance.

Later, when the tools were put away in the little shed by the sloop, he asked, "You wouldn't care to take tea with us, Douggie?"

I was gratified by the invitation and followed him up to the little house. Haakon and I sat on the bench between the two palm trees while the two boys flopped on the steps of the house, displacing a flock of smaller children who studied us silently.

"Winnie-O," Haakon called. "You ain have some tea for us?"

An answer that I didn't catch came from inside the house, and Earlin ran inside, returning quickly with a tray which he held out to me — a large enamel-ware cup of hot milk and coffee, a thick slice of buttered bread and a cold piece of fried fish. We talked idly, watching the wave patterns refracting over the surface of the water, while the sun sank below the ridge across the bay.

At the outset when I visited the Mitchells, I simply watched the work, taking an occasional photograph and asking questions. Soon I was being asked to pass a tool or go for a nail, then to do this or that simple task, until, in the tradition of Tom Sawyer's fence, I was working full days and taking all my meals with the family. At no point did I ever state my purpose, and by like token, I was never asked just what I was doing. Slowly I came to realize that it never really occurs to a Bequian to wonder what a stranger is doing in Bequia. The people of Bequia know that their island is the only place in the world really worth living, and they charitably assume that the rest of the world has the good sense to share that opinion.

By the end of January, 1971, five months after the keel was laid, the vessel was "set up", *i.e.* all the frames had been shaped and fitted inside the rib-bands, and the bends and the beam shelf had been fastened to the upper ends of the frames. During February, as I insinuated myself into the project, the "beaming off" (fig. VII-2) was taking place. By March, I was working full time and we were fitting "knees" to brace the deck beams where they butted against the bends. The knees, short natural crooks approximating a right angle, were dressed on the ground and then held in place while a saw was used to make a final smooth fit. Two 5/8 inch holes were drilled through each arm of the crook into the adjacent timber and an iron pin dipped in pitch driven into each. The pins were cut as needed from a length of reinforcing rod and, when in place, were peened over a washer to tighten the joint, the whole assembly being called a bolt (a "screw bolt" is an expensive item in the islands and is generally used only when a joint must be closed over a greater distance — for example when the keelson is drawn down to the keel to lock the butts of the frames in place).

The work day began a little before eight in the morning, when one of the younger children rowed across the bay to fetch a carpenter from La Pompe

fig. VII-2. Beaming off. Uncle Nappy (left), Haakon (center), Orbin (right rear) and Earlin (right front). February, 1971.

who had begun to work on the vessel during the beaming off. The early hours of the morning were best, and the pace of work was brisk. At eleven o'clock Winnie sent down one of the younger children with "breakfast," the main meal of the day, which we ate in the shade of the vessel. Afterward we lay talking (some of us) and dozing (others of us) until work resumed. The afternoons were hot as the sun beat against the hillside behind us, and the hours sometimes dragged until tools were put away at four o'clock and the carpenter was rowed back across the bay.

After the knees were all fitted, we began to fit the "scarlings" (the fore-and-aft timbers which formed the deck openings for hatch, cabin and cockpit, companionway forward and "lazareet" in the stern). With the scarlings in place, half-beams could be fitted which completed the deck layout. The frames were cut off even with the bends, and finally the top timbers were shaped and slipped into place between the beam self and the bends, to form the framework for the bulwarks and the top rail.

The carpenter from La Pompe, named Napoleon Olliverre III and called Uncle Nappy, was a relation of Haakon's, but was nonetheless earning $5 EC/day, the going rate at the time. Uncle Nappy was also a great raconteur (as is, to a certain extent, every Bequian; stories familiar to everyone are told and retold with great relish in the telling — largely, I assume because of the absence of modern media in Bequia) and willingly set himself the task of initiating me into the joys of life in Bequia and the mysteries of boat-carpentry. He was especially proud of his ship-lap joint (fig. VII-3), which he insisted should be used on scarlings and coamings because it gave a caulking seam on both faces of the joint.

"Ship-lap and double lock," he intoned proudly each time he completed a joint and drove it tight.

One afternoon after work, Uncle Nappy invited me home with him for evening tea. There he introduced me to his wife and showed me a painting of the schooner *Emeralda* (fig. XXV-6), 51 tons, built in 1940 by him, and owned by him and his four brothers. In his lifetime he had set up and built 11 vessels including Haakon's and had given assistance on many others.

By early April, the hatch coamings and cabin trunk were completed, the mast partners and samson post were in place, and the top timbers were fitted (fig. VII-4). Down below, the outer sternpost was in place and the rudder case had been hollowed out and fastened to it.

The outer sternpost is a recent West Indian innovation for dealing with the problem of where to fit the propellor when an auxiliary engine is installed in a sailing hull. In yacht construction the propellor is generally fitted into an aperture in the rudder, which means cutting the rudder stock (the rudder stock is the axis on which the rudder swings and the backbone which gives strength

fig. VII-3. *Uncle Nappy and the ship lap joint.*
February, 1971.

fig. VII-4. Moving ahead on Mitchell's sloop.
From left to right: Orbin, Earlin, Haakon
and Herbie Olliverre. Friendship Bay,
Bequia. April, 1971.

to the rudder). Obviously, cutting an aperture weakens the rudder. In modern yacht construction, this problem is overcome by laminating the rudder or by using a welded metal rudder stock, but neither of these methods is available to island builders.

They choose, instead, to erect a second sternpost a short distance behind the first. The outer sternpost then carries the rudder case and rudder, while the inner sternpost is drilled for the stern tube and propellor shaft (fig. VII-5). The method is structurally sound, but has the disadvantage that considerable drag is generated by the large aperture and by the unfaired edges of the after sternpost.

During this period, Haakon became increasingly worried about securing the milled boards necessary for planking the deck and hull. His intention was to use silverballi *(Cordia alliorda)* from Guyana, but there were interminable delays in shipping his order. And there was no way to expedite matters other than sending an inquiry *via* the *Lady Angela* when she sailed twice monthly to Guyana.

While we waited, we worked at small jobs which were necessary but didn't give the satisfaction of changing noticeably the appearance of the vessel. On April 2, we cut a rabbet in the after face of the rudder case and set in the navel piece, a thick plank which fastens to the lower side of the transom frames and provides the only structural support for the transom stern. This seemed unsound to me, and I mentioned to Haakon the ledges that I had seen used in Carriacou.

"Oh," he said. "That why I see plenty Bequia vessel with the stern droop, but I never see Carriacou vessel droop yet. Must be why."

When the navel piece was in place, we added the "pointer," a straight, raking timber, mounted atop the navel piece and running up toward the extension of the top rail. Next in place were the "horn timbers" — small, inverted frames running from the tip of the pointer down to deck level, which form the characteristic oval shape of the transom.

The next morning, Uncle Nappy called me to come down for instruction in the proper method of rabbeting the keel. He began by beveling a small block of wood to use as a guide, cutting 1/8 inch off the edge (fig. VII-6). The guide was held flat against a frame as shown, and the rabbet was chiseled out so that the "garboard streak" would lock into the bevel. In addition to locking the garboard in place, this method provided a joint into which caulking cotton could be driven without forcing the garboard away from the keel, a common cause of leaking.

fig. VII-5. Schooner Sea Hawk C *hauled down for repairs. Owner Danny Crozier on right. Admiralty Bay, Bequia. February, 1971.*

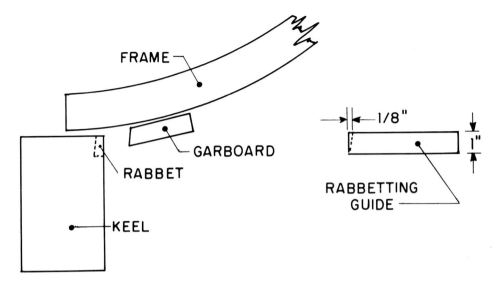

fig. VII-6. *Detail of rabetting guide used by Uncle Nappy.*

During the two months that I had thus far worked, the Mitchells had come to regard me as more good-natured than genuinely helpful. I was unable to take the hatchet and produce a surface as smooth as if it had been planed; I couldn't tell from the placid surface of the bay when sprat were running; and I sheeted the boom too close when sailing to windward. One day in April as we were having our "breakfast," conversation came round, as it frequently did, to the difficulties of getting supplies. This time it concerned a 7 HP outboard motor which had been out of service for several months because of a broken shift lever. I asked to see the motor and was surprised to find that the shift lever in question was in an accessible place and not very complicated. I went aboard *Eider* for some tools — a hacksaw, a tap and die set, a piece of bronze flat bar, an electric drill and a portable generator.

At first I had only the younger children as spectators, but by the time the simple task was finished, the gallery was full. When I turned off the generator, Charles, the spellbound youngest boy, was muttering, "Douggie is a magic man."

"Man, you got tools you ain touch yet," Earlin chimed in.

The Mitchells, though highly skilled and inventive in working wood, were deeply in awe of all things mechanical, and their estimate of my personal worth soared. Never have I achieved so much effect with so little effort; I became the person to consult on a host of subjects from broken tools and toys to authenticity of the twice-a-week Westerns shown against a patch of white-washed wall in Port Elizabeth. It was a definite boost for my ego; but far more importantly, it was later to provide me with the opportunity to make something more than a token contribution to the building of the vessel.

By this time Easter was at hand, and work stopped. Uncle Nappy had a visit from his son living in Canada, and the rest of us took a holiday.

Somewhat earlier, Orbin had happened to mention that on Easter Monday, the National Bar — grog shop and social center for the community of La Pompe — usually organized a boat race. When asked if he planned to enter, he replied that he didn't have the entry fee, so I took my cue and offered to put up the entry fee of $5 EC in exchange for an opportunity to sail in *Cedar Blossom*, a two-bow boat built by Haakon before his accident and used now by Orbin for fishing and lobster diving.

Which is how it happened that Easter Monday found me standing waist-deep in the sea, holding the bow of *Cedar Blossom* into the waves that were breaking onto Friendship beach. Bo-So, the other crew, was holding the stern, and Orbin was standing with the other skippers in a clump on the beach. Suddenly a shout went up, and Orbin sprinted toward us, splashed into the sea and tumbled into the boat. Bo-So and I gave a shove to the boat and did the same.

"Buss out the jib," Orbin shouted and began to haul in the mainsheet.

Bo-So yanked on the jib sheet and pulled the jib out of its loose knot around the forestay. The sails filled and we were quickly away. But somehow Bill Bynoe was a little quicker and already had a small lead as we stood out past the shoal patch off Pt. Hilary and began to beat up toward Hope Rock (fig. VII-7). Orbin perched on the gunwale with the tiller in one hand and the

fig. VII-7. *Bequia two-bow boats racing in Easter Monday Regatta. Friendship Bay, Bequia. April, 1971.*

mainsheet in the other, springing up in every little puff, then hauling off, occasionally pumping the tiller back and forth in sheer impatience. Bo-So held the jib sheet wrapped around his hand and sawed in and out, hauling in on the rise of each wave, easing out in the trough. Lacking other instructions, I crouched on the ballast stones and tried to stay out of the way. As we sailed, Bo-So kept up a constant barrage of advice, instructions and encouragement.

"Hold she. Hold she hard."

"No, no. Let she shoot out."

"Study, study."

"Go back, man, go back. Got to go back. He cutting we."

Sailing with a Bequia crew comes as a bit of a shock to any graduate of the William Bligh School of Maritime Manners. The tradition of an unimpeachable, unapproachable skipper, grim-eyed and aloof on the quarterdeck, making his inscrutable decisions unchallenged, has simply not taken root in Bequia. According to the Bequia Code of Unparliamentary Procedure, advice and criticism may be freely and constantly offered by all ranks from highest to lowest, regardless of the circumstances or the skipper. In all matters pertaining to the sea, Bequians are astonishingly and — when you get used to it — refreshingly democratic.

Despite, however, this free flow of information, we failed to gain on Bynoe and were a couple of lengths behind as we stood over Hope Rock and eased sheets to shoot through the narrow, surging channel between the rock and the island.

Once out of the tight quarters, Bo-So grabbed the bamboo pole that we had stumbled over each time the ballast stones were shifted, using it to "goose" the jib. As we ran back past Pt. Hilary, Haakon trotted along the shore, urging us to shift the ballast aft and "get she shooting". In spite of our efforts, we gained nothing on Bynoe on the long run down to the West Cays and nothing on the beat back to Friendship Bay. We "brought" second by the same margin that we had held throughout the race.

After the boat was hauled up and washed out, we went up to the house for "breakfast." I assumed the festivities were over until Haakon stood up, late in the afternoon and said,

"Well, Douggie, let we go. It be time for spree."

Which is how it happened that Easter Monday evening found me at the La Pompe National Bar where a "feast" had been set out for contestants, friends and relations — which included, in practice, all the males of the community. To eat, there was rice-with-peas-between, stew chicken, cornmeal mush (called coucou by white Bequians and fungee by black Bequians), West Indian potatoes and a salad of onions and Irish potatoes. To drink, there was "strong rum" (140 proof), Scotch whisky and Heinekens beer. It began to look as if my $5 entry fee was bread cast upon the waters.

The crowd was warm, noisy and friendly; everyone urged me to partake of the bounty and make myself at home. From a table near the open window a voice hailed me by name. A large man with a natural air of authority motioned me over and poured me a drink from his bottle. No introductions were necessary: Athneal Olliverre was already known to me by reputation and, apparently, I to him. Athneal and his brothers owned the whale fishery which operated from Petit Nevis, and Athneal himself was the head (and for that matter, only) harpooner. His manner was quiet and unassuming, and yet I felt somehow as if I were in the presence of an elemental force of nature. He seemed to know without asking that I would want to know about whaling, and so, without preamble, he launched into a description of that art as practiced in Bequia. After awhile, he beckoned me to follow and led me along the road to his home where he showed me the tools and trophies of his trade. As an aid to understanding the intricacies of his art, he was steadily pouring shots of rum, which we washed down with everything from beer to banana soda pop. When rum and conversation had imparted as much as Athneal deemed essential, he suggested that if I really wanted to know something about whaling, then awhaling I must go. The upshot forms the subject of the next chapter.

Meanwhile, back at the bar, the spree was in full swing, though the initial offering of liquor was exhausted. I bought my own bottle of rum (for $4EC) and set out to repay my obligations. Eventually, I found myself seated on a wooden bench looking out over a yard in which the small fry of the community were gathered to gawk. My neighbor was just assuring me that everyone was glad to make welcome "the fella what giving Haakie a help," when we were interrupted by angry voices.

A bench was overturned with a sudden crash as bottle and glasses went flying. Bill Bynoe jumped to his feet and began to announce in a high singsong voice what he was going to do to his adversary when he laid hands on him. Which was hypothetical for the moment, since both men were being restrained by their friends. However, disagreements quickly arose among the friends and sub-groups began to surge and shove. As the fight showed signs of becoming general, I eyed the open window, gauging the distance to the ground.

"No, no," my neighbor laughed. "Is not for you, man. Is only for show. They ain doing *you* nothing."

Cyril, a half-witted cast-away adopted by Bynoe, saved everyone's face by pushing his way through the crowd to seize Bill around the waist and wail piteously. Gradually the commotion subsided, then was abruptly forgotten when, on the stroke of 9 o'clock, the women who had been gathering outside resolutely invaded the premises and grabbed partners. Thus began the dance which was to complete the evening.

When it was time to go, I said goodnight to Haakon and prepared to walk back to Admiralty Bay where *Eider* was still, at this time, anchored.

"Douggie, you ain want Earlin to walk with you?" Haakon asked.

I gestured toward the crowd and laughingly repeated what my neighbor had said earlier, "They ain doing *me* nothing."

"No, no." he said anxiously, "Is dark moon tonight. You don't frighten of jumbies?"

I assured him that I would be fine and made my way back aboard without mishap.

The following morning when I rowed ashore for the walk over to Pt. Hilary, Haakon and Earlin were waiting for me. They had walked to town to buy several long lengths of purpleheart (*Peltogyne pubescens*). Ordinarily Haakon preferred to avoid retailers and retail prices (in this case, $.58 EC/board foot), but his lumber had still not come from Guyana and he did want to keep the job moving. We put the long planks on the deck of *Eider* and sailed around to Friendship Bay. That same afternoon we began to put down the covering boards (the outermost planks of the deck, which cover the upper ends of the frames), a tedious job requiring very few materials. Uncle Nappy had taken time off to plant his "provisions", so Herbie Olliverre, another carpenter from La Pompe, came to work.

With the covering boards in place, the top timbers could be "bolted" to the frames below, and the top rail could be mortised onto the tops of the top timbers. While Earlin and I worked at that, the others worked down below, fitting the keelson onto the top of the keel and drawing it down with "screw bolts" to lock the butts of the frames securely to the keel. Next, the bilge stringers were fastened along the insides of the frames halfway between the keelson and the beam shelf. With the addition of these members, the frames were rigidly locked in place and needed only the planking to have their full strength.

It was at this point that I was able for the first time to measure the vessel and draw lines, finding in the process a low spot in the area of the sternpost. It was this discovery, mentioned in Chapter II, which convinced me that my method of taking offsets was fairly sensitive.

One day after we had eaten the breakfast and were resting in the shade, the younger children of the family came down for a swim in the bay. Charles, the youngest boy, brought with him a little sailboat which he tried out in the sea. When I asked to looked at it and expressed my admiration, the two older boys ran back to the house for their models, and it was picture time (fig. VII-8).

These models, being made of the wood of the gum tree (*Bursera simaruba*), were called gumboats. They were shaped with a pocket knife and smoothed with a piece of rough stone. The ballast keels were made of lead, melted over a charcoal fire and poured into a beach sand mold. Much care and skill had gone into the shaping and decorating of these models, and all the boys had produced "by hand and eye" very sophisticated designs. It seemed to be part of a process by which they began to acquire adult skills.

In fact, the oldest of the three model builders had already begun to hang around the vessel after school, happy to run errands, fetch tools, and perform some of the simpler jobs. The older boys, both of whom had gotten their school-leaving certificates at fourteen, were rapidly acquiring skills and were

fig. VII-8. *The Mitchell children with their gum-boats. From left to right: Roderick, Charles, Alvie (rear), Dorthalie and Osrick. May, 1971.*

able workmen by the time the vessel was completed. The evolution from model builder to boat carpenter occurred so smoothly and naturally that no one seemed to realize that it was education and therefore distasteful. And at every stage, the children had the satisfaction of knowing that they were making a real contribution to the material welfare of the family.

It was during this period that Haakon decided to brace the stern with "ledges" such as I mentioned seeing in Carriacou. Two cedar timbers were fastened inside the frames of the counter stern and extended forward past the two stern posts onto the frames of the tuck. When pinned from side to side through the two sternposts, the full weight of the stern was cantilevered onto the sternposts and keel, making a very strong assembly. If this new method catches on in Bequia, then I will have become an agent of cultural diffusion.

By the last week of April, everything had been done in readiness for decking and planking, and still the materials had not come from Guyana. Haakon asked me if I would take Earlin down to Grenada to buy Douglas fir for making spars, none being available in St. Vincent. He was still planning to race against *Mermaid* in August and wanted to keep some part of the project going forward. On the trip down we kept company as far as the Tobago Cays with Orbin and Bo-So, who were going to camp there and dive for lobster for a month or so.

In St. Georges it didn't take long to discover that there was no Douglas fir of the length required. Everywere we asked, the response was substantially the same.

"No, we have nothing of the kind. No one builds schooners any more. No reason to stock the gear."

As long as we were in Grenada, it seemed like a good idea to check on the progress of the two schooners that I had earlier seen near Grenville. As Earlin and I walked through the little town, I noticed several long straight logs lying in the street near the little concrete jetty. I asked whose they were and was directed to a small shop owned by Hyacinth MacLaren, a Carriacou man and former schooner owner. The logs, we learned, had been cut in the government experimental forest at Grand Etaing and were destined to become the spars of the *Yankee Girl R*.

The logs were of Maho pine *(Thespesia populnea)*, a flowering tree called pine only because of its rapid, straight growth habit and its medium light wood. I had seen the quality of work that went into the *Yankee Girl* and figured that any spars good enough for Roberts were good enough for us. MacLaren warned us that, although the cost was reasonable, the trees were bought "where is, as is."

The following morning I stuffed some gear into a sail bag, and Earlin and I set forth in a bus, which immediately began to climb. The road wound upward past small, unpainted wooden houses propped against the slope of the land, each surrounded by its aureole of red-brown earth, kept bare and smooth by dogs, chickens and children. At the outer edge of this inhabited circle grew the trees of life — breadfruit, bananas, mango, avocado, nutmeg, cocoa — and beyond them, the tangled growth of tropical rainforest.

As we climbed, it grew steadily cooler until we entered the zone where the sun was obscured and the atmosphere became cloud and swirling mist. At the top, past all houses and other signs of human habitation, the bus pulled over and the driver informed us that this was what we had asked for — Grand Etaing, the lake lying in the crater of the volcano by which the island had been formed.

There was no one to give us further directions, but after turning around a few times, we struck a dirt track that went neither up nor down and followed it through a plantation of bananas to a clearing which held a small wooden hut and an open-sided shed. Under the shed, a bare-footed worker, in faded trousers rolled to the knee and a shirt too miscellaneous to button, turned the handle of a heavy grindstone while a comrade sharpened a cutlass.

We asked for the person in charge and explained what we wanted — mast, boom and gaff. There followed a period of reflection during which the foreman sucked his teeth and looked us over. Finally, he announced that the aforesaid timber came to just exactly $40 EC, a price so reasonable that it seemed indiscreet to inquire into either his pricing policy or the eventual destination of the money. When we had paid, he indicated, with a sweep of his arm, the area in which we were free to make our selection.

We followed the road in the direction indicated and entered a stand of Maho pine, growing in a network of ridges and ravines, where the only level ground was occupied by the road itself. The boom and gaff were not difficult; we found suitable trees near the road, and quickly felled and limbed them with an axe borrowed from the foresters. The mast was another story.

A tree able to yield a spar 36 feet tall and 8 inches on the butt was about the upper limit of size in this stand of timber, and we looked long and hard to find one. The only candidate we could locate was on the other side of one of the steep-sided ravines. Felling and limbing were no problem; neither was the first leg of the trip to the bottom of the ravine. From there we had only some 300 feet to reach the roadway, the only difficulty being that it was up a slope that would have been too steep to stand on without trees and undergrowth for a handhold.

Being not completely green as to the way things get done in the islands, Douggie the Magic Man reached into the sail bag and pulled out *Eider's* mainsheet and two double blocks. And confidently rigged a four-part tackle — one end hitched to the butt of the log, the other fastened to a tree part way up the slope. Of these there was no shortage. We were pulling downhill, and on the first heave, we straightened the log and got it started across the ravine. As we refastened our block to a tree higher up the slope, I felt very pleased with myself and was glad that a small crowd of laborers had gathered to watch our efforts. Again we heaved, and the log responded by advancing until it had bridged level across the ravine and jammed its butt firmly into the soft earth. It was no longer a matter of skidding the blamed thing; we were now pulling against the full weight, and the harder we heaved the more the butt dug into the side of the hill.

At this point the fundamental flaw in my plan became apparent: in a sort of hysterical reflex for tackling the hard part of a job first, I had hitched to the butt of the log. Now that it was well and truly jammed, it was obvious that if the log had been pulled from the smaller end, it would have been much easier to lift and unjam.

The laborers, whom I had been so eager to impress, at this point rallied around and, with the instinctive courtesy so often displayed by West Indians, refrained from commenting on my methods. Even with their help, it was still very near a draw match. We cut saplings to use as levers, shifted the tackle to a new direction, and gradually wriggled the butt sideways. Gaining an inch or two with each heave, we finally worked the butt to one side and pulled it far enough up the slope that the log began to skid again. Even so, the slope was greater than 45°, and it was heavy going.

It was past noon when we rested with the three logs lying by the roadside.

Earlin and I had had nothing to eat since early morning and had brought nothing. The laborers, in the comraderie of common hardship, shared with us their mid-day meal — an appetizer of bananas, a main course of bananas washed down with cold water, followed by a dessert of bananas. I relished every mouthful.

Even with the logs lying beside the road, we were not, as the saying goes, out of the woods. It was still a long way down a winding mountain road to the port; and the only link, we were told, was a trucker with the easily remembered name of Ivy Forrester. He lived in the last village passed before entering the cloud forest. An hour's walk and $100 EC secured for us the aid and ability of this individual, who assured us that unwieldy loads were all in a day's work.

We slung a block from the crotch of a convenient tree and lifted the butt of the biggest log while our friends provided the "Norwegian steam" to lift the smaller end directly onto the bed of the truck. After that, the boom and gaff were child's play. The mast and the boom both dangled off the bed in the rear and extended forward of the cab on the off side. It looked wildly precarious to me, but the driver was blithely confident. Earlin and I used the full 40 yards of the mainsheet to truss the load before crawling into the cab from the driver's side and bracing ourselves for descent and reentry.

On every hairpin curve I held my breath and gave it all the body english at my command, dreading the thought of reloading without our gang of well-wishers. My gritted teeth combined with the luck or skill of the driver saw us through, and with the last of the daylight we dropped our putative spars on the waterfront, an easy roll from the water's edge. The first stage of the journey was over, and in my relief and fatigue I had not yet begun to worry how poor *Eider* was going to bear such a burden.

My slowly reeling mind was just coming to grips with the prospect of *towing* the blessed things 40 miles hard on the wind when Earlin piped up.

"Look, Douggie. *Lady Angela* done tie up over there. Uncle Davis going tow she to Bequia land."

He ran off to make the arrangements while I sank down upon the log, my knees made weak by a sense of relief.

In late May, Haakon finally located some silverballi — in Bequia, of all places — a stock of some 1300 board feet which had been bought earlier by another Bequian for a project which had not materialized. The quantity was sufficient to plank the hull, and the prospect put new life into everyone. For too long, the work had gone slowly with little to point to at the end of the day or even the week. Now, for a pleasant change, the work went rapidly and the entire hull was planked in sixteen days. No small part of this speed was owing to my generator and electric drill. It was the owning and operating of this drill that enabled me to make a genuine contribution to the building of Haakon's vessel.

The planking began at the bends and proceeded downward to the turn of the bilge, before starting again at the garboards and coming upward (fig. VII-9). This is certainly not the strongest method of planking, since it leaves

fig. VII-9. Haakon Mitchell with recently planked sloop. Friendship Bay, Bequia. July, 1971.

several short planks in the critical zone between wind and weather. However, it is economical of time and material since most of the "spiling" (tapering and shaping) is left to be done on those few planks.

It was apparent to me even as a novice that planking had to consist of more than simply nailing planks of uniform width over the frames; the planks must be wider in the middle and taper toward the ends since the hull itself does this. Furthermore, the edges of each plank must pretty closely match those of its neighbors, so that caulking joints of uniform width will be formed. And a final constraint is imposed by the fact that a plank will bend across its thickness but not across its width. Any matching with the edge of another plank must be done by cutting, not by springing. Most of this was intuitively obvious; what came as a surprise to me was that a plank may taper, then widen before tapering again. The method for laying out this non-uniform curve, essential to the good fit of a plank, is called spiling, and it was the most technical aspect of boat carpentry (as distinct from boat design) which I observed in the islands.

The plank next to the keel, called the garboard, must be an especially good fit, and the day the garboard was fitted I made careful notes of the method. An especially good plank was chosen for the garboard — wide, straight-grained and knot free — and laid on saw horses conveniently near the hull. A long, straight batten was found, long enough to scribe a straight reference line the length of the plank. A cross mark was struck at the mid-point of this line and a corresponding mark made on the center frame of the hull. Then with a carpenter's rule, Haakon measured the distance forward to the centerline of the next frame and had one of the boys lay off this distance along the reference line on the plank and make a cross mark. This was continued both forward and aft until all the frames were represented by cross marks on the plank.

At this point a fairly important matter of judgement came up and was dealt with in the usual manner — *i.e.* with free-flowing advice, contradiction and comment. What was under discussion was the nailing of the batten to the frames. It had to be so positioned that its lower edge would correspond, in final placement, to the reference line on the plank. When the decision was made, the batten was bent across the frames from stem to stern post and nailed lightly, particular care being taken not to "spring" the batten, *i.e.* bend it from side to side.

Haakon went to the tool shed and returned with an old pair of dividers — iron with brass pivot and brass points. With these he began the "pricking" — gauging the interval between the lower edge of the batten and the rabbet in the keel, then transferring this to the plank at the cross mark corresponding to the frame gauged. When he had finished, there was a line of little holes, pricked by the divider points, which defined an edge for the garboard. The batten was removed from the frames and bent around the prick marks, so that a smooth curve was formed for the lower edge of the garboard. This line was cut with a saw and then beveled with a plane so that it would "hook" into the keel rabbet.

When the plank was ready to fit, Haakon solemnly returned the dividers to their place in the hut. The forward end of the plank was set into its place on the stem rabbet and securely fastened with cleats laid over the end of the plank and nailed into frame and keel on both sides. Using clamps hooked inside the frames, we gradually brought the plank down onto the frames so that holes could be drilled, and nails driven and clenched. If the plank was too tight against the keel, then Haakon had the boys slack off the clamp so he could "take a rub" with the plane. If, on the other hand, the joint seemed too open, a cleat was nailed to the frame at the upper edge of the plank, and a thin wedge driven between the cleat and the plank to close the seam a bit.

As successive planks were added, the lower edge of each was spiled to fit against the upper edge of the preceding plank. Both edges of all planks were beveled so as to form a "caulking seam", *i.e.* a seam wider on the outside so that cotton wick could be driven into the seam and tightened, without coming through on the inside.

With the completion of the planking, Haakon's spirits improved noticeably. The odds, initially against him, had now tipped decidedly in his favor, and the chances for a successful outcome had become rather good. As a further contribution to the lifting of spirits, the long-awaited purpleheart lumber arrived from Guyana, and the deck was laid without delays.

When the planking was finished, I made another set of measurements from which the lines in fig. VII-10 were made. The lines were fair and harmonious, and I began to share the general feeling that the vessel would be a fast-sailer. Aside from the obvious difference in the stern, the body plan of Haakon's vessel showed a strong resemblence to the whaleboats and other two-bow boats of Bequia in the moderately flat floors and very slight drag to the keel. Both of these traits reflect the fact that the two-bow boats rely on a centerboard for their lateral resistance, rather than on their "tuck". From the lines alone, it was clear that all of Haakon's prior experience was in building two-bow boats.

However, the tumblehome which is apparent in the topsides was a very unusual feature, one which I saw on no other West Indian vessel. This intrigued me and I tried, without making any leading remarks, to learn where Haakon had gotten the idea.

"Is tumblehome they call it," he announced proudly. "When I just a boy, I did sail to Barbados in my father schooner, and I see plenty Nova Scotiamen. They all having tumblehome and they plenty fast."

This remark, besides its importance to me in pointing to Nova Scotia as a design influence in West Indian sailing craft, was the first reference that I had heard Haakon make to his father. Once, Uncle Nappy had mentioned that Oily Cot had been owned by Haakon's father, Uncle Harry Mitchell, who bought it for its stands of cedar. I knew that Uncle Harry had been a schooner builder and a land-owner, and that he had been the father of Reg Mitchell, builder of the three-masted schooner, *Gloria Colita*. Under these circumstances, it seemed odd that Haakon should be so poor and so isolated in the community.

By the middle of July it was apparent, despite the speed with which the planking and decking had been done, that the vessel would not be ready for the Regatta in August. No acknowledgement of this fact was made, nor was there any expression of disappointment. Still, the rhythm of the work slackened noticeably. Haakon spent several days helping Winnie to work the ground below and to the side of the house for planting of "provisions." Corn and pigeon peas must be in the ground by late July in order to benefit from the rains that come when the Trade Winds lessen in August and September, the

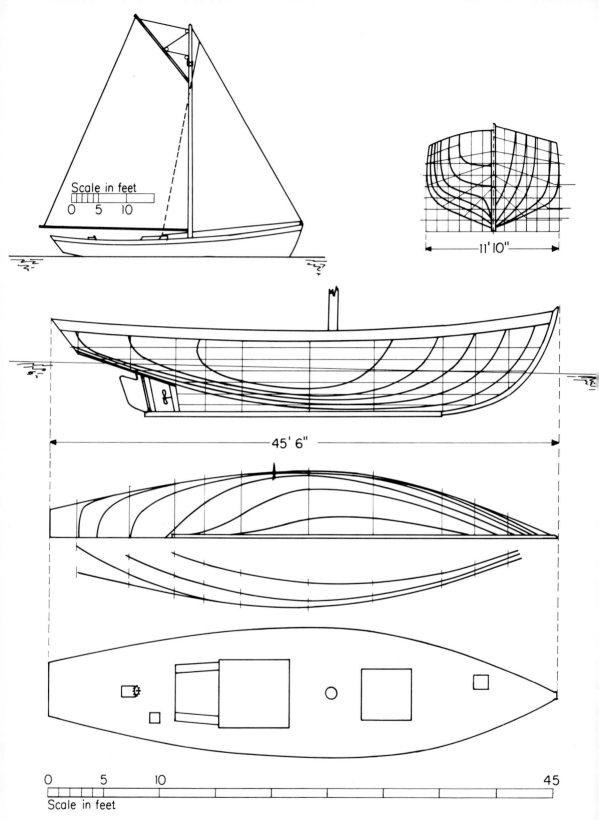

Scale in feet
0   5   10

11' 10"

45' 6"

0   5   10   45
Scale in feet

fig. VII-10.   Lines of sloop Skywave. Built 1971 by
Haakon Mitchell at Friendship Bay,
Bequia. Taken off July, 1971.

hurricane season. Orbin was sewing a new jib for *Cedar Blossom* so that he could enter the Regatta. Earlin and I continued alone on the vessel, setting the nails and filling the holes with a mixture of paint and Portland cement.

As Regatta time drew near, Haakon suggested that I take Earlin with me to Carriacou, then afterward go on to Grenada to pick up some further items of gear for the new vessel. I was ready for a break and decided to mark the occasion by holding a beach barbecue for those of my Bequia friends who would be racing in Carriacou. Which is how it came to pass that Earlin and I set sail from Bequia with one of Haakon's flop-eared sheep in the cockpit under our feet.

The following afternoon as we watched the first race of the series from the rocky islet called Jack a'Dan, I set about the preparations for my barbecue. Earlin helped me kill and butcher the sheep, but stood aside with a dubious expression on his face as I dug the pit and began somewhat clumsily to spit the sheep. Finally Earlin remarked,

"Douggie, plenty time I see white people cooking so. But it look to me like it have more sand than sauce."

A collage of previous barbecues flashed through my mind — of flies, smoke, ashes, roasted knuckles, and inevitably, sand — and I asked what he would recommend instead.

"Mutton pot," he replied, immediately and with obvious relish. And so it came to pass that, despite an exciting race aboard the sloop *Vaeta*, despite a memorable post-race spree with the Bequia sailors, despite the near sinking of *Eider* because of a broken sea-cock, my clearest and best memory of that year's Regatta is mutton pot.

The recipe for mutton pot is almost insultingly obvious. It requires mutton and a pot — a round, black iron pot which is a standard item of gear in any Bequia fishing camp or household. The pot is nestled in a driftwood fire and enough coconut cooking oil poured in to form a puddle in the bottom. Sugar is added — the damp, brown, unrefined sugar of the islands — to simmer in the oil until a rich, dark "colouring" is formed. Next the mutton, cut in chunks, is dropped in, a little at a time, and stirred until browned. Next onions are added ("cut fine, Douggie, fine as dust"), then potatoes, carrots and any other tuber that happens to be available, and finally garlic and red pepper. Then the covered pot is left to simmer while the rum bottle is passed from hand to hand and the sun drops below the sea horizon.

The recipe is simple enough, but the fullest enjoyment of mutton pot is a little more complicated. When the meal is "shared out" in shallow enamelware dishes, meat and vegetables swimming in the rich brown broth, it must be eaten reclining, with the left elbow in the sand, in a circle of firelight ringed by tents rigged from spars and sails, and preferably after a day of racing, fishing or diving for lobster. I know of nothing better.

When Earlin and I returned to Bequia after our trip to Grenada and a leisurely cruise back through the Grenadines, Herbie and Luke Olliverre had already caulked the topsides and begun work on the bottom. Earlin immediately fell in behind them, filling the caulked seams with a mixture of paint and Portland cement. I worked on top with Haakon, making sleeping shelves in the cabin and fitting the chain plates made from heavy pieces of mangrove root.

When Herbie didn't show up for two days running, Haakon said, with much sucking of teeth, "Is spree he going. He won't fit to work for a week now. You knowing anything about caulking, Douggie?"

I didn't, but with Haakon's coaching, I learned to hold the iron, feed the cotton wick and swing the mallet. Before long my seams were tight and even, though I was painfully slow in doing them. By early afternoon my arm was so tired that I had to stop. My efforts and limited success seemed to have broken some sort of spell because as soon as I laid down the tools, Earlin seized them and had a try. By quitting time. he was already better than I was, and we had more caulkers than tools. From that day Haakon dispensed with paid labor.

For the Mitchells, it was the planking which made the vessel a reality. But, for the community of La Pompe across the bay, it was the hollow booming of the caulking mallets which announced that Haakon was going to succeed.

"You know, Douggie," Haakon confided to me one evening after he had been to La Pompe for some errand, "When I did start, all is discourage me. They is tell me I will not succeed. Now is like they all want to be captain."

When the caulking was completed, we turned our attention to shaping the spars and fitting hardware; work was even begun on the engine beds. Then one afternoon, Haakon announced that he had some men coming after work to help us roll down a cannon from the old fort at the top of Pt. Hilary to lay out as a mooring for the new vessel.

My spirit recoiled from this desecration, and as we climbed the hill, I raked my memory for some heavy object which could be substitued for the otherwise doomed historical relic. Nothing came to mind, and I couldn't find the words to speak to Haakon of civic duty and historical preservation. When we reached the crumbled stone foundations of the small fort, I felt a surge of hope as I saw how heavy the half-buried cannon was. But five pairs of arms, conditioned from early youth to hard physical labor, made quick work of that hope. My heart ached as I imagined the little fort restored — picturesque and romantic on the rocky hilltop with its breath-taking view of the Grenadines to the south. While I was still groping for words, we lifted the muzzle and toppled the cannon toward the brow of the hill, then with one last heave, sent it rolling and lurching down the hillside toward the bay. The others rushed after it, shouting and shoving when it slowed.

Abruptly a realization swept over me. Yes, the rusty old cannon was a relic — a relic of an age of piracy and exploitation, of slavery and oppression. As a cannon, it had probably never done an honest day's work in its life. Now, it was being recalled from oblivion and given a useful function to perform. It was

108

fig. VI-11. Christening of Skywave. Friendship
Bay, Bequia. November, 1971.

going to be sunk to the bottom of the bay to provide a secure mooring for a vessel that was the key to a better future for a poor and struggling family. By the time we reached the shore, I was yelling as loudly as anyone.

Early in November, Earlin asked me in the offhand manner which I had finally learned meant something of importance was afoot, what I thought of the name *Skywave*. I replied that it had a nice sound and asked where he had gotten the idea. He said that he had seen it on a passing yacht and asked my help in painting a name board for the stern. And this constituted the official announcement that the time for launching had come. Word was sent out on the coconut telegraph that the big event would take place on Sunday, November 21.

Haakon, though not a church-goer, was careful to observe all the conventions and arranged with Father Adams, the Anglican priest in Port Elizabeth, to bless the new vessel on the Saturday before launching. On Friday, Haakon explained to me that a vessel must have godparents, and asked me if I would "stand" godfather. I was, and still am, deeply gratified.

On Saturday afternoon, Father Adams came as far as possible in a Land Rover, then walked down the hill accompanied by two acolytes who carried the small cross, a vessel of holy water and an altar cloth. The Mitchells, a few close friends and I climbed to the deck of the vessel, where we stood while the blessing was taking place. An altar was arranged on the main hatch; the priest read from the Book of Common Prayer, then sprinkled holy water over the bows. One of the younger boys unfurled the name banner and the new vessel officially became *Skywave* (fig. VII-11).

fig. VII-12. Skywave, *cut down and ready to launch. November, 1971.*

After the ceremony, I approached Father Adams, eager to learn my duties and responsibilities as godfather.

"Very simple," he replied cheerfully, "If the vessel sinks, you must raise her."

There were other duties as well, as Haakon informed me later that evening when he handed me several banknotes, and said, "After the cutting down in the morning, Douggie, you must put some money in the purse (suspended from the sternpost) to encourage the others to make a little offering. They might be 'shamed, but if they is see you going, they would be encourage."

"You mean you want me to prime the pump," I laughed.

"That is it, that is it," he agreed. "You must use politics with some of these people. You know how."

Early on the big day, the first ones stirring were Winnie and her helpers, who were making final preparations to feed the expected crowd. Soon after, Haakon and the boys were busy, tending to last minute chores — laying out the kedge anchors, stropping the hull with a heavy cable, and smearing anti-fouling paint on spots where the shores were removed.

By mid-morning, enough people had arrived that the "cutting down" could begin. In fact, there was no cutting involved; a dozen men simply set their shoulders under the starboard bilge and held the weight of the vessel while the last of the shores were removed. Then, the vessel was leaned gently onto sand-filled burlap bags that had been placed amidships on the starboard side. These, in turn, were slashed and the sand raked out until the vessel had come to rest on the rollers (fig. VII-12). In these and the subsequent proceedings, it was Athneal Olliverre who by common consent took charge, he being the person most likely to turn a gang of merry-makers into an effective labor force.

Skywave had been built on a low bank a few feet above the level of the water, so the actual launching was more a matter of controlling and restraining the weight of the vessel than actually moving it. Getting the hull to the water's edge was simply a question of easing the check lines that were run from the sternpost to convenient trees on the hillside above. There was one anxious moment — when someone on the check line slipped and the vessel lurched sideways, nearly sliding off the rollers — but when rollers had been shifted, the hull was in an even better position.

As the bows reached the waters of the bay, the excitement of the crowd mounted to a frenzy (fig. VII-13). Rollers were heaved down the slope to be placed under the bows, men splashed and yelled in the shallows, and screaming

fig. VII-13. **Skywave,** *hauling into the shallows.*
November, 1971.

111

fig. VII-14.   Afloat at last. Skywave *in foreground,*
Eider *in background. November, 1971.*

children swarmed everywhere. Finally the vessel began to stir with her own
bouyancy, then rolled slowly and heavily to port before floating free (fig. VII-
14).

A crowd of children swam out and swarmed aboard, while the older boys
began to come and go in rowboats, carrying ballast stones from the shore.
Back ashore, the remainder of the day's activities were being organized. First,
the success of the new vessel was drunk in the prescribed manner: a tray with
bottles of whisky and rum, a glass and a pitcher of water is presented to the
guest, who pours his own measure, tosses it off and then pours the chaser, rin-
sing glass and mouth in one economical operation before the tray is offered to
the next person.

Meanwhile, Winnie and her helpers had arrived with three dishpans of
food to begin the "sharing out." One pan was heaped high with mutton, brown
and pungent, the second held rice with pigeon peas and the third was filled
with boiled tania. Plates were filled and carried to the little groups that had
formed where there was shade. The men were served first, and the women
came later to serve themselves. As plates were emptied, they were rinsed in

the sea and returned to service. Later in the afternoon, the mast was floated out and stepped, using the halyards of another sloop brought from across the bay (fig. VII-15). As she floated there on the sparkling waters of Friendship Bay, newly rigged and ballasted to her waterline, *Skywave* must have been the realization of Haakon's every dream. And yet he was very subdued in his hour of triumph, simply commenting, "It true, you know, what they say: and a man have friends, he ain need money."

fig. VII-15. *Stepping the mast of* Skywave.
November, 1971.

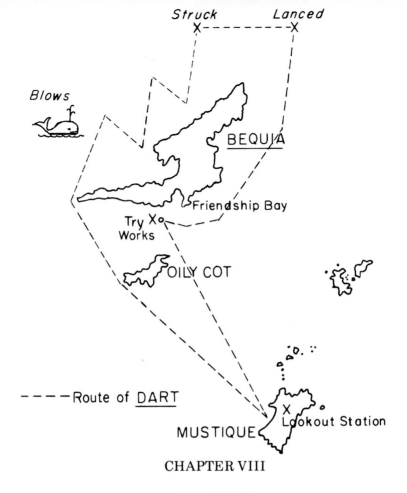

CHAPTER VIII

BLOWS!

After *Skywave* was launched, my official pretext for remaining in Bequia disappeared, and by rights I should have been on my way. But there was always something new and interesting to do, and I lingered another four months — helping to rig the new sloop and get her sailing (fig. VII-1), hunting wild sheep on Oily Cot, gathering bird's eggs on Savanne or simply sharing the routines of daily life with people whom I had come to admire intensely.

If it had been only these idyllic pursuits, my conscience would have prevailed; it was Athneal Olliverre's invitation to go whaling that really held me. The original invitation had been made in the convivial atmosphere of the La Pompe National Bar the preceding Easter, and I went out one time late in the season primarily to get a feel for the sailing performance of the whaleboats (7 nautical miles in 45 minutes; 9.4 knots in an open boat with a waterline length of 26 feet; a startling speed coefficient of $k = 1.8$). But by then it was so late in the season that there was very little chance of even sighting a whale, and it was not really like whaling at all.

It seemed highly unlikely to me that Athneal had really meant to set out in pursuit of the largest animal in the seas with a greenhorn in the boat. However, at the launching of *Skywave* in November, he repeated his invitation

114

fig. VIII-1. Skywave *under sail. Admiralty Bay,*
Bequia. January, 1972.

for the season beginning in mid-February, and I decided that if the whalers were willing to risk it, then I was too. Even so, my courage was at low ebb that morning in late February, as I made my way down the beach toward La Pompe in the pre-dawn darkness.

Early as it was, preparations on the two whaleboats were already well along. The canvas cover was off the tub amidships where 100 fathoms of heavy rope lay neatly coiled. The first harpoon was in its chock, its canvas-sheathed toggle jutting forward over the bow, while the other harpoon and three lances were tied along the starboard gunwale. Spars, sails and shrouds were bundled together and laid across the thwarts. Lard pails with tight-fitting lids, containing food and fresh water, were stowed here and there in the bottom of the boat.

Athneal greeted me matter-of-factly, then turned back to supervising the stowage. When all was ready, both crews laid hold of the first boat. With arms and backs straight, we lifted, then heaved, at the grunted command. Then again, until the slender double-ender slid down the beach and into the bay.

The steersman scrambled aboard and shipped the long steering oar, sculling to keep the bow into the waves, while both crews returned to launch the other boat. Then we began wading back and forth in the water, trundling out the ballast stones. Athneal motioned me to a place on the port side of his boat, the *Dart*, and with a shove we were away, scrambling quickly aboard to run out the long sweeps.

The man behind me indicated a seat and an oar, and it dawned on me for the first time that I was not just along for the ride. I lodged my oar between the wooden thole pins and seized the handle. Again there was a grunted command, and we began to pull away from the drag of the breaking waves and out into the bay. It took a couple of strokes for me to adjust to the slight hesitation that occurred as the oar slid, then thudded against the thole pin at the beginning of the stroke and again at the release. But the adjustment came quickly, and for the first time since college, I was grateful for those long hours spent rowing on the Charles.

When we had pulled far enough offshore to have sailing room, there was another grunted command, and the oars were quickly unshipped and stowed. One man steadied and guided the butt of the mast while the others lifted from astern. When stepped, the mast was first secured by the forestay to which the jib was sewed, then on each side by the shrouds. The mainsail, already lashed to the mast, was knotted to the boom and run out, while the peak was hoisted on the sprite. The lower end of the sprite was fitted into a short piece of rope, called the snotter, which was looped around the mast, and the sail was stretched into an efficient airfoil by two men thrusting the sprite upward while a third slipped the snotter up the mast to hold the tension.

The steersman, Joseph Ford, fitted the rudder onto the pintles, slipped the tiller into its slot and reached for the mainsheet. The jib was sheeted and in less time than it takes to tell, the *Dart* was sailing. A few yards away, the *Trio* (pronounced try-o) was carrying out the same transformation. The early morning breeze filled the sails, and the bows rose to the first Atlantic swell. The crew shifted their weight to the weather gunwale as spray began to splash back over the bow. I checked the plastic bag covering my camera and wondered again if I had been wise.

"Give she a touch more board," Uncle Joseph said, and the man nearest the centerboard box shoved on the iron lever controlling the board until he got a nod from the steersman. As soon as we had cleared the headlands, Athneal climbed into the gunwale and began to scan the gray surface of the sea (fig. VIII-2). We were sailing a close reach, out toward the island of Mustique which lay on the Grenadines Bank, 7 miles to the southeast.

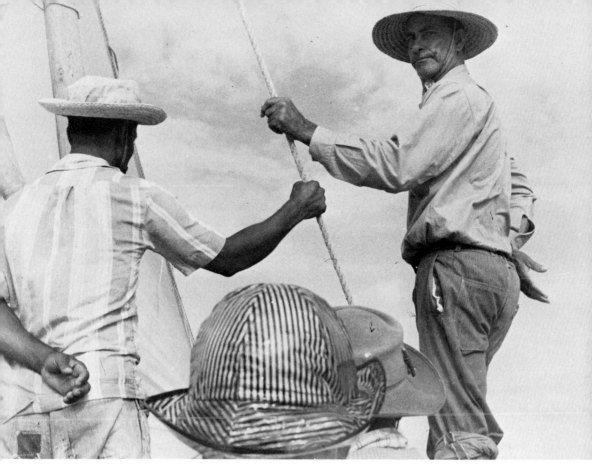

*fig. VIII-2. On the lookout for whales Athneal
Olliverre on the right. March, 1972.*

The humpback whales which the Bequia whalers hunt calve somewhere in the South Atlantic in December and begin to appear in the Grenadines in small family groups in February. They remain in the area until the latter half of April — feeding, resting, and tending the young. It is this sojourn in the Grenadines which makes possible a shore based fishery such as the one in Bequia.

This much Athneal had already explained to me, and it seemed logical that we should be out sailing where the whales might be expected to appear. Therefore it came as a bit of a surprise when we anchored in a small cove on the lee side of Mustique and climbed past a small collection of houses to the top of the island. From the summit there was a commanding view of the sea for miles in all directions, and I began to understand the plan of action.

One of the younger men climbed to a fork in the lone tree that grew on the scrub-covered hill and scanned the sea with a pair of binoculars. Meanwhile a fire was started, and a coffee pot appeared from some hiding place in the rocks. Soon all six of us were lounged around the hilltop, letting the sun and the coffee chase the chill of our pre-dawn sail. Someone passed around one of the lard pails, and we each helped ourselves to a handful of *farine* — a coarse meal made by grating and parching the cassava root.

117

"Look me hey!" Uncle Joseph shouted, gesturing in the direction of Bequia. "Someone cutting the glass. Look away, over Kenneth's."

There it was, on the hillside above La Pompe, a waver, then a flash as someone held a mirror to the sun and moved it until the beam caught us.

"Yes, yes," Athneal replied, excitedly. "Kenneth cutting glass." He hurriedly began to unfold the oilcloth wrappings of the parcel he had carried up from the boats, revealing a walkie-talkie — the gift, I later learned, of an American well-wisher.

What followed was a garbled interchange carried out in shrill West Indian dialect shot through with the usual squeals and crackles of the air waves and punctuated by sudden silences as the operator on the other end pushed and released the "transmit" switch in a purely random manner. I couldn't understand a single word, and apparently neither could Athneal, as he fired off questions, instructions and, finally, invective in a voice that rose steadily in both pitch and volume.

"Wait," one of the men exclaimed. "Look me hey! Glass cutting down Moonhole. Must be whale in the Channel."

"Let we go then, boys," Athneal shouted, wrapping up the walkie-talkie and starting for the boats.

We scrambled down the hill as fast as the rocky path, lunch buckets and other gear permitted. Inside five minutes we were back in the boats and under sail, on a broad reach and making our best speed for the southwestern tip of Bequia.

"Clean, sweet wind, man. Clean, sweet wind," Uncle Joseph sang out exultantly, as the excitement of a speedy chase galvanized the crew. The two boats were fairly evenly matched, and *Dart* was only some 50 yards ahead of *Trio* by the time we had sailed the 10 miles to the West Cays (fig. VIII-3). As we approached the narrow pass, a man scrambled onto a wave-splashed rock and stood waiting.

"Not far, not far," he shouted, with a sweeping, back-handed gesture toward the channel, nine miles wide, which separates Bequia from St. Vincent to the north.

We swept through the cut and hardened in the sails. Someone hammered down the centerboard as we came on the wind and drove into the first head sea. No one spoke now as we pounded into the steep waves, each man hoping to be the first to spot the tiny puff of gray-white vapor which betrays the whale. The man tailing the jib sheet played it in and out as the bows rose and fell. The man opposite me in the stern worked steadily with a gourd, baling the water that was now coming more or less constantly into the boat.

We stood north on the starboard tack until we had a clear view past North Point and up the channel. Then Athneal swung his arm back, palm down. Uncle Joseph leaned on the tiller and *Dart* came up into the wind. With the jib bundled around the forestay and the mainsheet loosed, we lay hove-to, all way off, riding the waves easily without splashing. A few yards to leeward, *Trio* did

fig. VIII-2. In hot pursuit, whaleboat Trio in
background. Off Bequia. March, 1972.

the same.

Athneal slipped the canvas sheath off the gleaming bronze barb of the harpoon and motioned for the line. From the tub amidships, the line was handed aft and taken once around the snubbing post by the steersman's knee, before it was passed forward to the deep, lead-lined notch in the stem head. Athneal shoved in the wooden pin to prevent the line from jumping out, then knotted the line solidly to the short nylon strop of the harpoon iron. When all preparations were made, the waiting began.

"Blows! Blows!" The eerie cry, almost a howl, came from the other boat. The wisp of vapor hung over the sea surface long enough to see that we had overstood. The whale was astern and farther out in the channel. Quickly, Athneal handed back the jib sheet; Uncle Joseph was already overhauling the mainsheet with great sweeps of his arm. We bore away on the other tack.

119

The whale spouted again, and this time everyone saw it — more gray than white, but easily lost among the breaking wavetops. Twice more we saw the spouts as we swept down toward the whale. As Athneal wedged his knee into the harpooner's chock and groped for the harpoon, the flukes of the whale appeared, lifted into the air and then slipped massively down into the deep.

"Clean flukes!" someone intoned on a mournful note.

"Is a yearling only," Athneal said. "But plenty fat. Let we go back, Joseph. He going up with the tide."

We went onto the starboard tack and began beating our way up into the east, trying to gauge where the whale would surface after his twenty minute dive. The seas were becoming higher and steeper now as we worked our way into the tidal stream that sweeps along Bequia's north shore.

"Blows!" I sang out and pointed to a spot well out ahead, earning a nod of approval from Athneal. We continued to sail since we were too far away for an approach. The whale spouted five times before sounding, and we now had a better idea of his direction and rate of travel as he fed in the ocean depths.

Again we beat into the wind, this time for about ten minutes, before Athneal gave the signal to heave-to. Tension mounted as the long minutes of the dive stretched on. Then a slick appeared on the water's surface forty yards off the starboard bow. This time the vapor cloud was accompanied by an explosive *whoosh*. There was no hail this time; we were too close. By good luck, the whale lay with its massive head toward us (a boat approaching from either side is easily seen by a whale; a boat approaching from astern risks injury from the powerful flukes).

Softly, almost gingerly, each man went about his job. Any bump or scrape, magnified through the bottom of the boat, could send the whale sounding to safety. The sheets were lightly held, just enough to keep the boat gliding toward the shiny black mass. Athneal wedged his knee and tested the weight of the harpoon to loosen his arms.

Whoosh. This time we were so close we could smell the warm, stale air expelled from the whale's lungs. Softly, Uncle Joseph slid into place the long steering oar, more effective in close quarters, where it may be necessary to turn the boat half around with a single stroke to avoid the dangerous flukes. Three other men had quietly gotten out paddles and were moving us slowly closer to the shiny black body. Then, with one smooth, unhurried motion, Athneal lifted with his right arm and surged forward with his whole body, arching the heavy harpoon up and over the back of the whale where it struck and buried itself to the wooden haft.

Suddenly, everyone was in motion. A broad sweep of the steering oar turned the boat to the side, out of immediate danger. The shrouds were hurriedly loosed, and the mast and sails thrown in a heap back along the thwarts. Uncle Joseph, with a quick tug, lifted the rudder off the pintles and left it floating at the end of a short piece of line.

From the whale, nothing — a long moment of empty time while an animal weighing 30 tons gathered the strength to struggle for its life. Then the dark shape of the tail began to move and a slick formed at the surface of the water. The flukes lifted clear and the heavy body of the whale began to slide down-ward into the sea: deep into the sea to escape; down until the choking need for air should force it back to the surface.

While the others worked to prepare the boat for the struggle, Athneal moved rapidly to clear the line and make sure there would be no fouling. As the dive began, the men crouched in the bottom of the boat to protect themselves from the smoking, hissing rope that followed the whale down into the sea. Abruptly the stern lifted, and water began to rush in over the bows. The line was not running free and the whale was dragging us with him.

"Slack, Joseph, slack," Athneal screamed.

Uncle Joseph grabbed for the baling gourd and, in the nick of time, splashed water on the snubbing post, cooling the line and easing its run.

After a period of time that seemed endless, though I suppose it was only a few minutes, the line slowed and we could sense that the whale had stopped sounding. As the strain lessened and then disappeared, line was taken in to be piled loosely in the bottom of the boat; the whale would not sound that deeply again.

When the whale blew and sounded again, line was paid out very slowly, most of the strain being eased by the boat moving across the surface of the water. After sounding three times, each time for a shorter interval, the whale became winded and simply swam at the surface of the sea, towing us behind him, betraying his failing strength by smaller and more rapid spouts. Now the men began to overhaul the line in good earnest, drawing us closer and closer to the whale. Athneal slid one of the lances out and took up his position in the bow. The whale was almost still in the water now, and Athneal motioned us closer and closer. With the lance braced across his chest, he lunged with his whole weight, driving it into the whale's side, just behind the left flipper.

Abruptly, the whale was alive again, thrashing wildly. Athneal, still grip-ping the lance, was lifted clear of the boat and thrown into the sea. Uncle Joseph's quick action with the steering oar saved the boat, and Athneal scrambled back aboard. Twice more he lanced, until all three lances were in the whale, which had still not made its death spasm.

"The bomb lance," someone called. "Use the bomb lance." Others nodded agreement. They wanted to end the struggle quickly by using the old brass blunderbuss with its exploding projectile.

"Lance going to get him, boys," Athneal laughed. "Is only a small one. Let we save bomb lance for big one."

He lifted his left foot onto the stem head and motioned us to close with the whale again. At first I was puzzled. What did he intend to do without a lance?

Then, with a single flowing movement, Athneal rose to balance for an in-stant on the gunwales before leaping toward the whale. He landed with both feet on the shiny back and hurled himself onto the last lance, driving it into the whale with all his weight.

The whale made a convulsive dive, and Athneal was left swimming again. But, this time the line stayed slack and the whale floated slowly back to the surface, all life gone. Later, Athneal explained to me that the third lance had been well-placed but had not gone deep enough. When he drove it in, he was counting on cutting the spinal cord and paralysing the whale.

Everyone was shouting at once as they helped Athneal back aboard, relieving the tension which had been building since early morning. Then, as the excitement died, the other boat came along on the other side of the whale, and preparations began for getting the whale back to the try works on the small island of Petit Nevis, located a few hundred yards off La Pompe.

First, a cut was made in the floor of the mouth and a rope passed through to lash the long, heavy lower jaw closed. Otherwise, it might hang open, increasing drag as the whale was towed and causing the whale to fill with water and sink.

It had been wearisome to have to beat while chasing the whale, but now we were in the fortunate position of lying to windward of the try works, permitting us to sail home rather than having to row with the whale in tow. Since the whale was relatively small, he was simply lashed alongside the *Dart* for the sail home. Two hours brought us into the lee of Petit Nevis where the whale was hauled onto a rocky ledge just below the level of the water.

A large, noisy crowd had already gathered, coming and going in a fleet of fishing boats. The cutting up began immediately with the usual instructions, advice, counter-advice and incessant bickering over precedence and perquisites. The blubber was cut into large sheets and pulled ashore with ropes. Then the butchering began (fig. VIII-4), with an excitement which somehow came as a surprise to me.

My notion of whaling, principally gleaned from *Moby Dick*, was that the value of a whale lay in the oil and in the bony plates that line the mouth of the baleen whales (of which the humpback is one). Not so on Bequia, where no one wears corsets and no one uses whale oil lamps. Some oil is still rendered in the large iron pots housed under a nearby shed, but the only market in recent years is the Lever Bros. soap works in Trinidad, where the price is no more than that paid for coconut oil, *i.e.* not worth transporting to Trinidad.

The principle value of the whale in Bequia lies in the meat. Whaling is just another form of fishing — with a longer line and a bigger hook. The meat itself is red and somewhat coarse-grained, without a trace of fat or gristle anywhere. It looks like the largest, most sumptuous beefsteak ever seen. The first time I had whale steak, I went about preparing it just as I would have beef, pan-broiling an enormous thick piece in a lightly greased skillet, while rubbing my hands together and chortling in anticipation. The first bite was heaven, rich and delicious, almost sweet. The second was a little less to my taste, and after the third bite I ate no more.

It was not until I began to board with the Mitchells that I discovered the proper way to cook it. The meat must be cut in small chunks, fried in a

fig. VIII-4. Butchering a humpback whale at the
tryworks on Petit Nevis, off Bequia.
March, 1972.

generous amount of the rendered oil and then added to a pot of rice and pigeon peas. In this combination, it is delicious. However, tastes in meat are largely cultural, and any wholesome meat comes to have a value in a protein-poor economy such as St. Vincent.

As our whale was cut up, the meat was brought ashore and arranged in piles of about 5 pounds each, and was sold more or less continuously for the remainder of the day (fig. VII-5). Some people bought meat for their own use — to be cooked and eaten fresh or to be preserved by covering the cooked meat with freshly rendered whale oil, in which condition it will keep for 3-4 months — and others bought larger quantities which they spread to dry on their roofs and sold in St. Vincent for $1 EC per pound.

The twelve whalers share equally in the profits from a whale, while Athneal and his two brothers each have an additional share as owners of the boats and the try works. However, the season is short and a season's catch

fig. VIII-5. Whale for sale, Petit Nevis. March, 1972.

does not usually run to more than 4 or 5 whales. In addition, it is difficult to dispose of the meat profitably since there are no cold storage facilities in either Bequia or St. Vincent, meaning that the entire carcass, which may yield as much as 20 tons of meat, must be sold in a few hours. In fact, many of the customers simply wait for the end of the day and count on pilfering what they need as the whalers grow weary of waiting.

The rewards could not be very substantial, since all the whalers have other occupations during the off-season. And still they go out, day after day during the season, buffeted by wind and waves, blistered by the sun, sitting cramped on a hard wooden seat for up to eight hours at a stretch — not to mention the element of risk. The motive behind the whaling must be more than economics. Perhaps it is that Bequia is consummately a sea-faring island, and whaling is the greatest contest of the seas.

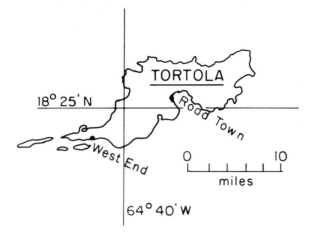

CHAPTER IX

HOMEWARD *VIA* TORTOLA

When at last my conscience renounced the gentle rhythm of life in Bequia, I resumed my journey northward and homeward in a relaxed mood — calling on friends here, adding a photograph there, but doing nothing in the least energetic, since my project, already much extended, had been completed by the launching of *Skywave*. There was only one small inquiry that remained to be made — a simple detail, easily dealt with.

Since it was a Tortola-built boat, the *Flame*, that had first aroused my interest in West Indian boatbuilding, it was simply a matter of thoroughness to make a stopover in Tortola. That it would be a short stopover there was no doubt; I knew, from excursions to the British Virgin Islands made while teaching in St. Croix, that boatbuilding in Tortola was already a thing of the past. The most there was to look forward to was a nostalgic conversation or two with former builders.

I knew the name of the man in West End who had owned the *Flame* before she came to St. Croix, and he in turn was able to direct me to the builder, who had weathered the decline in Tortola boatbuilding by turning importer and wholesale grocer (an important position on an island which produces nothing). Which is how I came to enter the business establishment of Leo Smith, on the main street of Roadtown.

Business was slow in the middle of the afternoon, and Smith, a clear-complexioned man of uncertain age, readily fell into conversation. To my preliminary inquiries about boatbuilding, he gave a rueful shake of his head and replied, "Them days is gone. Gone forever." We thereupon had a round of crocodile tears — mine because it meant there was nothing for me to do: his because, I suspect, he was just as glad to earn his living less strenuously (fig. IX-1).

fig. IX-1. *Shaping a boat timber with an adze at
Trellis Bay, Tortola. 1966. Photo by
Edwin M. Doran, Jr.*

With unswerving devotion to duty, I began to question him on those
points of design and construction that I had come to regard as important: the
proportion of beam to length used in Tortola, how he had learned his trade,
where the traditions of boat carpentry had originated. As he pondered my
questions, a far-away look came into his faded blue eyes.

"It have a next fella come here some time ago asking all them question,"
he replied, slowly and consideringly. "Then he go 'way and write a book."

My heart raced, and all I could hear was the pounding of the blood in my
ears. Had I really been so dumb? Had I spent nearly two years re-inventing the
wheel? I *had* run a quick check of the literature at the University of Puerto
Rico before setting out. Their collection, however, was sketchy, and I had done
the search in great haste, simply assuming that my inquiry was original
because it *felt* original. Now, my house of cards — very dear to me, however
flimsy — apeared to be falling in.

Evidently my deep chagrin was effectively masked, because Smith continued cheerfully to tell me about "that next fella" — how he had measured,
how he had photographed — blithely driving the stake ever deeper into my
scarcely beating heart. Slowly I collected myself enough to inquire if he
remembered the fella's name.

"Oh, yes," Smith replied. "He send me the book. Let we see and I can find it." Whereupon he drove me to his house, beautifully sited halfway up a steep hill overlooking the harbor, quietly pleased to share with me the affluence of his present circumstances and his worldliness in having overseas friends. While he searched, I sat on the verandah, consoling myself, as I have done before and since, with the enchantment of sunlight, sea and islands. All too soon he returned, triumphantly waving my nemesis in its plain brown wrapper: *The Tortola Boat: Characteristics, Origin, Demise.* By Edwin M. Doran, Jr. Supplement to "The Mariner's Mirror", Vol. 56, No. 1.

My heart sank even further at the crisp title and no-nonesense format. It was obviously a scholarly work, and not, as I had briefly hoped, a *pot pourri* of sentiment and folklore put together for the tourist trade. Smith was obviously much attached to his momento, and so, with solemn pledges to return it soon, I crept back aboard *Eider* to read the monograph and lick my wounds, intrigued in spite of my disappointment.

Professor Doran had visited Tortola for several months in 1966 — photographing, taking off lines and talking with builders at a time when there was still some active boatbuilding on the island. His work was detailed and precise: I was fifteen years too late, but read on with great interest. In addition to the field work done in Tortola, the author, a professional geographer and culture historian, had researched extensively the historical aspects of the Tortola boat type.

With quickening attention, I came to the section on "Origins" which concluded with the statement, "Once we have reached this point little more, unfortunately, can be said about the origin of the Tortola boat. Our basic problem here is the lack of knowledge about other West Indian boat types. Essentially no other lines plans of West Indian craft have been published and our ignorance of their detailed characteristics is almost complete."

My spirits rose now as rapidly as they had sunk before. Not only did Doran's work provide me with the lines of vessels no longer available for measuring, but also there was the exciting discovery that I had been doing what a professional in the field considered to be a necessary next step. That very afternoon I wrote to Professor Doran who replied, immediately and encouragingly, from Texas A & M University, where he was the head of the geography department.

After his sojourn in Tortola, he wrote, his principal area of research had shifted to the watercraft of the islands of the western Pacific with the result that he had never extended the work he began in Tortola. This was perfect as far as I was concerned — not only was I still exploring virgin territory, I was not even encroaching. As it happened, I was at this time about due for a visit with my mother in Oklahoma, which gave me the opportunity to consult personally with Professor Doran.

Until this time, I had planned simply to submit my drawings with brief notes to some learned journal devoted to Caribbean studies. Now, during two days of conversations with Doran, it emerged that the material thus far collected could form the basis for a broader treatment in a field — new to me — called marine anthropology. Thus far, I had concerned myself with only a few representative sloops and schooners. What was needed was information on *all* the watercraft of the region along with performance date and historical information where available.

Not only did Professor Doran encourage me to pursue the topic, he also kindly put at my disposal his monograph, photographic negatives, reprints and bibliographic materials on the subject. And he pointed out to me an important historical source that had been under my nose all along — the *Registers of Shipping* that are kept in the Harbor Master's Office of all formerly British islands.

The realization that much remained to be done had the unusual (for me) effect of producing a sense of elation, rather than depression. After all, *Eider* was still in the Antilles, and there are many things worse than sailing from island to island in quest of boat types and historical records. Especially since I now had the assurance that my inquiries were not mere personal eccentricity, but could be considered, at least in some circles, a useful sort of enterprise.

And that, Gentle Reader, is how I became a marine anthropologist, which patent I confirmed by purchasing several notebooks, a fifty-foot measuring tape, a Pitot tube for estimating boat speed, a hand-held anemometer and one thousand business cards upon which I styled myself: "Douglas C. Pyle, M. Sc., Marine Anthropologist." For this final affectation, let me offer a word of explanation: of the one thousand cards (most of which remain in my possession and make handy grocery lists) only fourteen were used in the course of my researchers, and they were crucial. In the frequently formal atmosphere of West Indian officialdom, a degree or a title may open doors that would remain closed to mere honest inquiry (but are the West Indies unique in that respect?). In any case, the cards cost $9.00, which divided by 14 works out at 64¢ for each occasion that a card provided the necessary entree, a remarkable value by any standards.

Meanwhile, back in Tortola, my metamorphosis into a marine anthropologist was still in the future, and I rocked gently at anchor, enjoying a period of euphoria which is unique to those occasions when a crisis has come and gone without serious harm. Sufficient unto the day was the fact that the watercraft of Tortola had already been characterized, and I had the afternoon off.

From Professor Doran's monograph I have included two sets of lines which seem best to typify boat construction in Tortola. The first set are of the sloop *Yolanda* (fig. IX-2), built about 1930 by Leo Smith, the lines being taken from the builder's half model in 1966. This vessel is similar to both *Skywave* and *Mermaid* — in beam-to-length ratio, in the sharp floors of the midsection, in the overhanging stern and in the moderate drag to the keel. There are individual differences in the shape of the stem and the transom, but it is

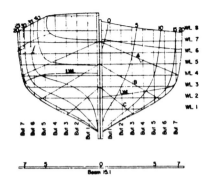

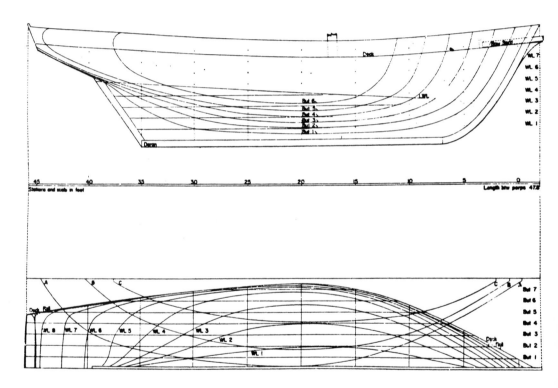

fig. IX-2. Lines of sloop Yolanda. *Built 1930 by
Leopold Smith at Roadtown, Tortola.
Taken off 1966 by Edwin M. Doran, Jr.*

clear at a glance that all three belong to the same family of inter-island
sloops, a type which is remarkably constant over a considerable span of time
and distance.

By contrast, the *Sea Queen* (fig. IX-3&4) has markedly different characteristics — a beam-to-length ratio of 1:3, a rounded mid-section, noticeable
hollow in the lower waterlines, no overhanging stern, extreme drag to the keel,

130

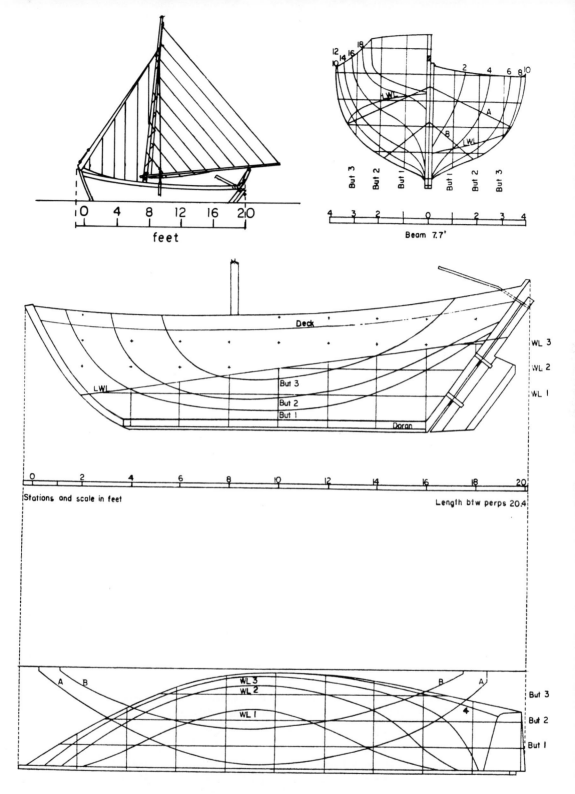

fig. IX-3. Lines of Tortola sloop Sea Queen. Built 1959 by Osmond Davies at East End, Tortola. Taken off 1966 by Edwin M. Doran, Jr.

fig. IX-4. Sea Queen *on the hard at Roadtown, Tortola. 1966. Photo by Edwin M. Doran, Jr.*

fig. IX-5. *Tortola sloop getting underway at East End, Tortola. 1966. Photo by Edwin M. Doran, Jr.*

pronounced or "moon" sheer and a leg-of-mutton mainsail (fig. IX-5). It is these traits which, taken all together, characterize the type known as the Tortola sloop (the transom stern and the moon sheer of the Antigua fishing sloops are recent and conscious copies, cf. Chapter 16).

The distinctiveness of the Tortola type was intriguing and gave me my first taste of the joys of life as a marine anthropologist: interisland trading vessels which had occupied my attention up to this point, show such similar characteristics that a common ancestor or design influence is easily inferred. Not so for smaller and purely local watercraft, which are usually unique to an island or group of islands with recognizable ties. Finding some clue to the origins of these purely local types became one of my principle preoccupations during the second phase of my inquiry.

The 68-foot schooner *Pride of Tortola*, represented in Doran's monograph, deserves comment without requiring to be reproduced here. Though built in Tortola for a Tortola owner, this schooner was actually built by MacDuff Richardson of Anguilla, who has already made his appearance in this narative. As a matter of fact, it was while working in the Virgin Islands that Mac received the blow to the head that was said to account for his unconventional views on current affairs and a certain unreliability in his professional capacity.

133

In any case, the exchange of boatbuilders between boatbuilding communities does give a clue as to why interisland trading vessels should be broadly similar while smaller craft retain their distinctive local traits.

It was curious that the simple fact of designating myself a marine anthropologist caused me to consider in a new light these and other observations that had previously seemed unrelated and without meaning. For example, I had been aware even before leaving St. Croix that there was no evidence of any indigenous boatbuilding activity in the U.S. Virgin Islands. My initial reaction was a shrug of the shoulders, and only later, when I had seen similar patterns elsewhere, did the underlying reasons begin to take shape.

St. Croix, a relatively small island with no near neighbors, had in the past a pure plantation economy. Manufactured goods arrived and sugar left in ships belonging to the Danish West India Company. There was simply no employment for locally built watercraft. The situation in St. Thomas was similar, though in this case the economic fortunes of the island turned on its free port status and its functions as a transshipment point. The result, however, was the same in that European vessels dominated shipping; a very limited local commerce was carried on in vessels built in Tortola.

These and other reflections, induced by my contact with Professor Doran, caused me to redefine my objectives, and I embarked on a new course of study which might be called "musical islands." During this phase, I sailed the arc of the Lesser Antilles four more times, measuring watercraft that had been missed earlier and searching for evidence, historical or oral, of earlier activity. Interestingly enough, I found that my first trip, guided only by hearsay and instinct, had nevertheless included all the islands that had active maritime industries. On the other hand, I did measure many types of watercraft previously overlooked, and discovered traces of earlier boatbuilding in areas no longer active. Also, many details and insights formerly unnoticed or disregarded were added to my notes.

The Lesser Antilles constitute a cultural mosaic of bewildering complexity. There are, of course, the obvious differences produced by colonial acquisition and administration, as well as differences in climate and economics engendered by different rainfall patterns. There are, however, other differences not so easily explained. On some islands, Carriacou for example, there is an awareness of African descent which extends to a detailed knowledge of tribal origins. On others, such as Martinique, many of the people are fiercely Europeanized — to the extent that can only occur in a post-colonial society. In some communities in sight of the sea, most people do not swim and are afraid of the water. In others, all ages swim and water sports are popular. On some islands, political administration is malicious or lackadaisical or both. On others, government functions well, even remarkably well.

Boatbuilding, as an aspect of material culture, shows in the islands the same mosaic quality, and is similarly unyielding to analysis. On some islands, like Anguilla, with few natural advantages, there is continuous and conspicuous boatbuilding. On others, such as St. Martin, advantages abound but no established tradition exists. As my interests broadened to include the origins and design influences in boatbuilding traditions, it became almost as important to know where building had not taken place. This meant looking on all the islands, even when I was reasonably certain that I already knew the answer.

Before it was over, I had visited all the islands except Barbuda and Tobago. My itinerary was shaped by wind, weather, regatta dates, and often by pure personal whim. As a consequence, my notes for this period are a kaleidoscopic succession of people, places and events. In an effort to present the information more clearly, I have disregarded time sequence, choosing instead to deal with the islands in geographical order from north to south, beginning in St. Martin on Bastille Day, 1974.

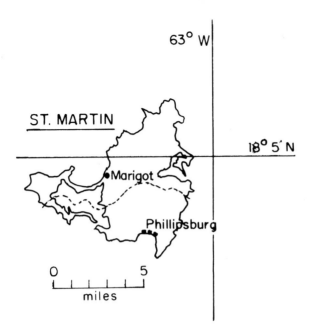

CHAPTER X

ST. MARTIN

The island of St. Martin lies south of Anguilla — across a channel only four miles wide, and yet the contrast between the two could scarcely be more marked. Anguilla is low, flat, isolated, has no all-weather harbors and no stands of trees suitable for boat timbers. St. Martin, on the other hand, has a backbone of rugged volcanic crests, a number of protected harbors, timber resources and a superficial prosperity resulting from a booming tourist industry. Both islands are dry — about the only shared condition, unless one counts as similarity certain political peculiarities.

In the case of Anguilla, it was recently her distinction to secure, in a surge of genuinely local sentiment, the blessings of independence by detaching herself from the independent *State of Nevis, St. Kitts and Anguilla* and re-attaching herself to the British crown — admittedly an unusual solution in the political climate of today's Caribbean.

The peculiarity of St. Martin is of longer standing and different sort — half of the island is Dutch and the other half French, creating a European frontier some 7 miles in length on a tiny island thousands of miles from Europe. Local tradition ascribes this split administration to the fact that the island was originally settled by a Frenchman and a Dutchman, who initially shared the island without benefit of politics, there being scarcely enough of it to quarrel over. Later, however, the situation was thought to require the clarification of established sovereignty and avowed allegiance.

No other solution being found, the two men ultimately found themselves back to back in the dawn's early light on a deserted stretch of beach not far from the site of the present airport. On signal they began to pace, each measured tread carrying them farther apart and closer to the moment of resolution. Step by step they moved across the wave-smoothed sand — until shortly after noon they had gotten so far apart that they had actually begun to draw closer. By four o'clock they had met on the windward side of the island, thus establishing the eastern end of the boundary line which was to run straight across the island from the point of departure to the point of encounter. It is further said that the Dutchman stopped for a siesta during the heat of the day, thus accounting for the slightly larger portion accruing to La Belle France.

However it may have come about, the southern portion of the island, officially Sint Maarten, is administered in Dutch by Dutch civil servants with the advice of a locally elected council. The northern portion, called St. Martin, is administered in French by French bureaucrats with the advice of no one. Meanwhile, the daily life of the island is carried on in English (of Caribbean inflection) with little regard for the niceties of administration or frontiers and few objections or difficulties from the authorities. The low level of official interference may simply be because there are few taxes to be wrung from such a dry island — additional evidence, if any be required, that aside from the possibilities of tax collection, military conscription and the garnering of votes, most governments have little concern for the doings of their citizens.

On one of my early visits to Anguilla, I heard of a fishing boat regatta held in Marigot Bay every year on the 14th of July. In 1974, as the first stop on my new program of "musical islands," I made shift to celebrate Bastille Day as it should be done — on French soil, with French bread and red wine, if available. This would provide, thought I, an excellent opportunity to measure the boats of Sint Maarten/St. Martin foregathered for the regatta.

On the evening of the 13th, I anchored close to the long curving beach that stretches westward from the little town of Marigot and scanned the shoreline for boats. It proved comparatively easy to select the boat that would represent the island in my study — there was only one boat in view over the whole sweep of the bay. It was clearly a racing boat because there was a group of men gathered around, rigging and trimming the freshly painted hull.

I rowed over to scrape acquaintance and ask permission to take off the lines, finding to my surprise a friend in the group. NoNo Richardson, whom I had known in St. Croix, had come back to St. Martin to race his cousin's boat, the *Alma Gloria*, in the regatta. NoNo was something of a sensation in St. Croix yacht racing circles, where he skippered a small yacht of no special distinction, invariably managing to out-foot and out-point all competitors. If you can do that consistently, you can bring home a lot of silver, which NoNo regularly did, frequently being the only black face at the after-race award dinners. NoNo's presence in St. Martin meant that I was assured of getting lines and performance data, as well as having a favorite in the regatta.

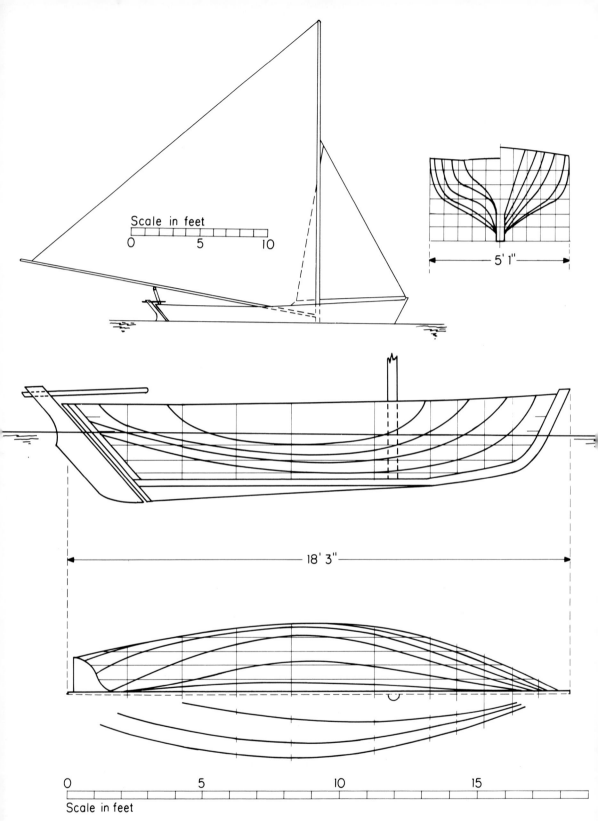

Scale in feet
0   5   10

5' 1"

18' 3"

0   5   10   15
Scale in feet

fig. X-1. Lines of fishing boat Alma Gloria. Built
by Philbert Richardson at Marigot Bay,
St. Martin. Taken off at Marigot Bay,
July, 1974.

The lines of the *Alma Gloria* (fig. X-1) show a close resemblance to the Anguilla beach boats in the strongly curved forefoot, fine entry, marked drag to the keel, sharp floors and the easy run carried onto the transom stern. The rig also is similar, with its leg-of-mutton mainsail and jib hoist at two-thirds of the mast.

The next morning, NoNo was out to tune the boat and came alongside *Eider* to pick me up. The breeze was very light in the confines of the bay, too light for the *Alma Gloria* to develop her full potential. Nevertheless, the figures indicate a weatherly craft with a good turn of speed.

Point of sailing	Angle off the wind	Wind speed in knots	Boat speed in knots	Leeway angle	Boat speed - wind speed
Close-hauled	45⁰	8	5.9	10⁰	.74
	40⁰	10	5.2	10⁰	.52
Beam reach	100⁰	8	5.7	5⁰	.71
Broad reach	115⁰	10	5.4	5⁰	.54
Running	180⁰	6	3.7	—	.61

As NoNo put the *Alma Gloria* through her paces, I noticed that he was carrying bags of sand for ballast, instead of stones. When I asked, he grinned and explained that on the down wind leg he planned to leave the sand dry and keep the boat light. On the beat back to the finish line, he would wet the sand and increase the ballast according to wind conditions prevailing at the time.

By the time we had finished the performance trial, the rest of the contestants had arrived — as it turned out, all the rest were from Anguilla. A crowd had begun to gather along the sea wall in front of the town, and the race committee, meeting in a dockside grog shop, dispensed with the ever troublesome issue of handicapping by assigning all entrants either to the 18-foot class or the 24-foot class.

Soon the smaller boats were gathered for the start, arraying themselves along the sea wall with sails set, crew in place, and stern held by the skipper, standing waist deep in water. At the starting gun, the skipper and as many well-wishers as cared to get wet pushed, swam, splashed and shouted the boats into motion, each seeking to be the first to clear the sea wall and get clean wind.

The afternoon was bright and hot, and the breeze continued very light. The boats were still closely grouped as they passed among the anchored yachts where I watched (fig. X-2), but racing downwind in light airs never settles anything. The race would be decided on the long beat back from the leeward mark, and it was then that I looked for NoNo to show his stuff.

When the smaller boats were all down the bay, the larger class was started. After they had swept through the anchorage, there was nothing to watch, so I began idly to compose a paean of praise to NoNo, terror of St. Croix and now, scourge of St. Martin.

fig. X-2. NoNo Richardson skippers the Alma
Gloria (foreground) in the Bastille Day
Regatta, Marigot Bay, St. Martin.

As the small boats reached the leeward mark, I could just make out a
change in the shape of their sails as, one by one, they rounded the mark and
came close-hauled. Now, the tiny white triangles began to glide effortlessly
back and forth across the smooth expanse of the bay, slowly drawing closer.
I strained to pick out the *Alma Gloria*, but it was impossible to distinguish
one white hull from another against the shimmering surface of the sea. The
boats were well up among the anchored yachts again before I could be sure
that NoNo was not among them. After half a minute of anxious searching,
I located the *Alma Gloria*, close under the shore as NoNo had planned, but
completely out of the race.

As I pondered the implications of this for yacht racing in St. Croix (what if
the Anguillans came to try their skill where NoNo was already unbeatable?),
the leaders in the class were closing for the finish, designed in this regatta to
avoid any possibility of argument over first place. A stake boat had been
anchored off the sea wall where the race started. Affixed to the stem of the
stake boat was a small Tricolor, waving merrily in the breeze. As the two

leading boats closed with the stake boat, a crew member lay in the bows of each, held by the ankles and stretched to his full length. Amid a crescendo of shouts from the shore, the boats feinted, then one edged inside the other and *Quick Step* of Anguilla snatched the flag. There being no second flag, there was no second place. Winner take all.

The larger class was won by *Saga Boy* (cf. Chapter 13) belonging to Emile Gumbs of Anguilla. Apart from the *Alma Gloria*, all the entrants in both classes were from Anguilla. This preponderance at the regatta foreshadowed the conclusions reached when I extended my inquiries to the matter of interisland vessels.

In the past the inhabitants of St. Martin supported themselves in part by killing wild cattle that roamed the island and preserving the meat with salt produced in the shallow lagoons on the leeward side of the island. Salt and bully beef were then sold to passing ships, many of them fishing schooners from New England and Nova Scotia. I can only suppose, when remembering those steep hillsides covered in dry, thorny scrub, that the purchasers of this bully beef must have had very good appetites and even better teeth.

Eating habits aside, what interested me was that local boatbuilders, as a result of this commerce, would have had ample opportunity to see and copy the schooner type. This influence, coupled with natural harbors and the timber resources of St. Martin, might have fostered a maritime industry — at some point in the past, even if there were none at present. With this in mind, I tackled both French and Dutch administrations in search of ship registrations.

My inquiries produced brows knit in concentration, shaken heads and shrugs, but no vessel registrations. I did happen onto a man named Williams whose father had built fishing vessels some thirty years earlier, and a young woman whose father had told her of two schooners, the *Anna* and the *Leontine* built in 1915-16 by John Connor Vlaun. It was only later when examining the *Register of Shipping* in St. Kitts that I began to have a clearer picture of this earlier activity.

Over the years since 1838, when the St. Kitts *Register* was begun, there were scattered entries for vessels built in St. Martin (also Saba, St. Eustatius and St. Barts) and brought to St. Kitts to be registered. Those from St. Martin were either built by Anguillans for Anguillans or, if the residence of the builder was given as St. Martin, by someone with an Anguilla surname (for example Richardson, Connor, Williams, etc). My conclusion was that these were, in reality, Anguilla vessels, even though built in St. Martin for access to materials or for some other convenience. And further, that the scarcity of boat-building in St. Martin resulted largely from having a near neighbor where, by historical accident or other contingency as yet unfathomed by me, a thriving maritime culture already existed.

However plausible this may be as explanation that there is little boat-building in St. Martin, it offers no help in understanding why there has been longstanding and continuous activity in Anguilla. There was nothing I could do about the inadequacy of my explanations other than to keep plugging and hope that if I could gather the facts for all the islands individually, then some intelligible pattern might emerge for the whole.

Onward!

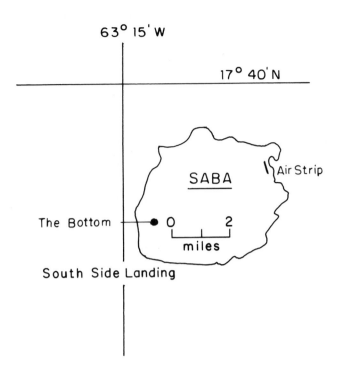

CHAPTER XI

SABA

In my earliest conversations and inquiries about boatbuilding, references to the island of Saba were made repeatedly and in tones of respectful awe. The tone of awe was explained by my first glimpse of the single volcanic cone which forms the island — rising, as it does, from 2000 feet under the sea to soar another 3000 feet into the atmosphere. The shoreline is everywhere steep-to, and there are no anchorages. At one spot on the southern side of the island, the pilot book grudgingly concedes, "landing may be effected by small craft, with local knowledge, in fair weather."

"If there are no anchorages and landing is difficult, then why — or how — would boatbuilding be done?" was my skeptical reaction. However, the rumors were persistent and insistent: boats and even schooners had been built in Saba. As for the obstacles to such endeavors, "Well, Sabans are just more determined than the average run of folks." In defiance of all common sense, it was asserted that vessels had been built high on the side of the volcano and lowered down the face of the cliff for launching. These rumors were so persistent and circumstantial that I became curious in spite of my skepticism.

143

fig. XI-1. Up, up and away. DeHaviland STOL
takes off from Saba airstrip. March, 1970.

My curiosity about Saba remained academic as long as getting there required landing in the fashion prescribed by the pilot book. Fortunately, while in St. Martin, I discovered that there was another, and perfectly acceptable, way to visit the island. As it happened, an enterprising Saban had recently found a shoulder of nearly level ground on the windward side of the mountain and had boasted that he could build an airstrip if only he had a bulldozer. The Dutch administration managed to put a small 'dozer ashore at South Side Landing, whereupon the aforesaid Saban gouged a road across the island and proceeded to keep his end of the bargain.

All very well, but a sizeable hurdle still remained since, for all the ingenuity in the world, the landing strip was almighty short. In fact, a new type of aircraft, designated the STOL (Short Take-Off and Landing), was developed by DeHaviland for this run and was just getting put into service in the early 1970's, when I was there. The fare from St. Martin to Saba, a round trip distance of 50 miles, was $30 US, the most expensive air mileage in the Caribbean, but cheap compared to the emotional cost of anchoring in 50 fathoms poor holding, on the rocky, wave-pounded flank of a volcano, even an extinct one.

Cheap it seemed, until we banked for our landing in a stiff crosswind, and I looked down at the landing strip,which appeared no larger than a tennis court. I am well aware that appearances may be deceiving to the inexperienced eye, but in sober truth the wheels jarred onto the landing strip while I, seated just behind the wing, was still staring down into the foaming sea below.

After deplaning, I stood alone beside the strip and watched while the airplane taxied to the end of the runway and lifted slowly into the air before striking out for St. Eustatius (fig. XI-1). I stood for a time, pondering the ingenuity of mankind in its quest for mobility, then set forth to retrace the historic route of the bulldozer, winding up the steep side of the volcano through the swirling mists while above me loomed the unseen summit, hidden in the wind-driven clouds (fig. XI-2).

The effect was a little unsettling — a few minutes earlier, in St. Martin, I had been sweating in the sun while around me people bustled and traffic snarled. Now I stood in the middle of the road, made clammy by the mists and the hidden sun, and there was no one to be seen — no cars, no people, not even any telephone poles by the roadside for company. I hiked the main thorough-fare in lonely splendor, climbing upward toward the little collection of houses known as Hellsgate. There, people stood in their doorways, smiling and speaking to me, helping to restore a sense of reality.

At another group of houses called Windward (fig. XI-3), the road stopped climbing and began to circle, following the side of the mountain for a distance before dropping down into the crater where lay the main settlement of the island, called, with commendable economy, The Bottom. At the near edge of the settled area, a young man lounged in the doorway of a small, neat house exactly resembling all the other small, neat houses in sight. I had been lucky enough, he informed me, to locate — on my very first try — the Old Inn Club.

fig. XI-2. Cloud-obscured summit of Saba. March, 1970.

145

fig. XI-3. Community of Windward, Saba. March, 1970.

I entered his establishment, asking for and getting in the following order: a cold bottle of beer, a meal, plain but filling, and information on boatbuilding. The beer and food came from a small room at the back of the house and were served to me in a small room at the front of the house. The information on boatbuilding came from a small house across the road wherein dwelt the publican's father, Bertil Chance, a shipwright and carpenter.

Chance, then already in his eighties, was born in St. Martin and had lived for many years in St. Barts before coming to Saba 36 years earlier. He told me of vessels built in Saba, and when I asked how they were launched, he replied that the lower ends of the ways along one side of the completed hull were sharpened so that they drove slowly into the sand, bringing the hull gently to rest on a bed of planks and rollers. Then, a tackle (he pronounced TAY-kell) was rigged from a kedge anchor to haul the vessel into the water.

From these recollections he drifted into tales of hurricanes and other extraordinary happenings, mostly centering on the occasion when high winds swept his privy into a field two hundred yards away. After the eye of the hurricane had passed, the winds changed and the privy was picked up and returned to its foundations. During the following hour, my repeated attempts to return to the subject of boatbuilding failed, though I became something of an expert on the aerodynamics of the West Indian backhouse.

After saying goodbye to Chance, I walked down the steep, winding road to

South Side Landing, where a strip of rocky shingle 50 feet long and 10 feet wide was tucked into a fold in the volcanic cliffs. There was no sand. At one end, a tiny customs house had been built, just in case. Nearby, two rugged surfboats were pulled up beyond the reach of the waves. It was apparent at a glance that there was no room to build anything larger than a rowboat — much less to launch in the manner described by Chance. I could only conclude that the passage of time had collapsed his experience of launchings elsewhere, probably St. Barts, onto his memories of Saba. In any case, the rumors about Saba had all agreed that launching took place by lowering the vessels down the cliffs.

As I weighed these matters in my mind, a small freighter put a line onto the Texaco mooring buoy and began preparations to discharge cargo. A Land Rover was swayed up and over the side, then lowered onto a small raft made of empty oil drums and rough lumber. One man sat at the wheel of the Land Rover, while another waited at the tiller of an outboard-powered surfboat.

Pushed by the surfboat, the raft left the side of the freighter and moved sluggishly toward the shore, pausing just beyond the point where the incoming waves began to crest. Several waves passed under the motionless raft while the man in the Land Rover waited. When he saw his moment, he yelled to the boatman, who stirred the outboard to maximum effort and brought the raft onto the cresting wave. The wave gathered power, and suddenly the raft was rushing forward, pulling the surfboat behind it. As the raft grated onto the rocky beach, the driver gunned the engine and the Land Rover surged off the raft, all four wheels spinning and fighting for a grip on the slippery stones.

For an anxious moment, the pull of the receding wave held the struggling vehicle. Then, the front wheels gained traction, pulling vehicle and driver up the beach just ahead of the next wave. Through the whole sequence, I stood dumbfounded: seeing is believing, but somehow my imagination would not stretch to encompass a bulldozer.

Long after my visit to Saba, as I tried to add historical depth to my inquiries, I found references to Saba in a couple of traveler's accounts. Charles Stoddard, writing in 1895 in *Crusing among the Caribees*, remarks that "true to their Dutch ancestry, they [the Sabans] are sailors and boatbuilders. Up in their mountainous crater they build the staunchest fishing boats that sail the Caribbean Sea and when these are finished, they lower them down the side of the mountain with ropes and launch them in the ocean." Somewhat later and more briefly, Sir Frederick Treves comments in *The Cradle of the Deep:* "Saba is a boat-building island. Boats and small craft are built in The Bottom and lowered over the side."

However, neither author did anything more exacting than view the island from the deck of a passing cruise ship, so their accounts merely establish that the hearsay evidence about boatbuilding in Saba is of greater antiquity than I had earlier supposed. It was not until I examined the abstracts made by Professor Doran of the Tortola *Shipping Registers* that I finally got some hard data. In 1859 the schooner *Augusta* — 66 feet LOA, 49 T, built in Saba by

Benjamin Horton — was brought to Tortola to be registered. There were other vessels registered to a Saban owner and built elsewhere, but of all the entries that I surveyed — for Tortola, St. Kitts, Antigua, Montserrat, St. Lucia, St. Vincent or Grenada — this was the only vessel actually built in Saba.

Accordingly, I surmise that the folk history of boatbuilding in Saba developed in the following manner: Benjamin Horton, an unusually determined individual (possibly an ancestor of the bulldozer operator), against all advice and common sense, built a schooner in The Bottom and lowered it, not over the cliffs (the "cliffs" of a volcanic cone, as any geologist or geometrician can tell you, do not overhang), but down the steep valley now followed by the roadway, to South Side Landing, where it was launched. Even in this attenuated form, Horton's accomplishment was so memorable that it would have quickly become enshrined in the folklore of the island. Then, with the passage of time and frequent retelling, this singular event became pluralized, until finally whole fleets of vessels were popularly supposed to have been built and lowered over Saba's cliffs into the foaming sea below. That, at least, is the version that I favor.

However, in the matter of seafaring, the Sabans are secure from all corrosive skepticism; beyond any doubt, they *are* seafarers. There is little, if any, employement on the island and most Sabans who leave follow the sea.

The log of the whaling ship *Cicero* records a stopover in Saba while the captain, a Saban, visits his family. And more recently, there was my own encounter with Capt. Ben Hassel, master of the *Frances W. Smith*, shortly after arriving in the West Indies (cf. Chapter XXIV).

There is no doubt, then, that Saba is an island of sailors who would undoubtedly build boats if only circumstances were a little more favorable. In the meantime, the island forms another curious fragment in the Caribbean mosaic — an island of seafarers who do not build boats.

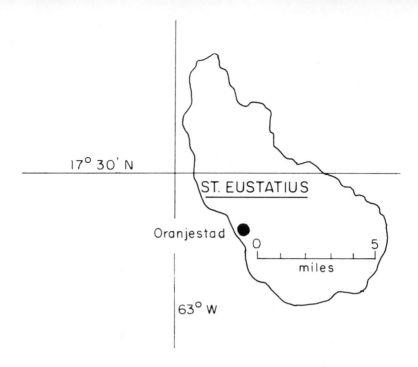

CHAPTER XII

ST. EUSTATIUS

The twin peaks of St. Eustatius (Statia) are easily visible from Saba or Sint Maarten, and the three islands together form the northern group of the Netherlands Antilles. Between the gently sloping volcanic cones of Statia lies a saddle of nearly level land, eight square miles in all, which forms in its lee a large and well-sheltered roadstead (fig. XII-1). The foreshore of this anchorage is edged with the ruined shells of buildings whose size and grandeur seem out of character with the peaceful, unfrequented roadstead of this small and arid island. Behind these ruins on a stone bluff, the small town of Oranjestad huddles under the wing of a small comic-opera fort.

The overall impression is that a once large and prosperous island has sunk into the sea, leaving a fringe of its former grandeur at the water's edge while the ruined inhabitants fled to the remaining high ground to re-establish themselves in dramatically reduced circumstances. The reality of this catastrophe is more political than geologic, but no less bizarre.

During the 1700's, as England and France struggled for primacy in Europe and the New World, the American colonies of both were required to trade only and directly with the mother country. Since the economic interests of the colonies did not always exactly coincide with those of the mother country, trade between and among colonies flourished in defiance of regulations. To give color of legitimacy to this intercolonial trade, sugar and rum from Martinique, for example, were shipped to Statia, where they were "purchased" by

149

fig. XII-1. *View of the roadstead at Oranjestad, St. Eustatius. November, 1970.*

neutral Dutch entrepreneurs, warehoused briefly ashore and then sold to a merchant vessel, perhaps from New York or Boston, which had sailed to Statia carrying lumber or salt cod. It was the little fort on the bluff that first saluted the new Stars and Strips ensign flown by an arriving merchant ship, constituting the first official recognition of the new nation.

The convenience of this arrangement had, of course, monetary value, and Statia waxed prosperous beyond the resources of its eight arid square miles. The Dutch were neither the first nor the last in the Lesser Antilles to prosper as neutrals. In fact, in the larger arena of world history, neutrality has been so frequently profitable — (Sweden or Switzerland for example in either World War I or II) — that it is surprising that the possibilities are not more frequently exploited. In any case, Statia became one of the busiest and most prosperous ports in the Antilles at this time.

Into this Eden of gently illegal endeavor, Admiral Rodney burst in 1781 like an avenging angel. The garrison of the little fort, hopelessly outgunned by Rodney's West Indies Squadron, struck their colors within the hour. Thereupon, Rodney and the Squadron romped and stomped through the roadstead, taking a gratifying number of prizes. This glorious action in defense of mercantilism should have secured for the victorious admiral the homage of an admiring populace and the rewards of a grateful government, in addition to what he had already copped in prize money.

What Rodney did not realize, or realized but discounted, was that the wealthy planters of nearby St. Kitts, not content to leave wholly to the Dutch the joys and benefits of neutrality, were maintaining their own factors and agents in Statia. Consequently, a great furor occurred in Parliament; what Rodney had seen as the enforcement of the Navigation Acts and, just incidentally, an opportunity to recover from extensive personal indebtedness, was construed in Parliament as a violation of the neutrality of St. Eustatius. The remainder of Rodney's naval career was dogged by this bitter dispute.

This strange concatenation of economics and politics first created, then destroyed, the docks and warehouses whose ruins along the shore constitute the high water mark of Statia's prosperity. Inland, a few ruined windmills indicate that at some time in the past someone raised a little cane, but when I saw the island, things were in a state of complete stagnation. In consequence, "doing" Statia required little effort and, since I found only two items with which to assuage my unappeasable appetite for marine anthropology, very little time.

Halfway up the steep little road that climbed from the waterfront to the town, I found a vessel under construction (fig. XII-2). The builder, instead of

fig. XII-2. Hard chine vessel in frames at Oranjestad, St. Eustatius. November, 1970.

using grown frames of West Indian white cedar, was using frames made from two sections of 2x8" lumber, the sides and floors being nailed together at the turn of the bilge. The result was a hard chine hull which, though arkward in appearance, was undoubtedly quicker and easier to frame and to plank. At a glance, I decided that however interesting such an experiment might be, it was not a traditional West Indian type and did not require to be measured.

Two years later on passage from St. Barts to St. Croix, I called again in Statia, where I found the hard chine vessel lying in the roadstead (fig. XII-3). Whatever the savings in time and material, the finished vessel was, alas, just as ungainly as might have been predicted. I felt fully vindicated in my decision not to preserve these lines for posterity.

After visiting the fort and walking around the little town awhile, I stopped for refreshment in Charlie's Bar, conveniently located in the lobby of the once-a-week movie house in the heart of downtown Oranjestad. It seemed as good a

*fig. XII-3. Hard chine vessel anchored off Oran-
jestad, St. Eustatius. May, 1972.*

place as any to make inquiries about a maritime past; in fact, it was exactly
the right place since Charlie himself had once sailed aboard a whaling vessel.
In April of 1917, he told me, the *B.S. Woodruff* of New Bedford had called in
Statia and taken crew before sailing to the Western Ground after sperm
whales. However, the threat of U-boats cut short the voyage (the United
States entered World War I on 6 April 1917) and the crew were returned to
Statia in September of the same year.

It is fascinating at any time to reach into the past through some personal
contact, and in this case unusually so, since I was actively looking for contacts
which might have influenced the design of West Indian sailing craft. And here
was such a contact, dropped into my lap, wrapped and tied with pretty ribbon.

Later, on a trip through New England and Nova Scotia, made to verify
some of these contacts, I visited the Whaling Museum in New Bedford, Rhode
Island, hoping to learn what type of vessel the *Woodruff* had been. I was
directed to a bound register of all known American whaling vessels, but to my
disappointment my search through the W's produced nothing even faintly
resembling the name "Woodruff." Then I was informed, to my relief, that
ships are always indexed alphabetically using the first letter of the registered
name, so I turned to the B's. Still no luck. I stood idly riffling the pages of the
register while absorbing the loss of such a promising lead. Something caught
my eye, and turning back three pages, I discovered an entry for the *Arthur
V.S. Woodruff* of New Bedford, 105 feet LOA, 155 Tons, built 1888, rigged as
a tern schooner, J.A. Tilden, Master and owner.

My mind ranged back to the cool, dark interior of Charlie's Bar. There had been no mention of "Arthur — of that I was sure, but it would not be unusual for the crew to shorten a name. As for the "B" — well, better ears than mine have confounded "B" and "V" in the West Indian dialect. In other respects, the *Arthur V.S. Woodruff* fitted nicely the specifications of a vessel employed in the Atlantic fishery at the close of the whaling era. And furthermore, a tern (three-masted) schooner was just the type of vessel suited for inter-island trading that might have been copied by a local builder or a returning sailor.

It was gratifying to pin down in a precise manner a possible source of design influence, but the difficulty was that — influence or not — there had never been anything more than very occasional boatbuilding activity in Statia. Presumably the reserves of timber, still on occasion exploited by Anguillans in search of frames, had existed in earlier times. And certainly, the potential for interisland trading would have been apparent on an island where commerce had once been so profitable.

On the surface, it would appear that in Statia all the elements necessary for a maritime industry had come together with, however, no permanent effect. Apparently some necessary element had escaped my analysis. In this regard, the information that I gathered in Statia contributed more to the question than to the answer.

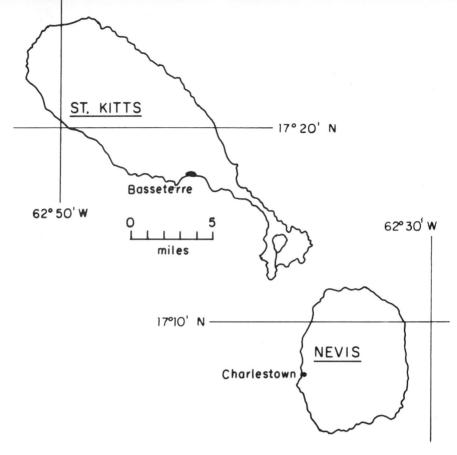

CHAPTER XIII

NEVIS AND ST. KITTS

The eccentric and uncomfortable motion of a small yacht at sea is a nuisance that I learned to tolerate in order to enjoy the convenience of traveling without leaving my home. However, rolling at anchor is something I generally consider to be beyond the call of duty. This I humbly offer as an explanation of why Nevis & St. Kitts got bypassed on my earlier trips through the Leeward Islands, since the pilot books and cruising guides all agreed that "neither island has a sheltered harbor, and a swell frequently sets into the roadsteads of both." Only when I found out that I was a marine anthropologist did my zeal drive me at last to call, first in Nevis, then in St. Kitts — and discover how much I had been missing.

Both islands are picturesque and inhabited by gentle people; and, more to the point for me, both harbored significant maritime lore: Nevis had a small, though active, boatbuilding center; St. Kitts had a series of *Registers of Shipping* dating back to 1838 — the earliest and most complete set that I was to find in all the Lesser Antilles. In addition, both are classic examples of volcanically formed islands. Nevis, in particular, rises to a single perfect cone (fig. XIII-1) whose summit, often robed in cloud, appeared to Columbus to be snow-covered and inspired the island's name (the Spanish for snow is nieves).

*fig. XIII-1.   View of Nevis, sailing lighter at anchor
off Charlestown, Nevis. April, 1975.*

The lower slopes of the island are wrapped around with the glossy, swaying green of coconut palms — except where the stone buildings of Charlestown peek shyly out onto the roadstead. Charlestown is the port, administrative center and sole emporium for the island, as well as the beginning and ending of the island's single road, which encircles the base of the volcanic cone. I was told that the island could be circumambulated in a day, and that seemed a reasonable sort of introduction to the place.

The fresh coolness of early morning lasted as far as Nisbet Plantation, once the abode of Frances Nisbet. The parish register of the nearby church records that in 1787 Frances Nisbet, widow, married Horatio Nelson, then Captain in His Majesty's Navy, stationed at that time at English Harbour, Antigua, just over the horizon to the east.

On the next leg of my journey, which was hot and dry, I fell in with a Nevisian whose son worked as a gardener in St. Croix. When we reached his home, he invited me in, refreshed me with cool water, and filled my arms with mangoes and bananas. I thanked him for his warm hospitality.

"Oh, that is nothing," he smiled. "If I coming to your country, is be just the same, won't it?"

I tried to hide my embarassment by asking if he wanted to send a message to his son in St. Croix.

"You tell him 'plenty howdy' from all he folks in Nevis, 'plenty howdy,'" he called, too courteous to give any indication of whether he sensed my deep chagrin.

fig. XIII-2. *Nevis sailing lighter headed home on Saturday afternoon. Off Basseterre, St. Kitts. April, 1975.*

Soon after leaving my friend's house, I reached the windward side of the island and was in the shadow of the cone during the long hot hours of the afternoon. Late in the day I stopped at a small guest house on the northeast coast for further refreshment. Falling into conversation, I talked until twilight, then accepted a jeep ride the few remaining miles to Charlestown, failing to that extent to complete the circumambulation, which had begun to seem a trifle strenuous anyhow.

The following morning I began my marine anthropology by measuring one of the sailing lighters (fig. XIII-2) built in Nevis, which are crewed by Nevisians and operate in the roadstead at Basseterre. All goods entering and leaving the still-active sugar economy of St. Kitts are landed by lightering, since the island has no deep-water pier. Some of the lighters are simple barges towed in strings by a tug belonging to one or another of the commercial establishments of the island.

fig. XIII-3. *Sailing lighters at anchor off Charlestown, Nevis. April, 1975.*

Others, however, work under sail, plying between freighter and pier during the week, then returning to Nevis for the weekend (fig. XIII-3). I was told that under the best conditions, these lighters can cover the eleven nautical miles between Basseterre and Charlestown in a little under an hour, sailing a broad reach — not a bad turn of speed for a roughly-built, full-carrying hull.

Of the four sailing lighters still in active service in 1974, one, the *Victoria* (fig. XIII-4), was hauled ashore for repairs, enabling me to take lines off

fig. XIII-4. *Sailing lighter* Victoria *hauled ashore for repairs at Charlestown, Nevis. April, 1975.*

this interesting and, as it turned out, unique type. The lines (fig. XIII-5) reveal a harmony and gracefulness that is not evident in the strictly utilitarian — not to say rough — construction of these vessels. A beam-to-length ratio of 1:2.5 is adequate testimony to the carrying capacity of these hulls. Nevertheless, the entry is fine and the run aft is smoothly developed, demonstrating that beaminess does not by itself preclude good lines.

The sailing lighters are, of course, undecked for ease in cargo handling, carrying only a single, fixed deck beam in the way of the mast and another removable one which is lashed into position amidship for longer trips. The *Victoria* was not rigged, so I drew a rigging plan from fig. XIII-3. The plan is essentially that of one of the local beach boats — a small jib and a leg-of-mutton mainsail with a gunter pole seized to the head of the sail, something of a cross between a gaff and a headboard.

Even though at times waves broke over the pier in Charlestown, the roadstead had been comfortable, and I set sail for St. Kitts hoping that the cruising guides had been unduly pessimistic. The sailing conditions could not have been better — fresh breezes and a close reach in sheltered waters brought me to Basseterre in a bouyant frame of mind. But alas, as soon as *Eider* was anchored and the mainsail furled, she began to roll uncomfortably, and I quickly decided to do some late afternoon sight-seeing ashore.

The town of Basseterre still retains in some quarters a sense of its Georgian prosperity; elsewhere it is pretty typical West Indian — unglazed windows and sheet metal roofs — and definitely on the quiet side. The bar and restaurant which I scouted out with some care, planning to make a long evening of it, began trying to close as soon as the sun was decently behind the mountain. The rest of the town was already shuttered and dark, so there was nothing to do but return aboard and grind my teeth in accompaniment to the many-throated serenade of a rolling yacht.

The following morning, desperate for something to do ashore, I acted on a suggestion of Professor Doran's and went to the Harbour Master's Office to inquire about ship registrations. The dusty office was on the second story of a nondescript building that stood at the head of the pier, its shuttered windows opened onto the waterfront below. I presented one of my cards and stated my business. The Harbour Master waved me cordially toward a large volume lying on a small table toward the back of the office. It was titled *Register of Seamen and Shipping* and a quick glance disclosed that it recorded on double pages of heavy paper the detailed particulars of all vessels that had been brought to Basseterre to claim the privilege of sailing under British colors. The earliest entry was in 1929, but when my interest became apparent, the harbor official indicated a stack of similar volumes, dusty like everything else in the office, lying on the lower shelf of a small book case. With increasing excitement, I lifted two more heavy volumes onto the table and discovered that the record of ship registrations was complete back to 1876 and in a smaller volume with a disintegrating binding there were abbreviated registrations back to 1838.

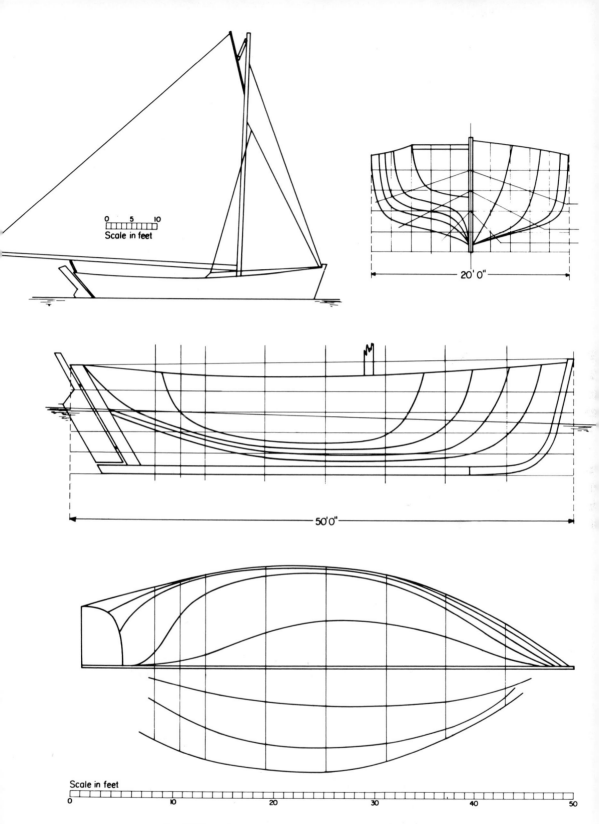

0   5   10
Scale in feet

20' 0"

50'0"

Scale in feet
0   10   20   30   40   50

fig. XIII-5.   Lines of sailing lighter Victoria. Built
1951 by George Mills at Charlestown,
Nevis. Taken off April, 1975.

Suddenly, the long night tossing back and forth in my bunk was worth it. Here in these heavy volumes was a comprehensive record of the boatbuilding activity of St. Kitts and her dependencies, Nevis and Anguilla, for nearly a century and a half, as well as occasional entries for Statia, St. Barts and St. Martin. As I turned the thick pages, the dry bureaucratic forms began to stir with the romance of the names: *Telephone R, Try Again John, Widow's Mite, Windrush.* And behind the hope, pride, whimsy and defiance of the names lay a wealth of concrete detail: builder's and owner's names, date and place of building, full measurements for computing tonnage, rig and structural details for identification. And on the right-hand page, scrawled diagonally across the lower half of the sheet, the date and the reason for closing the registration: Lost in the gale of 1922 at Basseterre, Sold at auction for £22.18.12, Foundered at Montserrat in 1926, Sold Dutch 1909, Wrecked at Dieppe Bay 1912.

Never could I have anticipated that the tedious alluvium of official thoroughness could be so absorbing. I was breathless with excitement, and in the thrill of the moment it seemed that the very importance of this information made it somehow likely that it would be denied to me. Abruptly, speed was of the essence, and I asked permission to use my camera and copy lens. It was then a matter of focus, snap, turn the page and do it all again, which went very fast to my great belief.

Only later, back aboard the still rolling yacht, did it begin to dawn on me that no real saving of time or effort had occurred. The five rolls of film still had to be developed, hung up to dry, cut into strips, stored safely for the rest of the trip, run through a micro-film reader and, finally written down in long hand. And all these chores had to be performed with the hindsight that the Harbour Master had been delighted to have in his possession something that was of interest to me.

It was not, however, everywhere the same. In some offices my advent was greeted with everything from suspicion to indifference, and nowhere were the records so extensive or so complete as in St. Kitts. In fact, it was very fortunate that my first contact with the *Registers of Shipping* occurred in St. Kitts, where a very slight effort was so richly repaid: if I had made my first try where the records were sketchy or begrudged, I would very likely have concluded out of indolence that the *Registers* were not worth consulting. As it was, they came to be one of my major preoccupations during my remaining time in the islands.

Apart from the *Registers,* there was very little marine anthropology that needed doing in St. Kitts. No large vessels had been built on the island for many years, as I knew from my sojourn in the Harbour Master's Office. There were, however, fishing boats that operated under sail (fig. XIII-6), as there had been in Nevis (fig. XIII-7). Fortunately, I had already measured a good example of a St. Kitts beach boat before arriving in St. Kitts, not the last time that this was to occur during my travels.

160

*fig. XIII-6. St. Kitts fishing boats off Basseterre.
April, 1975.*

*fig. XIII-7. Nevis fishing boat pulled ashore at
Charlestown. April, 1975.*

fig. XIII-8. St. Kitts beach boat Saga Boy *racing in Marigot Bay. St. Martin on Bastille Day, 1974.*

The *Saga Boy* (fig. XIII-8, 9), which belonged to Emil Gumbs of Anguilla, was actually built in St. Kitts and may be taken as typical of that island and Nevis. The lines and rig (fig. XIII-10) show the same characteristics as *Alma Gloria* (St. Martin) and *Bluebird* (Anguilla): sharp floors with lots of deadrise, pronounced drag to the keel, a fine entry, a beam-to-length ratio of 1:4, and a leg-of-mutton sail. There are, of course, slight individual variations — for

fig. XIII-9. Saga Boy *at home at Sandy Ground, Anguilla. January, 1971.*

162

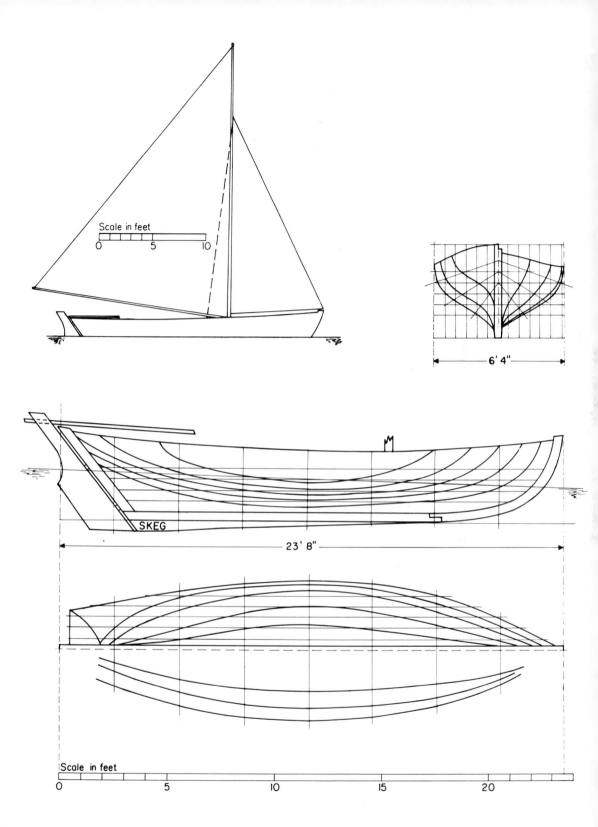

Scale in feet
0   5   10

6' 4"

SKEG

23' 8"

Scale in feet
0   5   10   15   20

fig. XIII-10. Lines of beach boat Saga Boy. *Built
ca. 1966 at Basseterre, St. Kitts.
Taken off January, 1971.*

fig. XIII-11. Saga Boy *in foreground.* Blue-bird *in rear, to the right. January, 1971.*

example, the differences in stem shape and in the sheer line shown in fig. XIII-11 — but it is clear that these craft are of the same basic type. In fact, the type is rather widely distributed in the northern Leeward Islands, being presently found in Nevis, St. Kitts, Anguilla, St. Martin and Montserrat, and might almost be called the Leeward Island beach boat.

My stopover in Nevis and St. Kits provided important information, but one night of rolling was about all that it seemed necessary to undergo. As soon as the *Shipping Registers* were photographed, I returned aboard *Eider* and considered my next move. The November day had gone cloudy, and the freshening Trades had backed a point into the NE. My next stop was St. Barts, but an immediate departure would have brought me to an unfamiliar landfall on what was likely to be a very dark night. The best course seemed to be to sail north in the lee of St. Kitts and anchor in Pump Bay for the night.

There followed an exhilarating sail — strong, gusting winds over flat water — with gray clouds swirling over the volcanic summit above and carefully tended cane fields for scenery. On the hill overlooking Pump Bay stood the once formidable citadel of Brimstone Hill which I visited in a drizzling rain. During the night the wind moved still farther into the NE and Pump Bay began to roll. Clearing off in the dark with strong winds and in unfamiliar waters didn't seem wise, so I clung to my berth and beguiled the dragging hours with visions of tomorrow's weatherly passage to St. Barts.

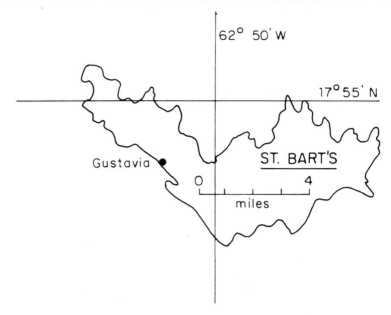

CHAPTER XIV

ST. BARTS

St. Barts was mentioned to me frequently as an island with a significant sailing tradition, and Gustavia was said to be an important schooner port. It was a little hard to believe at first glance — the tiny landlocked harbor appeared so entirely infused with the easy indolence of the tropics. And really, there was little apparent reason not to take things easy. An island of nine very arid square miles and 2500 inhabitants could scarcely be producing or consuming enough to generate even a modest amount of trade.

Two days at anchor in the placid inner harbor were enough, however, to persuade me that under the air of indolence lay an almost feverish (for the West Indies) level of activity. Sloops and schooners came and went, but stayed so briefly that there *seemed* to be almost no commerce. Small trucks and hand carts ranged among the shuttered stone buildings that surrounded the inner harbor. The focal point of this ant-like trundling was the small wharf at the harbor entrance where an odd assortment of vessels made brief appearances (fig. XIV-1).

In the small shops of the town, an unexpected array of luxury goods was displayed — perfumes, cameras, electronic devices, cigarettes of every conceivable brand and liquors of all descriptions at prices that made me dizzy (rum was 75¢ a bottle, Scotch whisky under $2). Had I known at the outset what later unfolded of the island's past, much fruitless foraging for evidence of boatbuilding would have been spared me.

The first permanent settlement on St. Barts was made in 1658, by Norman-French who eked out a living as subsistence farmers, unnoticed until 1740, when the English raided the island and dispersed the 660 settlers found there. In 1763, the island was returned to France and the former in-

fig. XIV-1. Trading sloop loading in Gustavia
harbor, St. Barts. May, 1975.

habitants reappeared from somewhere. In 1784, the island and its 739 in-
habitants were traded to Sweden in exchange for a French trading base at
Goteborg. The Swedes, in turn, created a free port in St. Barts, named it
Gustavia and soon began to profit from the embargoes that accompanied
the Napoleonic Wars. The Normans continued to work the land while 6,000
Swedish entrepreneurs arrived to operate the port.

This was the Golden Age of St. Barts, when as many as 2000 vessels annually cleared the little port. Goods arrived from all over the world, were
landed in the warehouses that sprang up around the port and were later re-
shipped with a new and unexceptionable bill of lading (exactly the same sort
of commercial legerdemain which brought prosperity to St. Eustatius in an
earlier round of European wars). When the Napoleonic Wars were over in
1815, Gustavia was abandoned by the 6000 Swedish entrepreneurs whose

fig. XIV-2. Schooner Ruth *anchored in the outer harbor of Gustavia, St. Barts. ca. 1950.*

warehouses, empty and ruined, stayed on as mute witnesses to the ever-turning wheel of fortune.

In 1874, France repurchased St. Barts and its 792 inhabitants, guaranteeing in perpetuity the free port status of the island. With the Swedes gone, the Norman-French began to play, on the smaller stage of the Lesser Antilles, the role that their Swedish mentors had played in the theatre of the world. Whisky from Scotland, cognac and wine from France, rum from Barbados, bourbon and cigarettes from the United States conveyed by steamer to St. Kitts, were carried in sloops and schooners to St. Barts. From the shuttered, half-ruined buildings along the waterfront, these goods eventually found their way to small, out-of-the-way bays and landing places up and down the island chain. Cattle, as many as 18,000 annually, were brought on the decks of schooners from Tortola, St. Croix and Puerto Rico to pass the night ashore in Gustavia before being reloaded and sailed to Guadeloupe and Martinique where they landed as French cattle, hence duty free.

Gustavia eventually became the home of the largest schooner fleet in the Antilles. Former captains and owners with whom I talked in the shops and cafes around the port could remember as many as twenty schooners and un-numbered sloops. Memories were still fresh of the stars of the fleet — the *Cachalot*, built in Florida; the *Nina*, built in Anguilla; the *Ruth* (fig. XIV-2), in Bonaire; the *Ruby* (fig. XIV-3), in Carriacou; the *Poctock*, in Brittany and so on.

167

fig. XIV-3. Schooner Ruby *anchored at Gustavia,
St. Barts, prior to 1955.*

Of all the vessels that figured in this folk history, only two were actually
built in St. Barts: the *Iselena* in 1910, by Romney and the *Inez* in 1915, by
Romney and Lédée. Romney is a common name in Anguilla, whereas family
names in St. Barts are Norman-French, leading me to believe that these two
vessels, even though built in St. Barts, were built with imported skills. Here
again, it seemed, was a seafaring island without the benefit of a boatbuilding
tradition.

Whatever its source of vessels, St. Barts was flourishing once more. It
was, if not a Golden Age, then at least an Age of Silver which continued until
1950, when it was discovered, quite by accident, that Gustavia was not, as had
been faithfully recorded in the pilot books and sailing directions for many
years, hurricane safe (fig. XIV-4). About half the fleet was destroyed on that
occasion, and the remaining vessels were demolished in 1960 by Hurricane
Donna.

On neither occasion were replacements bought or built, which effectively
ended the age of sail for St. Barts, though vessels from other Antillean islands
continue to frequent the port. The reasons for this collapse were twofold: on
the one hand, the French authorities, understandably disturbed at the size
of the fiscal leak created by these enterprising folk, began to exact industrial

standards of construction and safety which were impossible for sailing vessels to meet. And in the meantime these beached sailors had, with the faultless timing of true entrepreneurs, discovered the advantages and enjoyments of small aircraft.

Considered in the light of these facts, the extraordinary busyness of the little port becomes less perplexing, and the folklore surrounding this *bobol* (illicit) trade acquires a distinctly Caribbean flavor. Take, for example, the fact that the inhabitants of St. Barts, mostly fishermen and subsistence farmers, have the highest *per capita* income in the Antilles. And they have something even better than income — they have net worth (Raspail, 1966).

In 1955 when DeGaulle devalued the franc, returning one Nouveau Franc for each 100 Anciens Francs, the Treasurer of the Departement de la Guadeloupe visited St. Martin, which had no bank, to carry out this exchange. The sum of 70,000,000 AF was turned in by a population of 7,000. On this basis, the official then visited St. Barts prepared to exchange as much as 25,000,000 AF, judging this sum to be entirely adequate for a small, dry island with 2,000 inhabitants. Within 15 minutes of opening for business, his stock of

fig. XIV-4. Inner harbor at Gustavia after the hurricane of 1950.

169

Nouveaux Francs was exhausted. The Treasurer retired to Guadeloupe to regroup and returned the next day with triple the amount he had already exchanged. This sum lasted for just over an hour. He sent to Guadeloupe for an additional 2,000,000 NF and again ran out. When the exchange was finally completed, the island of St. Barts had coughed up nearly 1,250,000,000 AF — something like $2.5 million US at the time. This amounted to $1250, cash on hand in currency, for each of the 2000 inhabitants of the island. It was about this date that French policy toward the free port began to change.

On another occasion, one of St. Barts' leading citizens (though not yet Mayor and Deputé, *bien entendue)* was intercepted in the wee hours of the morning landing *bobol* in Martinique. His schooner and her cargo were seized and impounded, and a fine was levied as prescribed by law — three times the value of the contraband plus the value of the vessel, amounting to something over $100,000 US. French law, though stringent to a fault in other respects, does not regard smuggling as a crime — unless, of course, you fail to pay the fine. In consequence, our would-be importer remained at liberty for the rest of the night.

At 8:00 a.m. the following morning (N.B. the banks do not open until 9:00 a.m.) he reappeared at the Customs Office with the necessary sum in cash and paid the fine. He then superintended the reloading of the confiscated cargo, discovering in the process that ten cases of whiskey were missing. He thereupon ferreted out the Customs agent responsible, pressed charges and had the man imprisoned for theft. No wonder if official French interest in St. Barts increased.

Free port status, which in 1874 must have seemed such an easy and in-expensive way to provide for the island and its stone-poor inhabitants, was becoming a drain on the French Treasury too important to ignore. As a consequence, the Treasury let it be known in the early 1970's that "in perpetuity" in the original guarantee meant 100 years. When I last visited the island in 1974, a Customs agent had been installed in Gustavia and was quietly but pointedly issuing clearance papers to all vessels leaving the port. Another Treasury official had begun prowling the highways and byways of the island, making cryptic notations in chalk on houses and outbuildings (taxation on assessed value is a major portion of French internal revenue).

Such goings-on had an unsettling effect on the good folk of the island, who responded with predictable panache. First, they put out feelers to see if David Rockefeller, who maintained a little ol' hideway in St. Barts, was interested in acquiring an island and 2,500 loyal citizens willing and eager to turn out and cheer enthusiastically on birthdays and other state occasions. It is reported that Rockefeller declined the honor and opportunity, being dismayed (even he!) at the prospect of transporting drinking water from Puerto Rico for a thirsty populace, as is sometimes necessary in dry years.

This failing, the next move was to contact the Knights of Malta who, it develops, have the diplomatic privileges of a sovereign nation, including

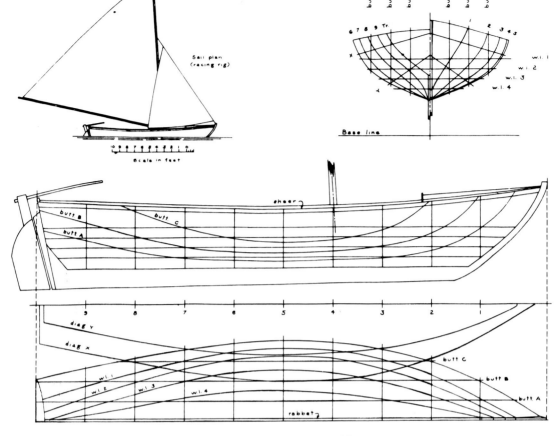

fig. XIV-5. St. Thomas fishing boat Glève. Built 1950 by V. Tacklin at Frenchtown, St. Thomas. Taken off by John Kochiss, 1963.

the power to issue passports, but have at present no fief, operating instead from offices in the Vatican. It was hoped that something might be worked out along the lines of Monaco or Liechtenstein — expensive but otherwise undemanding passports for those citizens of the world for whom taxes, laws and all the restraints of civilized society are merely an encumbrance to honest avarice. A workable and attractive scheme, I would have thought, but nothing came of it. Perhaps the Knights failed to see what benefits would accrue to them; or, more likely, they had scruples.

It is not my goal in setting down the above anecdotes to pander to the well-known and widely discussed weakness of the reading public for amusement and entertainment. The sole purpose of the foregoing is to explain why I am not astonished to find little evidence of schooner building in St. Barts.

Boatbuilding is slow, heavy work which has to be done in the heat of the tropic sun. It is work done by poor people and people forced by economic circumstances to provide their own employment. It is not work done by entrepreneurs, by people with capital who must move quickly to keep their resources employed to best advantage. Such people are consumers of vessels, not builders.

fig. XIV-6. Fishing boat Patsi, Gustavia, St. Barts. May, 1975.

In the matter of small craft, the situation in St. Barts is essentially the same. Neither of the two small craft which I include here was actually built in St. Barts, though in different ways both are typical of the island.

In St. Thomas, U.S. Virgin Islands, there live a group of people whose ancestors immigrated there from St. Barts in the 1870's (Highfield, 1979). These people live apart in a waterfront community called Frenchtown, speak French-creole dialect, and earn their living in part by fishing, using for this purpose a characteristic boat of which the Glève (fig. XIV-5) is an example. These lines were taken off in 1963 by John Kochiss and came to my hand by sheer good luck, sail-powered fishing boats having entirely disappeared from Frenchtown by the time I checked there in the 1970's.

The features of this type are beaminess, full and flaring bows, some drag to the keel and the leg-of-mutton mainsail. Since the people of Frenchtown have maintained for many years their cultural integrity, there is every reason to suppose that this boat type was brought with them from St. Barts, which is why the lines are included here.

The *Patsi* as she lay tied to the quay in Gustavia (fig. XIV-6) was the prettiest and most carefully built of the small craft that I found in the Lesser Antilles. Although she was built in Guadeloupe, and was referred to by her owner as a *canot saintois* (cf. Chapter XVII), her lines (fig. XIV-7) resemble those of the *Glève* to the extent that the two taken together establish by projection what the older boat type of St. Barts may have been. The same characteristics appear in a more pronounced form: greater beaminess, more flare to the bows, even greater drag to the keel.

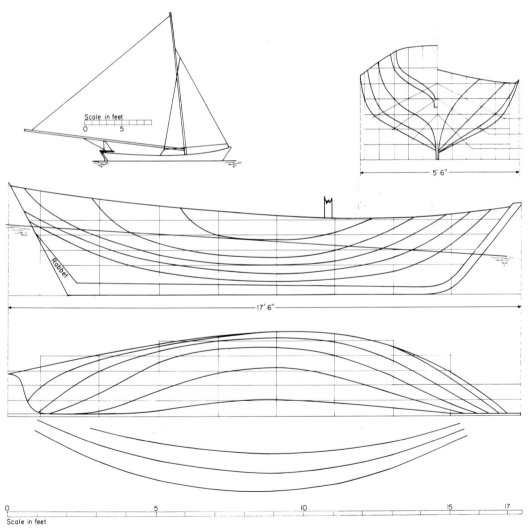

Scale in feet
0   5

5' 6"

17' 6"

0   5   10   15   17
Scale in feet

fig. XIV-7. Lines of Patsi. *Built by Bernardin Palmier at Pointe-à-Pitre. Taken off May, 1975.*

fig. XIV-8. Patsi *close-hauled off St. Barts. May,*
1975.

Since the *Patsi* was primarily used as a pleasure craft, the owner readily
agreed to a sailing trial in exchange for a portrait of his boat (fig. XIV-8, 9).
The winds were very light and the sea calm, making an easy and pleasant job
of collecting the data but limiting the speeds obtained. Nevertheless, the
Patsi showed a good turn of speed and was a delight to sail.

Point of sailing	Angle off high wind	Wind speed in knots	Boat speed in knots	Leeway angle	Boat speed - wind speed
Close-hauled	50°	4.2	2.9	5°	.69
	45°	6.6	4.7	6°	.71
Close reach	68°	8.0	5.2	3°	.65
Beam reach	90°	7.7	5.0	—	.65
Broad reach	135°	6.5	5.1	—	.78
Running goose-winged	180°	8.3	4.5	—	.54

There were many small sea-faring communities that I visited in the West Indies whose cultural integrity was precarious and whose future was uncertain; St. Barts was not one of them. The age of sail may have ended for St. Barts, but with flawless timing, former schooner owners and captains have become wholesalers and Cessna jockeys; the island has already moved into another era. Since there was never a great investment in traditional skills, the passing of the old order was undoubtedly rendered easier, occurring as it did without great loss of pride or integrity. Although St. Barts had little to contribute directly to my knowledge of boatbuilding, it did nevertheless provide one profound insight into human economic behavior: prosperity has an inhibitory effect on the sweat glands of the human brow.

fig. XIV-9.   Patsi running into Gustavia. May, 1975.

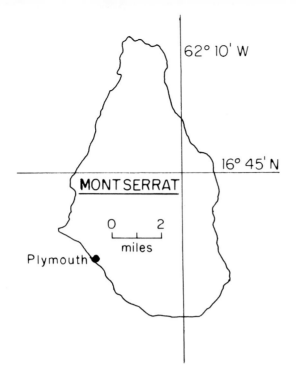

62° 10' W

16° 45' N

MONTSERRAT

0   2

miles

Plymouth

CHAPTER XV

MONTSERRAT

Many of the islands of the Antilles had seafaring reputations which reached me long before I visited them. Of these some were active boat-building centers, some had been active in the past and still others were seafaring but did no building. And then there were some islands, such as Montserrat, that were never mentioned at all.

My first visit to the island was pretty brief, the occasion being a passage from Martinique to St. Martin under conditions that got me to Montserrat just at first light, after sailing 144 miles in 20 hours, an average speed of 7 knots. Not very fast by the standards of the space age, but 7 knots was *Eider's* hull speed. The passage was made with double reefed main and the smallest jib aboard. The sky was overcast, but the conditions were not by any means stormy. It was simply the Trade Winds at full force — what are sometimes called the Christmas winds, since they begin around Christmas time and continue into March. It was the fastest passage that I ever made in *Eider,* and the only significance that Montserrat had for me at the time was the shelter it provided and the few hours sleep.

Later, when the island chain was being divided into islands where vessels were built and islands where they weren't, I visited Montserrat again. Despite my high resolve and consuming interest, the second visit lasted little longer than the first. There was, in short, very little marine anthropology to be done in Montserrat.

fig. XV-1. Montserrat fishing boat. April, 1975.

A small, steel coastal freighter and an island sloop lay at anchor in the roadstead off the town of Plymouth. Just beyond the jetty was a fish market where a few boats were drawn ashore. These boats no longer used sails, and their resemblance to the beach boats of the other Leeward Islands was so close *(cf. Alma Gloria, Bluebird, Saga Boy)* that I took the easy course and left them dozing contentedly in the sun. On other islands where outboard motors had replaced sails, I noticed that newer boats were frequently given a broader stern to provide extra buoyancy for the weight and thrust of the outboard. Here, however, the outboards were of such low power that the boats had retained the narrow transom of the sailing model.

In the Harbour Master's Office there was a single volume of the *Register of Shipping* which contained all the vessels ever registered in Montserrat. The earliest was the sloop *Vigilante,* built 1844 in Petit Martinique, and the most recent was the steel freighter *Gefion,* built 1952 in the Netherlands. Of 73 entries in the Register, 46 were of vessels built in Montserrat, though none had been built since the 1950's. Over the years the island had produced 63% of its own shipping capacity, and thus deserves to be considered an island with a seafaring past, though it was never important as a boatbuilding center and is not presently active.

fig. XV-2. Monteserrat fishing boat under repair.
April, 1975.

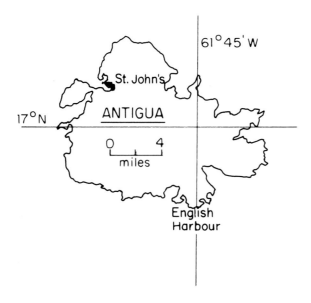

CHAPTER XVI

ANTIGUA AND BARBUDA

On my first trip to Antigua, I approached the island from the south in company with the yacht *Lancer,* also bound for English Harbour. We both left Guadeloupe at the same time, so it was natural that an impromptu race should develop. *Eider* was keeping up pretty well for an older design until there was a bit of an emergency, arising, I confess, from shoddy seamanship and poor judgement on my part.

Despite ample opportunity to learn better, I was still slow to realize that however tame conditions seem in the lee of an island, the channels tend to be rough, especially just at the edges. All the wind that you don't have behind the island seems to come sweeping around the north or south end. If, in addition, the tide happens to be running up the channel, then sailing is momentarily vigorous. On this particular morning, I had set the working jib and rolled down a shallow reef in the main, neglecting in my other preparations to lash adequately the genoa which was stowed in a bag on deck. When the first good wave rolled over the bow, the bagged sail washed the length of the deck before sliding gently over the side just out of reach.

I called to my wife to go into the man overboard drill which we had assiduously practiced in the early days of our trip: bear away sharply while overhauling and gybing the mainsail, run back a short distance before bringing the head into the wind and backing the jib — all gauged so as to bring the vessel up hove-to just to windward of the lost object. Practice

178

definitely pays, because her timing was perfect, and the genoa drifted under the lee rail just as intended. The bag was upside down, kept afloat only by the air trapped in the bottom. The wet dacron, stretched by the air bubble, afforded no grip, and the sail ducked maddeningly away from my lunge.

"It's going to sink," I wailed in despair. "Go 'round again. If I can't hold it, I'm going after it."

Nothing seemed important except that we were about to lose the only large headsail that *Eider* had. The second pass was just as good as the first, and my attempt to snaffle the bag, just as futile. Ignoring even the advice to hold the end of the mainsheet, I jumped for the sail bag, leaving my dismayed and long-suffering wife to perform yet another man overboard drill, this time in real earnest. She had one advantage this time: I was easy to find. As soon as I had my arms around the bag, I looked up at the retreating stern of *Eider* and began to yell.

"Go about. Get the damn thing turned around. Stop messing about and get back here."

Highly unreasonable of me since five seconds at most had elapsed since I took to the water, but from my new vantage point *Eider* looked to be a mile away. I stand ready to swear that the curvature of the earth was already perceptible over the intervening 50 yards. Fortunately, my wife kept a cool head and managed yet a third time to bring the boat back to the starting point. I got my left arm over the rail while the right still clutched the bag. The yacht seemed dead in the water until I laid hold of it, whereupon it suddenly seemed to tear along. My wife grabbed a handful of shirt with one hand while steadying the tiller with the other. And finally, with the extra effort of desperation, I heaved enough of the sail bag out of the water that she could get a grip, and between the two of us we rolled it into the cockpit. Then I got a leg over the side and, on the next roll of the vessel, managed to tumble back aboard — wet, shaken, and thoroughly ashamed of myself.

As a consequence of all these alarums and excursions, we were trailing by a good distance when *Lancer* began in the mid-afternoon to close with the line of rocky bluffs which form the southern coast of Antigua. As we approached the island, I searched with binoculars for the marks and alignments given for English Harbour in the sailing directions. Nothing was clear, but we pressed on in the wake of the other yacht, assuming that with their lead, they saw some landmark not yet visible to us. It was difficult to make out anything through the bouncing binoculars, but there seemed to be a line of breakers between *Lancer* and the shore. I took a quick glance at the chart, then looked up again to find that *Lancer* had let fly sheets and altered course drastically to port.

In a flash all was clear — *Lancer* had not made any better sense of the sailing directions than we had. However, from our position in the rear we could make the necessary corrections more easily and were able to smooth over the frustrations of the day by actually arriving first in English Harbour.

Anyone who has made a landfall there will affirm that blind faith in the sailing directions is necessary: you are literally within a stone's throw of the entrance before seeing the break in the cliffs which leads between the submerged rocks to starboard and the narrow spit of land to port. Once inside, the shelter and concealment are complete. I could only marvel at the luck or good management of the Royal Navy in making this the base for their West Indies Squadron. From this haven, secure from hurricanes and fortified against attack from sea or land, they were in a position to dominate the whole of the Leeward Islands.

With the passing of the sailing navy, the harbor and dockyard were abandoned and lay unused until after World War II, when an English yachtsman, Commander Nicholson, and his family called there on what was to have been a round-the-world cruise. Instead they settled in English Harbour, and out of their intuition and enterprise has grown today's yacht harbor and charter base. There, surrounded by the stately buildings of what is now called Nelson's Dockyard (cf. Chapter XIII), yachts and yachtsmen are sheltered, supplied and catered to. The Dockyard is so peaceful and picturesque, so complete for yachting purposes, that there is no need and little incentive to visit the rest of the island.

However, the *Mercantile Navy Lists,* published annually by the Registrar General of Seamen and Shipping for the British Empire, have significant entries for Antigua as early as the 1840's, indicating it to be an early center of schooner building in the West Indies. This is not surprising since the operation of the dockyard at English Harbour must have required the training and employment of local shipwrights. In an effort to substantiate this influence, on my third visit to Antigua, I ventured for the first time beyond the brown sandstone gateposts of the dockyard.

Outside the comfortable little enclave, the island — not surprisingly — was dry and desolate. Antigua, though not as flat as Anguilla, does nevertheless lack the mountainous heights which force the Trade Winds clouds upward and coax them into releasing some of their moisture. What did surprise me and then, when I saw the extent of it, actively depress me was the clutter and dilapidation of the landscape.

It might be that I am obsessively litter-conscious, but that seems unlikely — it's hard to live for several years on a small sailing yacht without developing a working tolerance for clutter. Neither do I think that I am imposing an alien standard on the island, because I visited other islands — Carriacou after three years of drought was as barren as the moon — which did not so affect me. In Antigua, the wasted land and the gaunt buildings seemed to be choking under a shroud of junk — empty bottles, cans and plastic wrappers; discarded appliances; abandoned buildings and vehicles — most of it the costly flotsom of our industrial century. It was frosting on the cake of despair, and yet I found it hard to feel sympathy. There was a tremendous debt of floors unswept, chores not done and repairs not made — a daunting backlog of promises not kept which needed discharging before the much

fig. XVI-1. *Fishing sloops in frames at St. Johns, Antiqua. April, 1975.*

needed work of development could even be attempted.

It was a distinct relief when the bus reached St. Johns, the capitol, which was nothing to write home about but was at least not actively depressing. Here as elsewhere, I relied mostly on random inquiry to locate vessels under construction because, by-and-large, boatbuilding attracts attention, and usually the public is as well informed as anyone. For Antigua, however, I had a better lead. At the suggestion of Prof. Doran, I had written to (the late) Howard Chappelle, then Curator of the National Watercraft Collection at the Smithsonian Institution, about my interest in West Indian sailing craft. He replied encouragingly and sent two little surprises: the lines of the *Glève* (Chapter XIV) and those of an Antiguan fishing sloop taken off by Jan Olaf Truang in 1961 as part of an FAO fisheries improvement project. Thus I had the advantage of knowing that vessels had recently been built in Antigua and quickly got directions to the workshop of Vincent Simon on the far side of the harbor.

Simon was easy to find but hard to talk to. On the bare ground between his shop and an open-sided school, there were two vessels in frames (fig. XVI-1),

fig. XVI-2. Fishing sloop nearing completion at St. Johns, Antigua. April, 1975.

and on the other side of the shop, another vessel of the same type nearing completion (fig. XVI-2). Simon himself was directing and coordinating the efforts of a number of workers at what was, for the West Indies, breakneck speed. It was a new experience for me to find a boatbuilder too busy to lay aside tools and talk indefinitely.

While waiting for this opportunity, I wandered around and confirmed that the vessels under construction were being built to essentially the same lines as those drawn by Truang (fig. XVI-3). For the reader interested enough to refer to the lines of the *Sea Queen* (fig. IX-3), the similarity of type is immediately apparent. A beam-to-length ratio of 1:3, the "moon" shear, pronounced drag to the keel and the leg-of-mutton mainsail are all shared characteristics.

By this time, Simon was able to chat with me a few minutes and related the following: that the present flurry of activity was the result of an FAO program which loaned money to fishermen for the construction of vessels and had also bought for his shop a band saw, a table saw and some other hand-held power tools; that the present generation of fishing vessels were much influenced by the Tortola sloop; that schooners had not been built on the island in his memory; and finally, that there was no timber and no boat-building on Barbuda. This last item was the most welcome of all since I had not been looking forward to the 30 mile beat through reef-encumbered waters to the island of Barbuda.

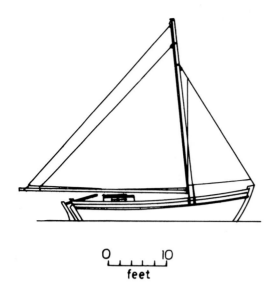

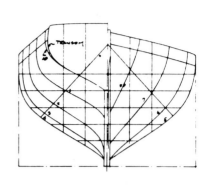

O | | | | | 10
feet

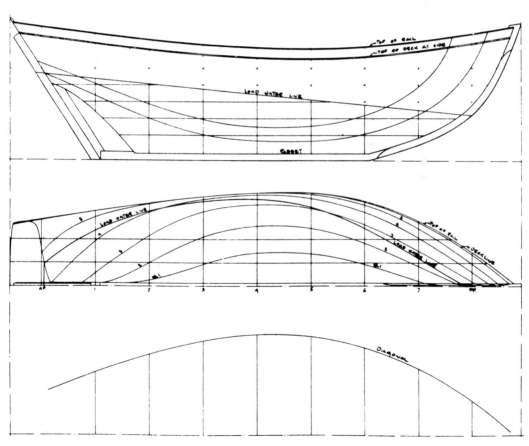

fig. XVI-3. Lines of Antigua fishing sloop. Built
1961 by Vincent Simon at St. Johns,
Antigua. Taken off 1961 by Jan Olaf
Truang.

183

When looking at a hull nearing completion, I noticed a detail in the garboard plank which I had not seen on any other island. The line of the keel rabbet was curved and carried across the deadwood onto the sternpost (fig. XVI-4); elsewhere, the practice was simply to fasten the butt of the garboard directly onto the sternpost. When asked about this, Simon replied that if a vessel took the ground, there was frequently trouble with leaking at this joint and that the curved rabbet avoided this difficulty. He was unable to say if this technique had been worked out in Antigua or copied from elsewhere.

In the matter of small sailing craft, Simon corroborated my observation at the fish market — no small fishing craft were in use, all fishing now being carried out in motorized sloops of the type built by Simon.

By the time of my final visit to Antigua, I had become fully aware of the importance of the *Registers of Shipping,* so after talking with Simon, the next item on the agenda was a little historical delving. As in other places, I went to the Harbour Master's Office, located in this case on the new deep water pier outside the town, where I found the current volume of the *Register,* beginning in 1946 and containing twenty-odd entries. For the earlier volumes I was referred to the old office which had stood on a now-decayed section of waterfront at the shallow head of the harbor. I found the old building but was informed by an onlooker that it had been vacant since the earthquake

fig. XVI-4. *Detail of construction, keel rabbet carried across deadwood onto sternpost. St. Johns, Antigua. May, 1975.*

(7 on the Richter scale) of the preceding July. He directed me to the present Customs Office in a nondescript government building where a series of mildly interested functionaries showed me a mildly interesting series of closets overflowing with boxes and folders of yellowing papers waiting quietly to crumble into dust. The *Registers,* large, heavy and stoutly bound, were not to be found among the debris.

Then, someone remembered that Mr. Darwin Flax, a retired civil servant, had once been interested in the preservation of government records. So I made another trek down a sun-scalded street, this time to a pleasant house on a quiet side street. There I learned that Mr. Flax had once participated in a project to unify all the records of the then West Indies Federation. He was also a member of a boatbuilding family that had come to Antigua from Tortola a generation earlier. But he was unable to help since the project for archiving had gone aground along with the Federation.

Inquiry at the local library and two more government departments entirely satisfied my yearning for dusty streets and stifling offices. The search officially ended at Brother John's with a bottle of Schooner beer, the *Registers* still missing in action. As a result, the necessary historical data had to be extracted at a later date from the annual issues of the *Mercantile Navy List* by a dull (names and personal information about builders and owners omitted) and laborious (vessels listed alphabetically by name for the whole British Empire) process.

The pattern which emerged was one which Antigua shared with other plantation islands: while sugar prospered, vessels were built; as sugar became unprofitable through the later half of the nineteenth century, boatbuilding slowed and then stopped. A brief flurry of activity occurred at the time of World War II, and finally, there is the present activity growing largely out of the FAO project.

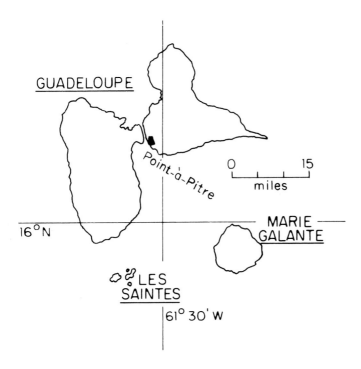

CHAPTER XVII

GUADELOUPE AND THE SAINTES

When talking with builders and others in the islands, I was frequently asked where I was born. Initially I sought to answer with the simple, unvarnished truth: "In Oklahoma." Blank stares were my usual reward in those benighted regions, where the musical stage is unknown; so I learned to add in the same breath, " — that's near Texas." The case of the Saintes is similar: on a map large enough to show the Caribbean in relation to North and South America, Guadeloupe is an island that can be found, being the largest of the Lesser Antilles. The Isles des Saintes are among the smallest, which explains why this chapter is entitled "Guadeloupe and the Saintes," even though in reality it is about the Saintes with only incidental references to Guadeloupe.

Les Isles des Saintes are another of those tiny enclaves that are interesting far out of proportion to actual size. The four inhabited islands of the group are rocky, dry, sparsely inhabited, and located on the edge of a fishing bank. Guadeloupe is high, verdant, densely populated and short of protein. And there you have it — *la raison d'être des Saintes*. They are nicely positioned for a local fishing industry, rather like Bequia in relation to St. Vincent or Carriacou in relation to Grenada. And like these two, the Saintes have their characteristic boat, called *le canot saintois*.

186

When anchoring for the first time in the little harbor at Bourg des Saintes, I had a fleeting impression that there had been some fantastic error in navigation. The little town with its prosperous, plastered houses and air of quiet repose seemed more Mediterranean than Antillean. The streets were paved with cut stones and free of litter, both conditions not seen even in the larger towns of the Commonwealth islands. At the head of the ferry dock was a small hotel complete with terrace and parasols. The main street was a boulevard shaded by chestnut trees.

Along the sand beach in front of the town the boats of the fishing fleet were drawn up in orderly array. All were *le type saintois;* that is to say, 6 to 6.5 meters (19 to 21 feet); hollow, flaring bows, extremely well finished, with one or two outboard motors on the stern and not a mast or sail in the lot of them. A single glance was enough to establish that the days of sail were over in the Saintes. Government loans to fishermen for the purchase of outboard motors (American or Canadian) had converted the fleet to mechanical power, modifying in the process the design of the stern. The fine entry and flaring bows were well-suited to a power-driven boat, but the stern was broadened for buoyance and the "tuck" was decreased, being no longer necessary to provide lateral resistance when sailing.

Older boats of the sailing model were easily spotted because of this difference in the stern, and fishermen readily boasted of the sailing abilities of this one or that one, seeming to regret the passing of sail. But nowhere could I find a boat that still had sails, so that a performance trial might be made or a sail plan drawn (it was later in my travels, though earlier in the book, that I found the *Patsi).*

For lines I chose the *France-Lise,* built by Georges Cassin in 1965 and reputed to be a fast sailer. Throughout the islands, reputations for fast sailing are made by sailing a particular passage, distance unknown, in a certain time which is easily and accurately known. When necessary I used the local yardstick of performance, converting it to knots by laying off the passage on a chart. For the Saintes, performance is reckoned on the passage from Boug des Saintes to Trois Rivieres, 7.56 nautical miles on a broad reach, which *France-Lise* had sailed in as little as an hour, 7.5 knots. Her lines (fig. XVII-1) show very clearly her kinship with *Patsi* (fig. XIV-7) in the fine entry and hollow, flaring bow, deep tuck and drag to the keel.

François Bocage (fig. XVII-2) was one of three builders then active in Bourg des Saintes. From him I gathered the following information on materials and methods: the stem, sternpost and frames are shaped from *poirier* (alias white cedar, alias *Tabebuia pallida),* formerly cut on the island, but nowadays in Guadeloupe. The keel is made from *bois du nord* (pitch pine or Douglas fir), and the planking is *acajou* (mahogony), available in Guadeloupe, which is ripped with a chain saw and planed by hand.

The main frames, called *les gabarits,* are set up at ⅓ and ⅔ on the keel, then ribbands, called *les lisses,* are bent around and nailed to the stem and the

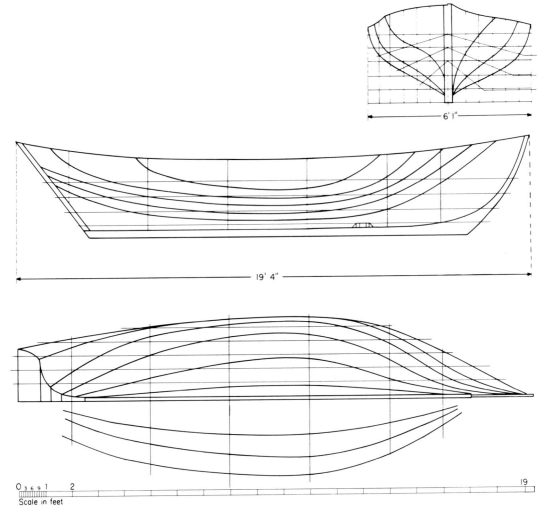

6' 1"

19' 4"

0 3 6 9 1   2   19

Scale in feet

fig. XVII-1. Lines of canot saintois France-Lise.
Built 1965 by Georges Cassin at
Bourg des Saintes. Taken off 1971 at
Iles des Saintes.

transom. The remaining frames are shaped and fitted inside this framework. Bocage learned his trade from his father and is presently teaching his son.

In all essentials, the traditions and methods of boatbuilding were the same in this French-speaking community as those prevailing in the English-speaking islands. The major differences are in design, as already noted, and in finish; le canot saintois was the most highly finished boat type that I saw in the Lesser Antilles. The frames and other members are shaped and planed on all faces, not just on the nailing face as is the practice elsewhere. In addition, scantlings are adequate but not exaggerated, as by some builders who will sometimes substitute excess of material for careful workmanship.

As we talked of changes in design brought about by the outboard motor, Bocage remarked that the fishermen use about 200 liters (25 gallons) of gasoline a day and buy a new motor every year. Even with gasoline at 20¢/liter, as it was then, it seemed an expensive way to go fishing. Since that time, the rapid worldwide rise in petroleum prices causes me to wonder

188

if any of these boats will be restored to sail propulsion. The technology is certainly not lost, because Bocage was able to give me, without pausing for relfection, the dimensions of spars, rigging and sails.

It was evident from the moment of anchoring off Bourg des Saintes that sloops and schooners no longer played any part in the commercial life of the island. All supplies and passengers were carried on the ferry that made several runs daily to Point-à-Pitre. However, the traditions of boat carpentry were so well established that it seemed worth inquiring whether there had been any schooner building in the past. On my first visit in 1970, inquiry about schooners yielded only shrugging shoulders and shaking heads. Something must have been wrong with the way I asked, because I discovered on a later visit in 1975 that there had been a shipyard, organized enough to have a name — *le Chantier de Coquelette* — where sailing vessels were built as recently as the early 1950's.

fig. XVII-2. *Builder François Bocage and sons at Bourg des Saintes. April, 1975.*

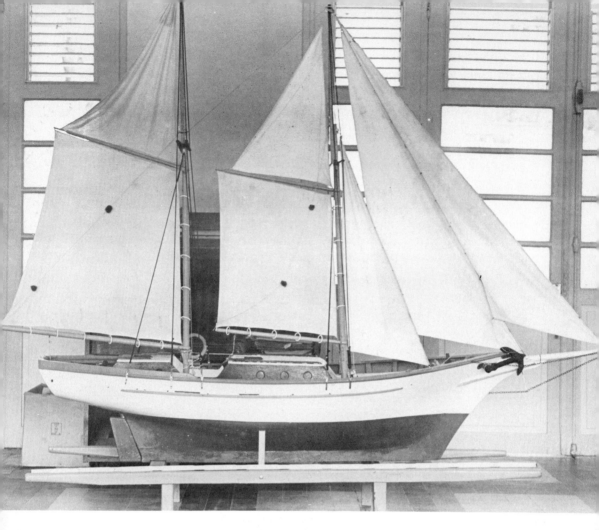

fig. XVII-3. Schooner model at Mairie. Bourg des
Saintes, April, 1975.

Thus encouraged, I went to the *Mairie* to see if any records had been kept of this activity. No such luck, but there was by pure coincidence a schooner model (fig. XVII-3) in the antechamber, built by one Théodore Samson. A simple model would not ordinarily have stirred me to great exertion, but Théodore Samson turned out to have been the owner of *le Chantier de Coquelette,* which cast a different light on the model.

Samson died in 1960, but his sister and a former employee were both still living, and from them I pieced together a reasonably complete account of such schooner building as had occurred. Both sources agreed that the first person to build schooners at Bourg des Saintes had been Bernard Agincourt, who took as a younger partner, Léon Samson, who became in time the father of Théodore Samson. The earliest vessel which could be called to mind was a 28 meter (91 foot) cutter built by Agincourt for the customs service about 1885, which sank in 1928. Agincourt and the two Samsons were all natives of the Saintes, and the elder two had no formal training. Théodore Samson, on the other hand, served an apprenticeship in a shipyard somewhere in France and could read plans and take lines off a half model. In his lifetime he built about 20 vessels, including those serving Marie Galante, an island to the windward of Guadeloupe. Samson's last construction, a motor vessel, was launched in 1960, the year he died.

In addition to his other creations, Samson had laid a valedictory hand to the model, *L'Etoile des Marins,* thereby giving it more than the usual significance. For taking off the lines, I had by this time moved even further down the road toward fully automated marine anthropology. This method requires only a short piece of electrical cable, a camera, a carpenter's rule and an assistant. The wire, held by the assistant, is bent to conform to the hull at selected stations, then photographed with the carpenter's rule in the field for scale (fig. XVII-4). Later the negative can be projected onto graph paper with the enlargement adjusted to make the ruler conform to the scale chosen, and the curve delineated by the wire is traced onto the paper, where it

fig. XVII-4. *Semi-automated boat-measuring.*
Bourg des Saintes. April, 1975.

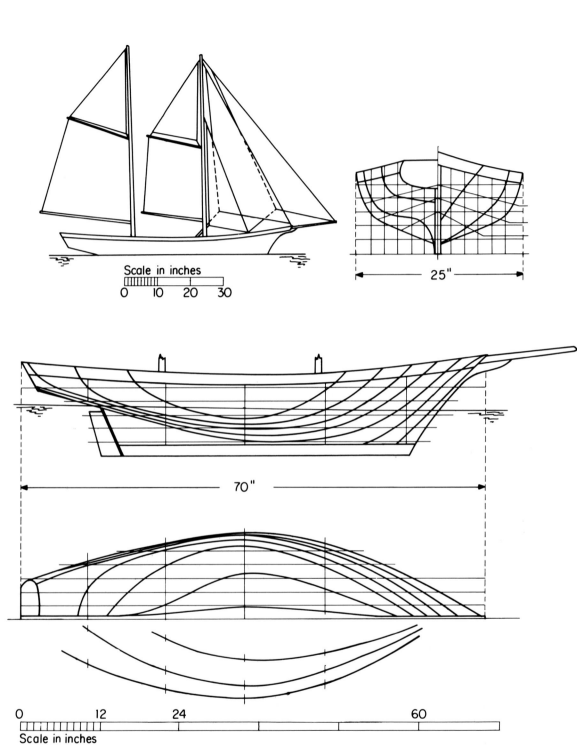

Scale in inches

0   10   20   30

25"

70"

0   12   24   60

Scale in inches

fig. XVII-5.   Lines of model schooner L'Etoile des
Marins. Built ca. 1959 by Théodore
Samson at Bourg des Saintes, Iles
des Saintes. Taken off April, 1975.

192

constitutes one of the sections of the body plan. The sheer line of the hull is similarly traced from a side view, and the deck plan is drawn from widths measured and recorded at the selected stations.

The method worked well, and the lines thus obtained (fig. XVII-5) fitted together with ease. No scale was given on the model, but the length of the model between perpendiculars was very near 180 cm. It seemed reasonable to assume that a scale of 6 cm = 1 meter was intended, corresponding to an original of 30 meters, which seemed to have been a common size for vessels built at *le Chantier de Coquelette*.

If it is assumed that Théodore Samson, who could read plans and take lines off a half model, was engaged in making a faithful copy of a representative schooner, then the following may be remarked: In overall appearance, schooners built at Bourg des Saintes were similar to the general run of West Indian and North American schooners, though somewhat beamier than elsewhere and having the flaring bow as a purely local trait.

Come we now to the subject of boatbuilding in Guadeloupe, wherein the larger island stands, as suggested at the outset, decidely in the shadow of the smaller. In short, nothing much was going on in Guadeloupe. I tried both in Basse-Terre and in Point-à-Pitre to find records of vessel registrations such as were routinely kept by the British colonial administrations. For my trouble, I got that peculiarly Gallic shrug of the shoulders that is somehow discernable even over the telephone. Local boatbuilding seems never to have attracted the attention of French officialdom except in its relation, real or imagined, to the nuisance of smuggling.

As for small craft, I found in the fishing villages of the leeward coast only rough versions of *le canot saintois* which have recently replaced the *gommier* (dugout canoe, cf. Chapters XVIII and XIX) according to anthropologist Jean Archambault, of the University of Montreal. Therefore the principal importance of Guadeloupe for the present narrative is that it provides a brief, very brief, introduction to two matters of increasing importance as we proceed southward: official French indifference to local maritime enterprise; and the persistance, in French-speaking communities, into the present or the very recent past, of the original type of Caribbean small craft — the dugout canoe.

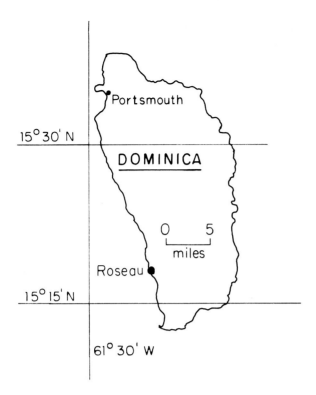

CHAPTER XVIII

DOMINICA

Dominica is a high, rugged island whose darkly forested volcanic backbone thrusts abruptly upward out of the sea — to summits of 4661 and 4672 feet within five miles of the shore. Here and there plumes of smoke ascend slowly from the flanks of the ridges where the charcoal burners are at work. Somehow this island always seemed mysterious and brooding to me. I felt, or perhaps merely imagined, an undercurrect of hostility on the few occasions when I went ashore. I was warned against going alone into the countryside. As a consequence, I know less about Dominica than any other island I visited and less than now seems desirable, especially about the *gommiers* (fig. XVIII-1) which are made on the windward side of the island.

The Carib Indians, who originated on the mainland of South America in the Orinoco Basin, were spreading rapidly northward and had occupied the islands as far as Guadeloupe at the time Columbus arrived in the New World. In fact, it was the threat posed by the all-devouring Caribs which caused the Arawak peoples living to the north to welcome the Spaniards as deliverers. Only when it was too late did they discover their mistake.

By all accounts the Caribs were as bloodthirsty a folk as ever chewed the *boucan* (a dried piece of a former enemy which was boiled up and chewed on the eve of a raid to put the warriors into the proper frame of mind): they continued to raid and harass even strongholds such as Antigua until well into the eigh-

194

fig. XVIII-1.   Gommiers at Portsmouth, Dominica.
April, 1975.

teenth century. The basis of this remarkable ability was the dugout canoe — up to 60 feet in length, carrying 50-60 paddlers, and capable of speeds of 16-18 knots.

The last stronghold of the Caribs was, not surprisingly, in the rugged fastness of Dominica, where there is still a reservation for their descendants and where dugouts are still made. Through excess of caution, I do no have first-hand knowldege of this primeval art, and must rely instead on other sources: for Dominica itself, on the description and photographs of M. Emile Hayot of Fort-de-France, Martinique (who advised me not to venture into the countryside); for Martinique in earlier times, on the account of Père Labat (Labat, 1724); and for the Tupi Indians of French Guyana, on an interview with M. Mario Mattioni, an ethnologist and curator of the Musée Départementale de La Martinique. All three accounts are so similar that there is little doubt that the methods still used in Dominica are aboriginal and essentially unchanged from pre-Columbian times.

The hull of a dugout is made from the trunk of the tree *Dacryodes excelsa* (called *gommier* in Dominica and the other islands where a French-creole dialect is spoken), still plentiful in Dominica, though scarce in Martinique since the turn of the century. After a suitable trunk has been felled and flattened on one side with ax or adze (iron tools being the only difference between modern and primitive methods), coals are heaped onto the flattened surface. After a time, the charred wood is scraped away and the process repeated until the hollow nears the desired depth. Then, several holes are drilled along the centerline of the bottom so that the thickness of the hull may be accurately

195

gauged. The hull is then worked to a final thickness of 3 inches in the bottom and 1 inch along the gunwales, the bow is sharpened and the stern cut square.

Next, the hull is "opened," thus transforming it from a simple pointed cylinder into a complex shape of astonishing hydrodynamic efficiency. To accomplish this, the hollow is filled with water which is heated by dropping in hot rocks (fig. XVIII-2). As the wood softens, the hull is opened by wedging temporary thwarts between the gunwales until the water cools and the wood sets to its new shape. This process is repeated using longer and longer thwarts until the final shape of the hull is achieved. It goes without saying that the terms "desired thickness" and "final shape" depend on the eye and experience of the builder.

fig. XVIII-2. Gommier being "opened" on wind-ward coast of Dominica. Photo by Emile Hayot.

In this unfinished state, hulls are frequently towed to Martinique and sold, selling in the early 1970's for $1000 to $1500 U.S. The hulls are then completed by the new owner, who adds one or two raising strakes, which are edge-nailed to the gunwales of the dugout and braced by widely spaced frames. Since the gommiers of Dominica had the same provenance as those of Martinique, I have chosen to relegate further details on these crafts to the next chapter, turning instead to the matter of schooner building.

Roseau, the capitol of the island, had a poorly sheltered harbor with foul bottom and poor holding, where on occasion I saw waves breaking over the concrete jetty. There was little to recommend such a place — to a boat-builder any more than to a yachtsman. Especially when a few miles to the north lay Prince Rupert Bay, one of the most beautiful stretches of sheltered water in the islands. Protected by the green heights of Morne Diablotin, this grand expanse of perfect calm stretches from Rollo Head in the south to Prince Rupert Bluff in the north. Lying in the northeast corner of the bay is the little town of Portsmouth, slumbering now, but once so lively that an American consul was stationed there.

196

fig. XVIII-3. Romulus St. Clair (Jack) Mitchell, seated at left. Photo property of Conrad Mitchell.

In 1913 when Robert Cushman Murphy called there aboard the whaling brig *Daisy,* there were 38 whaling vessels lying in Prince Rubert Bay (Murphy, 1947). According to Murphy, vessels of the New Bedford whaling fleet frequently transshipped their oil in Barbados, then sailed to Dominica to rest and refit, thus saving the time and expense of a return voyage to New Bedford. Apparently Prince Rupert Bay was chosen because there was little likelihood that crew would jump ship in a place where only other whaling vessels called. Also, it may be that there were fewer restrictions on how the resting whalers acted when ashore in such an out-of-the-way spot. There were, in any case, numerous conflicts and complaints, and the primary assignment of the American consul was to smooth over these difficulties.

fig. XVIII-4. Schooner Malta M *hauled ashore for repairs, ca. 1948. Photo property of Conrad Mitchell.*

Whatever its past glories, Portsmouth had pretty well quieted down by 1970. As soon as the anchor bit, I sat down and stared into the distance fascinated by the ant-like chain of workers, each with a stalk of bananas on his head, who emerged from a shed, walked the length of a long jetty and gangplank, then disappeared into the side of a gleaming white freighter, emerging by another door, bananaless. I don't know how long they had been at work when I arrived in mid-afternoon, but they continued until the ship sailed a 4 a.m. the following morning.

On the beach south of Portsmouth there was a small vessel in frames which, I learned in town, was being built by George Noel of Petit Martinique, a small island just to windward of Carriacou. It was hardly surprising, under the circumstances, that the vessel should resemble the Carriacou sloops.

The *Register of Shipping* kept in Roseau merely confirms this pattern: relatively few of the vessels registered in Dominica were built there; of these most were constructed by builders from Bequia, Carriacou, Petit Martinique, and in one instance, Montserrat. Presumably these builders were drawn from other islands by the abundance of timber available in Dominica.

Almost all of the boatbuilding carried out by a builder whose residence was given as Dominica was done by Romulus St. Clair Mitchell, called Jack (fig. XVIII-3, on left), who came to the island from Bequia and built 17 vessels between 1916 and 1948. The last of these, the *Malta M*, was photographed while hauled ashore for repairs (fig. XVIII-4). In the present generation, Conrad Mitchell, a son of Jack, has built three vessels, one of which, the *P M Bill*, is shown in fig. XVIII-5.

Here again, we are faced with the anomaly of an island which should have *some* boatbuilding, but which remains obstinately unaware of the force of my logic. The rugged terrain of Dominica makes coastwise commerce a convenience if not an acute necessity. There are timber resources in abundance, and at the turn of the century there was ample opportunity and inspiration for any local person who might have cared to interest himself in the ancient and honorable trade of ship carpentry. Yet the builders have come from elsewhere, and all but Jack Mitchell left when the job was done. It seems a little whimsical to suggest that they, too, found Dominica inhospitable, but I have at this point nothing better to offer.

fig. XVIII-5. Sloop P M Bill *owned by Conrad Mitchell of Portsmouth, Dominica. April, 1975.*

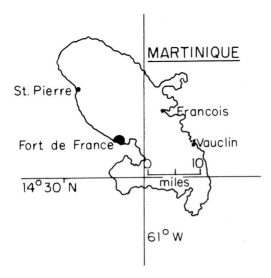

CHAPTER XIX

THE GOMMIERS OF MARTINIQUE

Martinique, with its cultivated landscape and civilized air, forms a startling contrast to the unsettled (and unsettling) ruggedness of Dominica, and yet the two, so markedly different in other respects, share an attachment for the *gommier*. Although volcanic and mountainous in geological structure, Martinique has rolling lower elevations which are gardened or grazed, while the uplands are planted to bananas, pineapples or coffee. Dotting this Mediterranean countryside are tiled and stuccoed dwellings, appropriately called villas even though thousands of miles from the Cote d'Azur.

In Fort-de-France, shiny Peugeots, Citreons, Mercedes and Fiats ply the streets, elegant shops display perfume, crystal and the latest Parisian fashions, outdoor markets overflow with tropical abundance while supermarket shelves are lined with French gastronomic delights. And threading its way in affluent haste through and among these symbols of the good life is a bustling population with the clothes, grooming and carriage of European urbanites.

In the aftermath of World War II, as European colonialism was phased out, the British chose divestiture and proceeded to grant constitutions and internal self-government to their Antillean possessions. The French moved in the opposite direction, absorbing Martinique, Guadeloupe and French Guiana into *la République Française* as full-fledged *départements*. It would be presumptuous and premature to offer any judgement on the outcome or desirability of these two courses of action, but for the present it is a matter of simple and superficial observation that the French West Indies march to a different drum than the Commonwealth Caribbean states.

*fig. XIX-1. Yoles racing in Fort Royal Bay,
Martinique. July, 1974.*

Bang in the middle of the glamour and glitter of aggressively modern Martinique, it is a little surprising to find still in extensive everyday employment the original (and in that sense, primitive) watercraft of the Antilles — the dugout canoe (fig. XIX-1). The *gommier* and its close relative, the *yole*, form the basis of the most intensive local fishing industry in the Lesser Antilles. In 1972 there were 2,656 of these craft registered in Martinique, of which 1,605 were full-time, and the remainder part-time, fishermen. Low-interest government loans for the purchase of outboard motors have completely mechanized the fleet, but all fishermen still carry spars and sails in case of engine failure.

During part of my time in Martinique, I anchored near the fishing village of Vauclin on the windward coast. Daily at sunrise, the fleet set forth in groups of two and three, the front half of the hull thrust cleanly out of the water by the 50-60 HP motor — reminding me of those aquatic birds which skim the surface of the water before launching into flight (fig. XIX-2). All were heading for the 100 meter banks which lie 10 miles to windward, where they spend the day trolling and hand-lining. In the afternoon, they return to sell their catch either directly to householders on the beach, or to jobbers in small vans who carry the fish across the mountains to Fort-de-France. Fishing ten miles at sea in these tiny craft is called by the fishermen, "aller à Michelon," a very apt expression though I have no idea where they heard of Michelon.

For measurement, I chose the *Après-Moi*, a three-man fishing gommier, based at Vauclin. The lines (fig. XIX-3) are simple in the extreme — the midsection is nearly a perfect semi-circle, and the bow and stern sections are nearly symmetrical. The lower waterlines are hollow both bow and stern, resulting in a highly efficient fusiform shape. As an instance of the efficiency of these hulls, there were in 1973 at the Carriacou Regatta two entries in the

*fig. XIX-2. Gommier (left) and yole leaving
Vauclin for the banks east of Martinique. January, 1975.*

"engine boat" class — one a conventional launch with a 50 HP Johnson outboard, the other a gommier from St. Lucia with a 25 HP Johnson. The race
committee, nothing if not expedient, decided in favor of convenience and
ran both craft in the same class, without handicap. Over the six-mile course,
the launch, with twice the power, managed to gain only a single boat-length
over the gommier.

The hull form of the gommiers is so streamlined that speed and efficiency
are hardly astonishing; what does come as a surprise is the seaworthiness of
these craft. For emergencies they carry a sailing rig consisting of an unstayed
mast, a bamboo sprit and a rectangular sail (fig. XIX-4) — very simple to sew,
set or stow. Not only do these craft fish offshore in almost all weathers, but
they also have a staggering carrying capacity. When I went to the Customs
House in Dominica to check ship registrations, I had to step carefully past the
sticky rivulets which oozed from a heap of bagged sugar which half filled the
outer office. The Customs officer, wrinkling his nose in distaste, told me that
the sugar had been impounded because duty was not paid (on sugar soaked
with sea water??). This sodden mass — a ton even before waterlogging — had
been brought from Martinique in a gommier the preceding day — 25 miles
across an open channel on the same day that I crossed with a double-reefed
main!

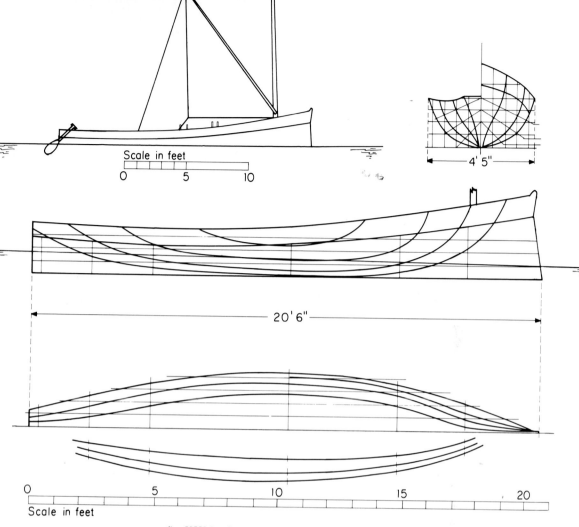

Scale in feet
0   5   10

4' 5"

20' 6"

0   5   10   15   20
Scale in feet

fig. XIX-3.   *Lines of gommier* Après-Moi. *Taken off at Vauclin, Martinique. January, 1975.*

fig. XIX-4.   *Gommier sailing with* mizaine *only. Trou de Cochon, Martinique. January, 1975.*

fig. XIX-5. *Alphonse Renoverre replacing a plank in a yole at Robert, Martinique. January, 1975.*

The true dugout, hollowed from the trunk of a gommier tree, is still the hull preferred by fishermen. However, as suitable large trees have disappeared from Martinique and become scarce in Dominica, the cost has risen; and a new type of craft, called the *yole*, has been developed. The *yole* has the dimensions and lines of a *gommier*, but is built from keel, frames and planks in the conventional European manner. At Trinité, a few miles north of Vauclin, I watched Alphonse Renoverre replace a plank in the bottom of a *yole* (fig. XIX-5). The tools and skills which he used in spiling a plank (marking and cutting a board so that the resulting plank can be successfully fitted onto the curved hull) were the same as those found in Bequia, Carriacou or Anguilla.

Despite the radical difference in construction, the two craft are very similar in form. When seen from a distance, only the shape of the stem distinguishes the two (fig. XIX-3; *gommier* on left, *yole* on right). In order to verify this judgement, I measured the racing *yole Goodyear* which I found at the village of Robert. The lines (fig. XIX-6) are virtually the same as those of the *gommier* — the same round mid-section, the same fore-and-aft symmetry, and the same hollow waterlines and fusiform shape.

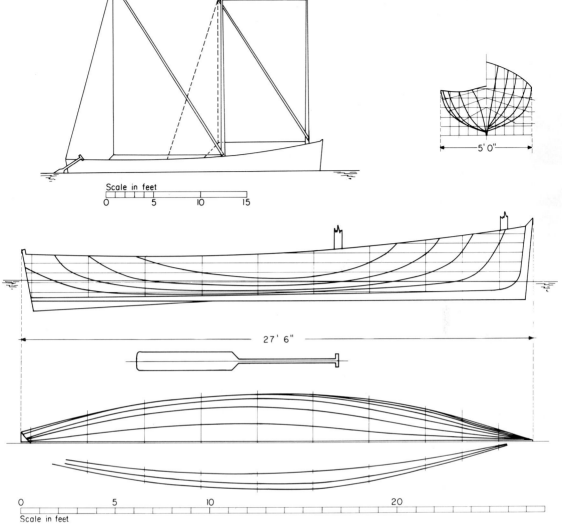

fig. XIX-6. *Lines of racing yole Goodyear. Built 1974 by Michel Meongyen at François, Martinique. Taken of September, 1974.*

The most striking difference between *Goodyear* and *Après-Moi* lies in the sail plan. In addition to the *mizaine* set forward, there is also a *grande voile* stepped a little forward of midship. This difference, however, has nothing to do with *yoles* and *gommiers*, but arises instead from the fact that the *Goodyear* was built for racing whereas *Après-Moi* was a fishing boat.

Sailing traditions in Martinique have been preserved in a manner typical of many societies that are in a period of rapid technological advance — skills no longer in demand are enshrined in the form of sport (*e.g.,* boxing and wrestling, the rodeo, the spelling bee). Some years ago an association of sailing enthusiasts was formed who have developed a calendar of some twenty races a year which are generally coupled with the Fête Patronale of one or another of the towns and villages along the coast - the Fête being an occasion of general merriment designed to bring folks into town to consume popcorn, peanuts and whatever else isn't selling well. For the purpose of

fig. XIX-7. Start of regatta for yoles at François,
Martinique. January, 1975.

drawing a crowd, what could be better than a fleet of white-winged *yoles* and *gommiers* lined up to race (fig. XIX-7).

Not realizing that anything of this type was going on in Martinique, I attended my first race quite by accident, but instantly formed the determination to acquire both lines and performance data. The lines were no particular problem (see above) since that could be done at any time and required no person other than myself. Performance data was clearly another matter because these craft do not sail except in races when it is all or nothing and requires a crew of 11-15, depending on the strength of the wind. My inquiries were not prospering until I discovered, again by accident, that Vauclin boasted a racing yole and my good friend Raymond Asselin was acquainted with the owner.

The arrangements were made for Thursday afternoon (half-day early closing by French tradition) and Raymond asked me to stop and see him before keeping the *rendez-vous*. He quietly gave me to understand that the opportunity to sail in the *Vini Ouê Ça* was a bit of concession (Raymond was well-liked by the fishermen of the village), and he gave me 200 francs ($50 U.S.) to buy a round of drinks. It seemed a little excessive to me — until I reached the shed on the outskirts of Vauclin where the *yole* was sheltered.

Gathered on the beach, engaged in the multitude of chores necessary to launch the sleek hull, was a squad of perhaps 30 men and boys of all ages and sizes. First, the sails and spars were brought out, laid on the sand and knotted together. Then about half the men laid hold of the hull, turned it over and carried it into the sea where they remained, holding it. The remainder began to step the *mizaine* and the *grande voile,* carrying the spars and sails as a unit and setting them into the canoe. Naturally this increased by a good amount the difficulties of holding upright the unballasted hull, and I was beginning to see the purpose of the 200 francs.

When all was ready, the crew scrambled aboard and we were pushed into deeper water as the sails were sheeted and the *patron* began to scull with the steering oar to carry us off the shore. There were eleven of us in all: three men forward on trapeze lines (there were no stays on either mast), four men with *bois dresses* (hiking poles), one man amidship to bail and handle the clew of the *mizaine,* another aft on the clew of the *grande voile,* the *patron* and I. For sails we had set the lightweather mainsail (380 square feet) and the *mizaine* (190 square feet), a total of 570 square feet of sail on an unballasted canoe with 5 feet of beam. For comparison, *Eider* with all sails set sports only 560 square feet on a hull displacing 9 tons.

As the breeze began to fill the sails, the *patron* leaned into the big steering paddle and brought the head farther off the wind. The crew scrambled to their positions and continued for the entire time we sailed to shift in and out, compensating automatically for even the slightest change in course or wind. The *patron,* in addition to steering with the big paddle, actually sculled more or less full time — three or four strokes to pull the head off the wind, then a brief rest while the yole surged up into the wind. This pumping action had the effect of countering leeway — so well that we made no more than 3° of leeway even with nothing under the hull. This practice makes the *patron's* seat one of the warmest in the gommier, and in a long race the place is rotated among the senior members of the crew.

To measure wind speed, I was using a hand-held anemometer with a small red ball for an indicator. After watching me hold the device up to the wind and squint at the bouncing ball, the *patron* asked me if he could get "one of those things to take the temperature of the wind." For speed through the water, I was using a Pitot tube with a top of 7 knots, completely adequate until that day. However, in the puffs of wind which never exceeded 12 knots, the indicator in the Pitot tube slammed up to the top of the tube and water squirted well over my head. The breeze was very light and we never even came close to the full potential of the *Vini Ouê Ca,* though I would have been unable to measure it if we had.

After I had made a series of measurements while beating, the *patron* motioned for me to take the steering paddle. I grinned and accepted readily this evidence that things were thawing a bit after the initial coolness the crew had shown toward me.

"*Vas-y, blanc,*" several of the men called as I took up the position and leaned into the paddle. The *yole* surged in response — it was for all the world like twisting the throttle of a powerful motorcycle. There were cheers of encouragement from the crew.

"*Encore, blanc. Encore.*"

Whom the gods would destroy, they first make mad. Again I leaned into the paddle, intoxicated by a double dose of power and approval.

Too late the *patron* shouted at me to ease up. Already the speed and the increased angle of heel had brought water rushing in over the lee bow, and we rushed upon our fate. Suddenly it was all over, and there we were — 11 men, 570 square feet of wet canvas, several hiking poles, paddles, baling gourds, my camera, instruments and notes — all swirling and bobbing in the sea.

I didn't know whether to dive for the bottom or swim for the shore, but the crew were shouting and laughing their heads off. In some odd way, the ice had been broken and it was all right. One man swam over with my camera looped around his neck. Another waved the Pitot tube aloft. The *patron* paddled over to assure me that even after forty years he sometimes capsized a canoe.

In theory, it is possible to right a capsized *yole* since the unstayed masts come out of the steps and float clear. Then the hull is easily righted and the crew cling along the gunwales scooping water out until the smallest member of the crew can crawl in an continue baling. As the canoe floats higher, more men crawl aboard until the hull is baled dry. Then the sails are hauled aboard, and with a little balance, and a lot of luck, the masts are restepped.

In practice, however, with a flukey breeze and a short chop, we were too near shore to bother with the process. An outboard-powered gommier came out and towed us back to Vauclin where the day's diversions were already on their way to becoming something of a village event — subsequently on a number of occasions when walking in Vauclin, I was stopped by strangers who inquired if I were really the man who sailed under the *Vini Oué Ça.*

The 200 francs, wet but still negotiable, bought a round of 'Petit ponch' for the crew and their friends and relations. I shrugged off soloicitous inquiries about my watch and the camera and expressed as my only regret that I had not gotten data for the downwind performance of the *yole.* The owner of the *Vini Oué Ça,* who had joined us at the bar after watching the performance trial from the comfort and security of the shore, suggested that I accompany him in the committee launch the following Sunday to collect additional data.

On Sunday afternoon, I drove down to Robert with the owner and crew of *Vini Oué Ça,* unsure how well it would work to try to estimate accurately the performance of the *yole* from a distance. The regattas that I had seen elsewhere invariably started downwind, ran to the leeward mark, then beat home, displaying only two points of sailing and those too far away to benefit the spectators. However, at Robert the course was laid out in such way that there was a beat, a run, two reaching legs, another beat and a run for the finish line — most of it in full view of the crowd on the shore. In consequence I did not lack for opportunity to collect data, especially since the committee launch followed the canoes very closely.

As race time drew near, the wind seemed to be increasing, so the crew, after some discussion, decided to set the smaller of the two *grandes voiles.* The freshening breeze proved to be temporary and *Vini Oué Ça* was badly undercanvassed and finished only sixth, first place going to *Goodyear.* After the *yoles* raced, there was a race for *gommiers* and for the final event, the *yoles* set their largest sail as *mizaine* and raced with that rig (fig. XIX-8). In

fig. XIX-8. Yole racing with mizaine only at
François, Martinique. January, 1975.

this event, *Vini Oué Ça* ran much better and was leading until she hit a buoy
on the reaching leg and was disqualified. The data collected on Sunday afternoon as well as that from my earlier outing are included in the following table.

— setting *grande voile* and *mizaine* —

Point of sailing	Angle off the wind	Wind speed	Boat speed	Leeway angle	Boat/Wind speed/speed
Close-hauled	55°	10 knts.	6.5 knts	3°	.65
Close-hauled	45°	12	7.5 (est)	3°	.62
Close-hauled	50°	8	6.5	2°	.81
Reach	90°	8	5.4	—	.68
Run	170°	8	5.6	—	.70

— *mizaine* only —

Close-hauled	45°	9	4.4	3°	.49
Close-hauled	45°	10	5.1	3°	.51
Reach	90°	8	6.5	2°	.81
Run	175°	8	6.7	—	.84

If the ratio of boat speed to wind speed may be taken as expressing the
efficiency of a particular craft in extracting energy from the wind, then the
range of values for the *yole* indicates that its efficiency is similar to the other
types of small craft which I was able to compare. However, there is a great dif-

209

ference in the much higher speeds of which the *yole* is capable. As it happened, I had neither the opportunity nor the equipment to measure performance in winds strong enough for full speed to develop, but on two occasions I saw *yoles* sailing at speeds which I estimated to be in excess of twelve, and perhaps as high as fourteen, knots. These were undoubtedly the fastest small craft that I saw in the Lesser Antilles.

In the form and construction of the hull, there seems little doubt that the present-day *yoles* and *gommiers* of Martinique and the *gommiers* of Dominica and St. Lucia are derived from the Carib dugout canoe. However, the origins of the unusual rig — two rectangular spritsails with the smaller set forward — are more difficult to establish, though much discussed.

In a paper entitled "Aboriginal canoes in the West Indies" (McKusick, 1960), the author repeats a passage from *The Voyage of M. Henry Challons* (Stoneman, 1603) containing the following account: one day off the coast of Dominica the voyagers were hailed by a Spanish priest who escaped from the Caribs by putting out from shore in a small canoe. The priest told his rescuers that he was the last of a party of three missionaries who were shipwrecked on the island some years before. His companions had been killed by the Caribs, but he was spared in reward for showing his captors the use of the sail.

In a paper entitled "Aboriginal Sail in the New World" (Edwards, 1965), the author makes a comprehensive survey of historical sources dealing with sail in the New World. His view is that Stoneman's account comes too long after contact to be very convincing. He does cite Oviedo (1526), a keen observer who traveled extensively in the West Indies as early as 1514 and speaks of the Caribs as accomplished sailors, However, Edwards feels that a single source is not sufficient to decide the matter and eschews conjecture.

Mario Mattioni, quoted in the last chapter, is quick to point out that both the Caribs and their predecessors, the Arawaks, spun and wove cotton (Columbus adopted the hammock from the Arawaks encountered on his first voyage). It seems to Mattioni so probable as to amount to certain that the Caribs, who were unquestionably seafarers, must have developed sails before European contact.

Desmond Nicholson of English Harbor, a student of Carib antiquities, holds the opposite opinion (Nicholson, 1975) so emphatically that he waves aside all debate which he says amounts to "playing at silly-buggers" (personal communication). The Caribs, lacking the delights of television and transistor radio, were prone, when in search of entertainment, to ramble down the coast for a few rounds of rape, burn and pillage. For this purpose, they loaded fifty paddlers in a sixty-foot canoe and went merrily off at 16 knots. What use, asks Nicholson rhetorically, have such folk for sails? Besides, most of the channels in the island chain are less than 30 miles wide, and the rest of the trip is in a windless lee where one might just as well paddle. An interesting point, I feel, which leads one to wonder if the development of sail is largely a commercial proposition in an effort to cut overhead.

Nothing that I was able to observe sheds any new light on the question of sailing canoes. It is, nevertheless, odd to find an undoubtedly aboriginal hull type so closely associated with an unusual rig that has no counterpart in any of the islands where canoe-type small craft are not used. There is another oddity about canoes — the persistence of the dugout in some form or another into the present or very recent past coincides pretty exactly with the continued use of *patois, i.e.* French-creole dialect. If only Guadeloupe and Martinique were involved, such coincidence would not be in any way remarkable. However, there are also Dominica, and as we will see in the coming chapters, St. Lucia, St. Vincent, Grenada and Trinidad (all nominally English-speaking, by the way), where at least some patois is spoken and where some form of dugout is found or traceable. This observation churned in the back of my mind a good while waiting for a formulation; when formulated, it was my hope that some great mystery would be solved. But nothing happened — the coincidence is certainly there and just as certainly, I don't know what to make of it.

One way and another, I spent a good bit of time in Martinique, and never saw a sloop or schooner. Interisland trading vessels no longer play any part in the economic life of the island since commercial relations are exclusively with metropolitan France, which supplies manufactured goods and buys bananas, pineapples and other tropical produce.

It was always possible, however, that boatbuilding had gone on at some earlier date, so I inquired. Nothing was available from official sources; the same indifference which I encountered in Guadeloupe also prevailed in Martinique. I did finally stumble onto the carcass of a ruined schooner hauled ashore near an abandoned sugar factory at Cosmil on the windward coast. It had been the property of the sugar factory, and was used during the Allied blockade of World War II to carry sugar around to Fort-de-France and return with fertilizer.

It sounds a bit odd to take to the seas during a blockade, but wars produce unusual circumstances as well as strange bedfellows. When France was overrun by the German Army in the early days of World War II, the French fleet was scattered in a number of overseas locations, including Martinique. Some commanders maintained an unbroken chain of command which wound tortuously upward to Vichy; others "surrendered" and became Free French; some scuttled their ships. The commandant in Martinique was Vichy, as they say, and technically an enemy of the Allies. However, it was part of no one's plan to attack or to break out; everyone's interests were best served by a bloodless blockade, which unfortunately left the island without gasoline for road transport, but did leave the sea lanes open for windpower.

The dimensions, lines and construction details of the ruined schooner at Cosmil all suggested a temporary solution to a temporary problem rather than the outgrowth of a traditional culture. Aside from the situation created by the blockade, Martinique has probably never had any great need for schooners. There are no smaller, off-lying island dependencies which might trade with the main island. If there were trade with the nearby Commonwealth islands, it would undoubtedly be carried in vessels built there, while trade with France goes by steamer.

Though indifferent to schooner building, French officialdom was showing a lot of interest in fishing craft, as I discovered in my inquiries. There was a program to develop and diffuse a new type of fishing vessel to be called the *yole amélioré.* The name suggests modified or improved, and a number of interesting possibilities flitted through my mind on the way to the yard where a prototype was being built. What I found fell sadly short of my imaginings; in reality, the *yole amélioré* was nothing more than a little Mediterranean putt-putt — a small, decked, diesel-powered, three-man launch able to spend two or three days at sea and costing more than an individual fisherman could afford. When I sought by questioning to understand the wisdom and necessity of this development, it emerged that official concern centers on something other than naval architecture and fisheries management.

With the present arrangement of *yoles* and *gommiers,* constructed locally and fairly easily affordable, the fishermen can run ashore anywhere and sell all their catch with no records kept and little tax paid. As might be expected, this worries the government no end. Records not kept! Taxes not paid! Harumph!!

Larger and more expensive vessels would mean that the fishermen had to organize into co-ops or, more likely, work for an owner/capitalist. Larger catches would have to be landed at government-operated fish markets, where records *are* kept and taxes paid. I was secretly gratified to hear that by and large the fishermen had seen through the smoke screen and continued to prefer their traditional watercraft.

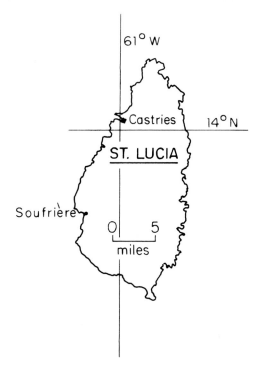

CHAPTER XX

ST. LUCIA

Early in my island-hopping days, someone advised me that channel crossing was best done by holding up close under the lee of an island, even tacking if necessary to work as far to windward as possible before entering the rougher waters and stronger currents of the channel. It was the implementation of this strategy which took me early one March morning into the dark calm of Chateau Belair Bay, lying in the lee of the Soufrière, St. Vincent's once and future volcano. The surface of the bay was smooth, but masses of cloud boiled and surged past the top of the volcano above. In the steep valleys that scored the sides of the cone, the silver flash of falling water here and there streaked the dark, glossy green. Ocasionally a small patch of coconut fronds marked a human habitation — one or two thatched huts in a small area of cleared ground.

The fishing fleet from Chateau Belair — small, two-bow boats of the Bequia model — was spread across the bay, tacking slowly back and forth, so dwarfed by the mass of the volcano that they seemed to change position without moving. There was a dreamlike immobility to the whole tableau which was soon left behind as we changed course and "let go" for St. Lucia.

The wind that had been pushing the clouds around high overhead was now at wave-top height. However, the strategy of working to windward was successful, and even in the steep seas of the channel, our course was free enough that little water came aboard. We were nearing mid-channel when something in the animated monotony of the waves caught my attention — a

213

fig. XX-1. *St. Lucia* canots at *Carriacou Regatta.*
August, 1970.

flash which was not a whitecap, a motion which was not part of the heaving sea surface. A few minutes later, there was another visual disturbance, this time from a different quarter altogether. As the disturbances became more frequent, they also drew closer, slowly revealing themselves as human figures clad in yellow oilskins and topped by woven hats with incredible high peaks. The figures seemed to skim the surface of the water at high speed, darting this way and that like disembodied spirits. When the full reality was finally disclosed to me, the figures were seated by threes, one behind another in a canoe so narrow and so low in the water as to be invisible at a very short distance. The figure in the stern was steering with the outboard motor; the one in the middle was baling. In the bow, lifted completely clear of the water by the thrust of the motor, the third figure peered forward and gestured from time to time, sending the whole rig swerving this way and that. This, as it happened, was my first encounter with a St. Lucia *canot.*

Several years later, an opportunity to measure a *canot* occured when a pair of them appeared at the Carriacou Regatta in 1971 to compete in the newly created "engine boat" class (fig. XX-1). These two craft, originally from St. Lucia, had been fishing for two years out of Kingstown, St. Vincent, which is how their owners happened to hear of the regatta.

The basis of the *canot,* like its counterpart the *gommier,* is a log, hollowed and opened, with a raising strake added atop the gunwale. The *canot,* however, is easily distinguishable from the *gommier* by the striking extension of the

214

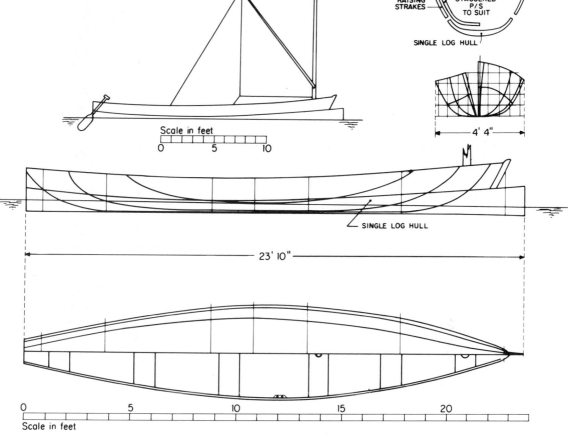

PLANK
RAISING
STRAKES

GROWN FRAMES
STAGGERED
P/S
TO SUIT

SINGLE LOG HULL

4' 4"

Scale in feet

0   5   10

SINGLE LOG HULL

23' 10"

0   5   10   15   20

Scale in feet

fig. XX-2. Lines of canot St. Bénédic. Built by
Joseph Hendricks, Soufrière, St. Lucia. Taken
off at Carriacou, August, 1970.

dugout into a sort of cutwater. There are other less apparent differences which
emerge from an examination of the lines of the *St. Bénédic* (fig. XX-2): the mid-
section is not so nearly round; the beam is 1 inch less though the hull (including cutwater) is 3 feet 4 inches longer; there is less freeboard in the bow;
the waterlines show less hollow and are less streamlined.

It is tempting to say that St. Lucia, being a little less French than
Martinique, has drifted a little farther from the original dugout type. That,
of course, is absurd since I can have no idea what the original type was. The
St. Lucia *canot* seems a little less developed, but this is probably owing to a
scarcity of large timber in St. Lucia. In fact, the *St. Bénédic* still performed
very creditably against a conventional, flat-sterned launch, as mentioned in
the preceding chapter.

It was this edge in performance which caused these *canots* to appear in
St. Vincent, where fishing was formerly dominated by Bequia boats. By
1974 the *canots* were offering such stiff competition that they had the Bequia
boys scratching their heads and building broader sterns to carry two outboards. There is a decided irony in the fact that at this very time, two-bow
boats of the Bequia model were replacing the sailing dugouts used along the
northwest coast of Grenada (cf. Chapter III).

215

fig. XX-3. St. Lucia fishing boat entering Castries harbor. April, 1975.

On a later trip to St. Lucia, I was in search of schooners and made for the major port of Castries, entering after dark, but with no anxiety since the harbor is deep and well-buoyed with a straightforward entrance. I followed the leading lights and proceeded to the quarantine anchorage as designated in the *West Indies Pilot* because I had been told that the authorities were strict about that sort of thing. After anchoring and stowing the sails, I turned in for what was left of the night, tranquil in the knowledge that Castries is the safest harbor in the islands. Just before dawn the heavens quietly opened and water began to pour from the sky.

There may be better music than rain on the deck heard from a dry bunk, but not wishing to be hasty in my conclusions, I lay abed until after nine o'clock to consider the matter. When at last I emerged into the sun-lit cockpit to get my bearings and plan the day's activities, I was dismayed to discover that *Eider* was anchored much closer to the shore than was necessary or safe in the dark. The anchor could scarcely have dragged in the windless night, and the directions for anchoring had been carefully followed. As I puzzled over the matter, the shoreline came even closer. When the first flies began to buzz around my ears, a great light dawned — what appeared to be the shoreline was, in fact, a great raft of garbage which had floated off the town's harborside dump and was drifting gently down the harbor.

Not a very auspicious beginning; but, undaunted, I got together my notebooks and set out to get clearance papers and, I hoped, information on schooner building. A bracing row through the garbage brought me to the Customs House — uncharmingly situated on the dilapidated waterfront whence came the debris — only to be told that clearance papers were now issued at the deep-water pier across the harbor. Doggedly, I made my way back to the

216

fig. XX-4.   St. Lucia fishing boat. Detail of sail plan.

dinghy and turned out the crowd of urchins who were merrily engaged in determining how many undernourished bodies it takes to sink the average dinghy. Ignoring their good-natured shower of rocks, I set off for the deep-water pier, where I gaily clambered up an oily piling — no ladder being available.

When finally I presented myself at the Harbour Office, I was hot and disheveled, but pluckily filled out the required forms, in triplicate without carbon paper, stating: draft forward and aft, what mails carried and how many cannon mounted.

"How long do you intend to stay," snapped the officer as I turned in the forms with $10 EC in harbor dues.

"Uh, well, uh, I don't know," I mumbled since I had no exact schedule, and the question caught me off guard.

"Aha!," the officer crowed. "You don't know how long you are staying. Very suspicious, Mr. Pyle. That makes me very suspicious."

Suddenly, it was all a little more than I had bargained for, so I availed myself of the option to make outbound clearance on the same form provided the vessel is leaving in 72 hours. That left exactly 71½ hours to copy the *Register of Shipping*, talk to any builders still around, interview the widow of Reg. Mitchell (cf. Chapter V) and take the lines off any fishing boats that might be found.

I do not solicit sympathy for the grim hardships of a boatmeasurer's lot; my only purpose is to explain why I was in a crashing hurry two mornings later as I rowed to the head of the harbor where the fishing boats (figs. XX-3, 4) were drawn ashore.

fig. XX-5. Builder Joseph Evans with canot Saint Peter. *Castries, St. Lucia. April, 1975.*

By herself at the end of the rank, I found the *Merci-Dieu,* just like all the others but looking a little unused. Ordinarily, I would have made inquiries and sought out the owner before setting to work, not only for reasons of courtesy and propriety, but also for such information as he might have about boat construction. On this occasion, my haste and sense of general ill-usage over-came my better judgement, and I set to work without further ado. Only two stations remained to be measured when the challenge came.

"Who say you come messin' bout de boat?"

The irate voice belonged to a man with the short pants of a fisherman and the indignant air of a boatowner whose boat is being measured without his consent. My luck was definitely out in St. Lucia.

"I was just making a few little notes because this boat has the best lines of any around," said I — because you never know till you've tried.

"Is a very technical thing, a mold and all. And you takin' a man mold, you must pay." Softsoap or not.

I groaned. The old shakedown again. Out of sight perhaps, but never out of mind. Any mishap, mistake or indiscretion must be amended by the payment of some sum of money — large or small, depending on the relative

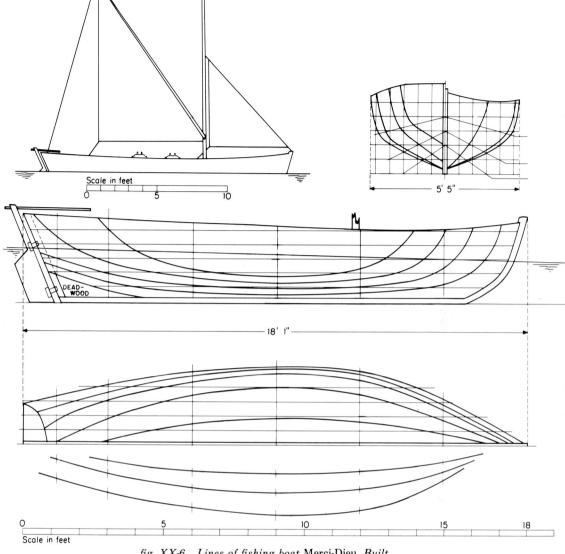

Scale in feet
0   5   10

5' 5"

DEAD-
WOOD

18' 1"

0   5   10   15   18

Scale in feet

fig. XX-6. *Lines of fishing boat* Merci-Dieu. *Built
by Joseph Evans at Castries, St. Lucia. Taken
off April, 1975.*

skills of trespasser and trespassee.

I apologized, explained, then apologized some more — and to my surprise, he became genuinely interested. Eventually he softened, told me his name was Joseph Evans, explained about the two types of small craft used in St. Lucia, and finally asked if I would like to take his picture beside another of the small string of fishing craft that he owned (fig. XX-5).

The lines and construction of the *Merci-Dieu* (fig. XX-6) show a generic relationship to the other beach boats of the English-speaking islands to the north: sharp floors, moderate deadrise, transom stern and slight drag to the keel. The really unique feature of this type is the hybrid rig: the proportions of the spritsail are the same as those of a *canot,* but the mast is stepped farther aft, permitting a small jib to be set. As Joseph Evans so concisely stated: "In St. Lucia, it havin' two kind of boat — *canot* and boat." That these two

219

divergent types occur on the same island and that the boat itself is a sort of hybrid undoubtedly results from the peculiar confluence of French and English influences which occurred in St. Lucia.

During the 17th and 18th centuries, as England and France staked out and then sought to maintain their claims in the New World, force was exerted by sending out The Fleet to do a little muscling. Said fleet left the mother country, sailed downwind across the Atlantic with the Trade Winds and passed downwind through the Lesser Antilles from southeast to northwest, before going to the Greater Antilles. From there they slipped into the Gulf Stream, to be carried northward along the North American coast into the zone of prevailing westerlies to return, ever downwind, to Europe.

Such was the sailing ability (or really, inability) of the warships of the period that an island left behind was inaccessibly upwind, especially if subsequently occupied by the enemy's fleet. Therefore the last fleet to leave Europe had a tactical advantage since it held the windward position after arriving in the Indies, and any alterations in political geography made in its name could not be amended until a year later at the very shortest. On the other hand, the later the fleet left, the greater its chances of getting caught in the Caribbean by the hurricane season. There was, obviously, ample substance here for the feint-and-parry so dear to the military mind.

One outcome of this game of blind man's bluff was that St. Lucia changed hands between France and England no less than fourteen times, before finally ending up on the English side of the board. Of course, all the islands of the Lesser Antilles — except Barbados — enjoyed in varying degree the attentions of the two rival suitors. However, St. Lucia holds the record for courtship, engagement, marriage and divorce, and it is hardly surprising that a form of dugout canoe here exists side by side with a beach boat derived from another tradition entirely.

St. Lucia was another of those islands that was never mentioned when schooners and schooner building were spoken of. Nevertheless, on the chance that there might have been some activity in the past, I wanted to check the *Register of Shipping*. The personnel in the Harbour Master's Office were cordial and helpful but there was, even so, a fundamental obstacle — the whole town of Castries burned to the ground in 1948. I began to understand why the town had such a drab appearance. And, of course, this meant that the records of ship registrations only began in 1948.

In the period since the fire, there had been a certain amount of boat-building centered in Castries, and the name of Malings Compton appeared frequently — first as a builder and later as an owner. The Harbour Master told me that Compton was knowledgeable on the subject and that he could be found at his store a few blocks from the harbor.

Malings Compton (fig. XX-7) was born in 1898 on the island of Canouan in the northern Grenadines, and there learned boat carpentry from his father before emigrating to St. Lucia in 1916. In all, Compton built eight vessels — the first in 1920, the last in 1952 and the largest (the *Albertha Compton*, 110

*fig. XX-7. Schooner builder Malings Compton in
front of his store in Castries, St. Lucia. April,
1975.*

feet, 120 Tons) in 1937. The methods which he described for the proportioning
and setting up of vessels corresponded precisely to those used throughout the
Grenadines. He did not, he told me, read plans, but Lewis Magras from St.
Barts, the other major builder in Castries, could.

The pattern of activity in St. Lucia was therefore similar to that found in
Dominica, Montserrat, Grenada, St. Kitts, St. Barts and St. Martin —
sporadic boatbuilding as local economic conditions dictated, with the builders
themselves coming from either Anguilla or the Grenadines.

As our conversation was drawing to a close, I asked Compton about the
origins of boat carpentry in the islands. This was the question that had drawn
shrugs, blank stares and obviously fantastic answers from one end of the chain
to the other — by now, my asking was purely perfunctory. Compton's answer,
however, was anything but perfunctory.

"Well," he said, throwing his head back reflectively, "this is the way it
came about. In 1838, when Sir William Snagg came out to take charge of the
island of Canouan..."

His information was so detailed and unhesitating, so concise and specific
that I immediately felt his account was significant. Later, in the most unexpected way, his personal account fitted with official records and with other
information from widely different sources to provide the key to understanding
and form the basis for a chapter on the culture history of boatbuilding in the
Lesser Antilles — a chapter that I had not known was to be written. Meanwhile, there were still three islands which were not yet included in my survey.

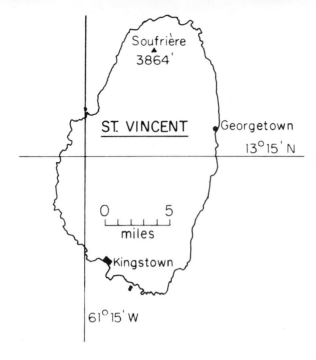

CHAPTER XXI

ST. VINCENT

During the time that Skywave was being built in Bequia, I occasionally had errands in nearby St. Vincent. If the errand was brief, then the most convenient method of conducting business was to get up before dawn, walk the three miles up and over from Friendship Bay to Port Elizabeth, and there-after to recline in luxurious ease on the deck of the mail schooner for an hour and a half while she thrashed her way across the nine-mile channel to St. Vincent. The mail contract at that time was held by the *Friendship Rose*, which left Bequia at 6 a.m. and reached Kingstown with the sun still behind the mountain — charging for this service a mere $1 EC.

This trip grew to be a great favorite of mine because it entailed, among other things, a belated breakfast at a little planks-and-tin snack shop that huddled just outside the gates to the dockyard. My unvarying choice was a mango, a fried egg sandwich and a large mug of coffee sweetened with con-densed milk — simple enough but a gastronomic delight after the pre-dawn hike and a lively sail in the early morning chill of the Trades.

St. Vincent is a lush volcanic island with a primarily agricultural economy based on bananas and arrowroot flour. Recently, efforts have been made to develop Caribbean markets for the island's abundant supplies of those tropical root crops locally known as "ground provisions" — tanias, dasheens, yams, edoes, sweet potatoes and cassava. In addition, St. Vincent is the ad-ministrative and commercial center for all of the northern Grenadines, and Kingstown harbor is still much frequented by sailing vessels (fig. XXI-1). This

222

fig. XXI-1. Schooner wharf. Kingstown, St. Vincent, March, 1975.

being the case, it seemed a good idea to inquire along the waterfront about boatbuilding.

"Oh, yes," came the reply. "It have a big vessel building over Indian Bay. Plenty big."

When I got to Indian Bay, sure enough, there was a large vessel on stocks (fig. XXI-2). Not only was this vessel large (90 feet), but it has some other unusual features as well. The bow was high and flaring in a way that I had never seen in a schooner before. An even closer inspection revealed that there was no sternpost; instead there was an enormous deadwood of timbers laid on top of the keel (fig. XXI-3, lower right).

One of the shipwrights was from Bequia and was glad to explain the unorthodox construction. The vessel was to be an "engine boat" fitted with twin engines — and twin propellor shafts on either side of the deadwood.

223

fig. XXI-2. Trading vessel under construction,
fishing boats in foreground. Indian
Bay, St. Vincent. October, 1970.

There would be a cargo mast but no sails, and the high bow was for punching head-on into the sea, something a sailing vessel is not able to do. Since the vessel was not intended for sailing and was far too large to be measured for mere curiosity, I contented myself with the odd photograph (fig. XXI-4).

Long before I had ever set eyes on a tropical island, the phrase "tropical waters teeming with fish" had been deeply etched into my mind by the romantic stories which are chiefly responsible for my version of the world. Consequently, it came as something of a surprise to discover, after a certain amount of snorkeling and spear-fishing, that this is not an entirely accurate picture. To be sure, a coral reef "teems with life," but only in the sense that a large number of *species* are represented, not all of which are fish and few of which are edible.

When was the last time that you tickled your tastes buds with sponge soup, then appeased your appetite with coral cutlets and topped it all off with sea urchin mousse?

The fact is that the world's large commercial fisheries are located in cold waters, or occasionally in mid-latitudes where there is an up-welling of cold, nutrient-rich water from the ocean floor. In the warm waters of the tropics, relatively little oxygen dissolves, there is no return of nutrients from the ocean depths, and consequently, little plankton and few fish.

In addition, St. Vincent, whose steep volcanic top is mirrored below the sea by an equally steep base, has almost no shelf and no onshore fishing grounds. Such fishing as there is is carried out in small two-bow boats (fig. XXI-2, foreground) of the Bequia model. Recently, *canots* from St. Lucia have begun to appear in St. Vincent; with their greater speed and range, they are able to go after the pelagic species such as bonito, dorado, mackerel and

fig. XXI-3. *Detail of construction, trading vessel*
at Indian Bay. October, 1970.

*fig. XXI-4. Detail of construction, trading vessel
at Indian Bay. October, 1970.*

various billfishes. The sum and substance of it, then, is that St. Vincent does not have at the present time any distinctive type of small craft.

Apparently this has not always been the case; Stedman Wallace, a knowledgeable Bequian, told me that until the 1940's, passengers and mail were carried daily between Georgetown and Kingstown in a 40-foot dugout canoe which was paddled, not sailed, the 24 mile trip being made in about 2 hours.

This accords well with the fact that there was a group of Yellow Caribs living in the northeast part of the island in the early part of this century (Fenger, 1958).

In the course of my inquiries up and down the island arc, I became familar with particular islands roughly in proportion to how much boatbuilding activity there was. The exception was St. Vincent, which became very familiar to me as the "big town" for Bequia, but where there were no new types of watercraft and little boatbuilding. The explanation is, by this time, rather obvious — to an even greater extent than Grenada, St. Vincent is eclipsed in maritime affairs by the Grenadines.

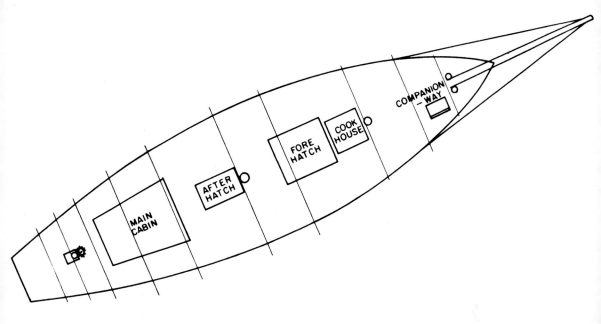

CHAPTER XXII

TRADING WITH THE *ROSARENE*

The quiet of the tropical morning had already been swallowed by the dusty cacophony of the dockyard as I picked my way through the minuet of backing trucks, stationary hand carts, swaying cargo slings and shuffling dockers. The captain of the *Rosarene* — a slender man wearing an unlikely felt snapbrim — had been pointed out to me by the Customs guard at the gate to the dockyard. I made my approach as the captain dismissed one man with a nod and set another to work with a pointed finger.

"I would like to get a passage to Trinidad, please. Haakon said to tell you . . .," I began, hoping to invoke the talisman of friendship.

"You must see the agent for that," he cut in with the harassed air of a man who doesn't intend to be bothered. "Is nothing to do with me."

Something had apparently gone wrong. Haakon had said to mention his name, and there would be no problem — probably not even any passage to pay. As I tried to explain further, Captain Hazell stepped onto the rail of the schooner and began to shout instructions to one of the men who was stowing cargo below decks. He didn't even give me a chance to ask who the agent was, but I was determined to make the trip, so asked the Customs guard again. He directed me to a dusty office on a side street a block away, where I repeated my request to a man behind the counter. He gave me a puzzled look.

"Why does a white man want to book passage on a schooner?" his manner seemed to say. "Not even West Indians travel by schooner any more." Not since interisland air service has become an integral part of island life.

fig. XXII-1. Schooner Rosarene *near Mustique,
bound for Trinidad. February, 1971.*

Somehow it seemed only polite to offer an explanation, but I was afraid
that my real purpose would sound romantic or eccentric. For practical reasons,
I had no wish to be regarded as either the one or the other.

"I need copper paint for my yacht and that is too heavy to carry on the
airplane," I offered, which was, in fact, true. Also, I wanted to see Trinidad
without having to take *Eider* into a large commercial port that was said to be
hot and uncomfortable. But the real reason was that I wanted to sample life
aboard one of the schooners that were still so fascinating to me.

Whether convinced or not, the agent began to write out my passage, $50
EC for the round trip and another $100 EC in bond — bond against my jump-
ing ship in Trinidad, he explained apologetically.

Hoping that Captain Hazell might thaw a bit at my perseverance, I returned to the dock, showed him my passage and asked when the *Rosarene* would
sail. He appeared to like the new state of affairs even less, and told me
grudgingly that when the schooner was loaded, she would return to Bequia for
the night and sail for Trinidad sometime the following morning. With that I
had to be content, and promised myself to be aboard very early since it was
evident that the captain had little inclination to delay his departure for the like
of me.

For all my purposes, avowed and unavowed, the *Rosarene* (fig. XXII-1)
was ideal, being very typical of the larger schooners presently trading in the

islands. She was built in 1946 by Armand and Samuel Hazell (who still own her; the captain is a cousin) and measures 86.5 feet between perpendiculars with a 22 foot beam and 60.28 registered Tons. She worked under sail alone until a Kelvin-Hughes diesel was fitted in 1971, *droguing* (carrying coastwise or short-haul) rice from Guyana to Barbados, general cargo between St. Vincent, Trinidad and Barbados; she has also on occasion had the mail contract for Bequia, Canouan and Union Island. At the time I made my trip, she was under charter to the St. Vincent Marketing Board to carry fresh produce to Trinidad twice a month. In fact, it was this produce which was being loaded that morning in Kingstown — 1150 bags of sweet potatoes in the hold and 460 bags of carrots on deck, being about 120 tons in all.

Wishing to take no chances with what I assumed was a highly flexible departure time, I was on the dock in Bequia very early the following morning. As it turned out, there was still cargo going aboard. Ahead of the foremast, a rough pen had been nailed together, and nine sheep, one very large hog and five smaller hogs were relaxing therein (fig. XXII-2). One of my only disappointments during the whole trip was that I was not present when the large hog was loaded.

fig. XXII-2. Schooner Rosarene. *Deck cargo. Bequia, February, 1975.*

fig. XXII-3. Schooner Rosarene, *rounding the West Cays, February, 1975.*

In addition to the livestock, there were the "traffickers" to be loaded and accomodated. These seven people, including one woman, paid round trip passage and carried small consignments of goods to be sold in Trinidad, where they bought other goods to be sold in Bequia. These seven, the eight crew members, the captain, mate, supercargo and another passenger were all as busy as ants, moving back and forth between bundles of belongings on the dock and the deckhouse at the stern, stowing parcels and contriving little nests for themselves for the voyage.

My position aboard was a little too ambiguous to engage in the predictable territorial encounters, so I perched on top of the deckhouse and watched the show, while listening to Lozina Kydd tell about her father who was a "whaler man" (cf. Chapter XV). Then, when the owner came aboard, I helped him repair a chafed place in the mainsail and seize on some reefing ties. Eventually, there was a crescendo of shouting, an acceleration in the bustling, and the engine roared into life. A little after 9 a.m. we backed through a black cloud of exhaust smoke and got under way.

As we motored down Admiralty Bay toward the West Cays, the crew went unhurriedly about their work, setting first the stem staysail, then the foresail, the jib and, finally, the big main, all while proceeding downwind — one of the advantages of gaff-rigged sails on hoops. When we rounded the Cays (fig. XXII-3), the sheets were hardened in a bit, and we began to thread our way across the Grenadines Bank toward Sail Rock, which lies on the eastern edge.

fig. XXII-4. Schooner Rosarene *over the Grenadines Bank. February, 1975.*

The long roll period and easy motion of the heavily laden schooner came as
a pleasant surprise. The decks stayed dry even though we were pitching
slightly into the seas which build up rapidly over the Grenadines Bank. In fact,
there was nothing to spoil a perfect day in the Trades aboard a windjammer
(fig. XXII-4) except the drone of the engine. However, as remarked earlier, to
have an engine in a commercial vessel is to create a compelling reason to use it.

Anyhow, the breeze was so light that we would scarcely have moved without the engine. As it was, we were proving again an important theorem in the engineering of auxiliary sailing vessels — the whole (speed through the water) is frequently greater than the sum of the parts (speed under sail + speed under power).

As we passed Sail Rock shortly after noon, the captain dived into his cabin and brought up a small wooden box, containing the compass, which he set on a small shelf by the companionway. The watch was set — four men in the captain's watch and four in the mate's — and thereafter a course of SSW was sailed for the mouth of the Gulf of Paria, called the Bocas. A bell also appeared and was set on the wheel box, where it was struck by the helmsman on the half hour, somewhat erratically at the beginning of the watch and with increasing precision as eight bells drew nigh.

There was little to do but watch the swaying gaff (fig. XXII-5) or ogle the

fig. XXII-5. Schooner Rosarene, detail of rigging.
February, 1975.

232

sheep, one of whom — presumably a male — was mounting the others — male and female, indifferently — at the rate of one about every five minutes, which he had been doing before we left Bequia and was still doing when we reached Trinidad. Even the crew, vastly amused at first, finally wearied of his *machismo* and began to throw things whenever he made another assault. I was dividing my attention between this sideshow and the green heights of Grenada, which were slipping past well down to leeward when the captain appeared at my elbow.

"I ain't know if you does eat our food, but the cook have a little something for you."

It had begun to dawn on me a short time earlier that I had neglected this rather fundamental matter when planning my trip, so I replied gratefully that I had frequently eaten Bequia food when I was working with Haakon.

"Oh, is you then," the captain exclaimed. "Is you that helping Haakon with the little sloop. If I did know that, we ain't worry with agent and passage and all. I putting you on the crew list and done."

He seemed genuinely embarassed that I had paid my passage and anxiously shepherded me back to get a plate of rice with a rosette of canned pilchards arrayed on top. He asked if I used pepper sauce, then dived into his cabin again and brought up his own bottle for my use. Apparently, only a real greenhorn goes to sea in the West Indies without an assured supply of this vital commodity.

At sundown we had a meal of "cocoa tea" ("in Bequia, it have three kinda tea — coffee tea, cocoa tea and tea tea") and a soup of pigeon peas with boiled plantains. Afterwards, the cook filled the running lights from a tin of kerosene and trimmed the wicks, after which the mate fastened them in the rigging. The compass was moved to a small shelf just above the captain's bunk, where it was also visible to the helmsman through a small port cut in the cabin trunk.

Darkness settled over the schooner, and the other passengers began to settle into the nests that they had thoughtfully provided for themselves along the lee side of the deckhouse. My place on the bench to windward, comfortable enough during daylight hours, was heeled just too much to lie down or even recline. As the hours wore on, my night became a kaleidoscope of shadowy images: the helmsman, face dimly lit by the glow of the compass light, leaning forward to peer into the dark; the captain disappearing into his cabin after prowling restlessly around the darkened decks; a sailor balancing on the lee rail, hand on the shroud while he emptied his bladder; a groggy passenger, dislodged by a lurch of the vessel, grumbling and worrying at a small parcel; the flare of a match mating with the glow of a cigarette. Thus the hours passed. The striking of the bell seemed at times to hasten the passage of the hours; at others, to impede.

At 1:30 a.m., the helmsman grunted something through the window and the captain roused to peer forward into the night. The Bocas Light, a 10-second flasher, had come up right on course, and Captain Hazell was noticeably easier. At 5:00 a.m. we reached Bocas del Dragon, the entrance to the Gulf of Paria, having sailed 140 miles in 19 hours 15 minutes, an average speed of 7.3 knots. As we entered the narrow channel between Trinidad and Monos Island, the captain perched on the weather rail just outside the deckhouse and shouted his commands to the helm.

"Steady now, steady so."

"Down, go down now. Keep she down."

There is another channel, wider and easier to navigate, on the other side of Monos Island, but it is much trafficked by tankers and other heavy shipping; schooners prefer the narrower pass even though the wind is often flukey, as it was for us. The crew quickly got the sails down while the captain continued to relay his instructions, now using the terms "port" and "starboard" instead of "up" and "down" to indicate direction.

Once through the narrow channel, we motored east across the Gulf of Paria, glassy smooth and slightly obscured by early morning haze. Large numbers of tankers and freighters lay at anchor, just visible in the haze. There was not a breath of air moving, and a sticky heat lay over the bay. Already, the impression was forming that Trinidad is not, either geographically or economically, part of the Antilles.

Inside the deckhouse the captain, frequently licking the end of his pencil, was preparing crew and passenger lists. His nervous attention to this ordinarily routine chore called to memory certain outraged talk in Bequia about some schooner captain who had recently been jailed for some minor (in the Bequia version, at least) irregularity in immigrations procedure and was still in prison.

When we tied up at the Quarantine Dock well outside Port-of-Spain, it became even more apparent that immigrations was no empty formality, as in other islands. First, we were lined up and conducted to a bare room where we waited while the schooner was searched. Then one of the officers returned to go over the lists, each person stepping to the other side of a white line painted on the floor as his name was called. When I answered to my name, the officer glanced up quickly.

"What is the purpose of your visit?" he asked, scowling ferociously.

In my chattiest and most confiding tone, I replied that I had come to buy some bottom paint. That was the line, after all, that had worked in St. Vincent.

"It says here the purpose of your visit is tourism." He waved my landing card and scowled even more ferociously.

"I, er, um. . . " Alas, Captain Hazell and I had not consulted on that particular point, and there seemed little point in trying to tell the Immigration officer that I was a friend of Haakon's.

Trinidad has a problem with illegal immigrants from poorer islands, and to a certain extent, I sympathize with the difficulties thereof. However, I would be double-dipped and deep-fried before I ever thought of immigrating, illegally or otherwise, to his country, which I was rapidly beginning to view in such

234

terms as "smelly" and "squalid" and "dinky". Even so, there seemed little purpose in pointing this out to the man; I was having enough trouble, just playing it straight.

"You make me very suspicious, Mr. Pyle," he growled, doubtless imagining that this remark was new to me. "I shall record, 'Purpose of visit not clear.' " He scrawled in his ledger, scowled a scowl to end all scowls, then waved us back to the schooner.

By the time we were under way again, the sun was burning through a lens of humidity, and it was breathlessly hot. We motored through the gray-brown water toward Queen's Wharf at the head of the harbor. There all the schooner traffic of the Windward Islands seemed to be seeking accomodation (fig. XXII-6). The scene was nightmarish: 19 schooners or schooner-size vessels crowded onto 400 feet of dock. Other vessels were anchored off, and others still circled, waving and screaming for space. Vessels on the inside cast off and fought their way out. Vessels on the outside immediately shoved bowsprit and bows into the tangle, trying frantically to shoe-horn their way to a place on the dock. And all this frantic maneuvering went on in the sticky, choking heat. It looked as if it might be a good little while before we saw the clear waters and blue skies of Bequia again.

fig. XXII-6. Queen's Wharf, Port-of-Spain, Trinidad, February, 1975.

fig. XXII-7. Secured at the wharf, Port-of-Spain. February, 1975.

The *Rosarene* circled a few times, did a little screaming of her own, and a rift miraculously appeared in the wall of hulls, spars and rigging. We nudged and edged, edged and nudged, trimming up the main boom to clear the small steamer astern while jamming our bowsprit past the boom of the vessel ahead (fig. XXII-7). We finally came to a berth on the inside. I later learned that our apparent good fortune was owed to being a government charter; otherwise, it is not uncommon for a vessel to wait one, two and even three weeks to get alongside for loading.

Preparations began immediately for unloading, and as the crew threw back the tarps and started to work, Capt. Hazell drifted over to me and said, "In Trinidad, they having all kinda people. They does tell you a thing, and then someone waiting to hold you. Is like a gang they having. Best you rest the nights 'board the vessel while we here."

I was touched by his concern and grateful for the hospitality, and thanked him accordingly. In any case, I had no intention of leaving the vessel and missing one minute of the dockside circus that was surging and swirling all around us. The crew of the *Rosarene* had already begun heaving the 86 lb. bags

236

of carrots off the deck and laying them on the rail. There, the bags were picked up by one or another of the oddest assortment of workers imaginable — all ages, sizes, races and sexes were represented. They came and went between the rail and the waiting carts and trucks, seeming to work for no one and toward no particular end.

It took me half the afternoon to grasp the fundamentals of the system — these people who swarmed around the side of the ship were not being paid; they were "helping" to unload the vessel simply for the opportunity to be present if anything broke or spilled. From time to time someone would grab a handful from a bag not tightly tied. The captain and mate watched, but did not interfere unless the pilferage became too obvious. What the dockers could glean, they immediately sold to one or another of the fraternity of small entrepreneurs who set up shop as close as propriety permitted. With cash in hand, the workers then nipped smartly over to the grog shop, conveniently situated on the dock, where they quickly invested their earnings in cigarettes (sold singly as well as in packs) or in 140 proof rum (sold by the shot only). Economic velocity — the rate at which money changes hands within a system — is regarded by some as an indicator of economic well-being. However, no great degree of well-being seemed to arise from the dizzying economic velocity in operation on the Trinidad dock.

With the carrots out of the way, the hatch covers were taken up and the cargo gaff was hauled up the foremast. A diesel winch at the foot of the mast was started after a short session of grunt-and-tug, and the mate took his place on the tail of the line which ran up to the gaff and down into the hold. Three of the crew worked down in the hold throwing the 175 lb. bags of sweet potatoes onto the cargo sling (the crew of eight which had seemed large to me on the trip down began to look skeletal). When the sling was filled, the mate deftly threw four turns of rope onto the spinning drum of the donkey engine and tailed it. The sling rose squealing and swaying out of the hold until high enough to clear the rail. There the mate paused, holding just enough tension on the tail to keep the load aloft, while a man on the dock swung the gaff outboard by means of a vang attached aloft. Then the line was let run, and the load eased neatly onto the dock. In the whole sequence, the margin between success and catastrophe depended entirely on the mate's strength, timing and experience. I would not have worked in the vicinity of that cargo sling for all the sweet potatoes in St. Vincent and half the bananas to boot.

Fortunately, the crew were made of sterner stuff (much sterner, when one recalls that not only had they loaded all that cargo, but had also stood watches the night before); and by 7:30 p.m., when they knocked off, most of the 1150 bags of potatoes were out of the hold. The job was completed the following morning in a couple of hours, the hatch covers replaced and the decks washed down. Whereupon, the crew dived down the forward companionway and reappeared a short time later all rigged out for a turn ashore, it being by now Friday afternoon. The captain and supercargo did some maintenance, including a little caulking from the inside to slow a leak that had appeared on the trip down. Then, after a further warning to me about the hazards of Port-of-Spain by night, the captain left in a taxi for quiet weekend at the home of friends outside the city.

After two nights on the narrow wooden bench inside the deckhouse, with the mosquitoes and sticky heat for my covers and the all-night blare of transistor radios for my lullaby, I got busy and located a hostel for foreign seamen operated by the Anglican Church. From this base, made bold by the twin luxuries of a cot and a shower bath, I ventured forth during the following days (daylight only) to find the evidences of boatbuilding which form the substance of the following chapter.

Ten days after arriving in Trinidad, a Monday, I stopped by the schooner to see how loading was going. Nothing was happening. The captain told me that the agents were looking for the cargo — not looking for *cargo* — but looking for *the* cargo! The cargo for the return trip was already consigned, had already been paid for, but the agents simply could not *find* it. So, for two more days, while they looked, the schooner and her crew sweltered and other vessels waited for space at the dock.

By Wednesday I was feeling pretty bleak; what there was of boatbuilding in Trinidad I had seen, and my life of ease at the Mariner's Club had begun to pall, particularly in view of my sundown curfew. Though I never confessed it to Capt. Hazell, I did go out early one Sunday morning when there was no one in the streets except a dry and withered woman who offered to sell me the small baby she held in her arms. It was a nice little baby, as I recall, and the price quoted was not unreasonable. But the experience left me shaken and I yearned for Bequia.

Suddenly, on Wednesday afternoon, with a rush and a roar, cargo began to appear and be loaded (fig. XXII-8): 500 sacks of cement, 200 M-T oil drums, 1500 clay building tiles and 850 cartons of crackers. In all, forty tons of goods were loaded in about three hours and the schooner secured for sea. There remained only our outbound Immigrations clearance.

Two officers came aboard for this formality which was no mere formality. One read the names from a master list while the other laid on hands and conducted each person personally across the deck. And guess whose name was not on the passenger list, presumably because "purpose of visit not clear." There ensued another round of fierce scowling (all applicants to the Immigrations Service must be screened on the basis of a Standard Scowl) which ended, to my relief, in our summary dismissal.

As we motored toward the Bocas, the reason for the afternoon's flurry of activity became apparent. The narrow pass used by the schooners is unlighted, and very tricky by dark. We threaded our way through just before sunset and set a course for Pt. Saline Light, on the southeast tip of Grenada. On the outbound trip we passed "over" (to windward) of Grenada, while on the return our course took us "under" the island and in the lee of the Grenadines. The Trade

fig. XXII-8. Schooner Rosarene, *loading M - T drums, Port-of-Spain. February, 1975.*

Winds are usually a little north of east, so the return course was meant to be an easier point of sailing.

On this occasion, the wind was south of east, and we were able to sail through the night with sheets started. At one point I was awakened by the flapping of canvas and the sounds of feet on the deck. The jib halyard had chafed through, and had to be repaired the following morning while we were in the lee of Grenada (fig. XXII-9).

The cement we carried was consigned to Union Island, so we held up close under Carriacou when making for Clifton, the reef harbor on the windward side of Union. The sea was calm and the mate was at the helm as we eased sheets and ran down toward the harbor mouth. At this point, Capt. Hazell came out of his cabin and glanced around, then burst into violent activity. He screamed at the helmsman to "bring she up, man," sent another man running forward as lookout and ran himself to cast off the peak halyard of the big mainsail. Only when the peak was broken down did the schooner begin to answer the helm and swing up into the wind.

239

fig. XXII-9. Schooner Rosarene. *Aloft for repairs in the lee of Grenada. February, 1975.*

I never saw the shoal and have no idea how close to it we came, but it was not simple nervousness on the captain's part. There is a shoal patch, called Gran de Coi, lying in the approach to Clifton harbor, which breaks in blowing weather but is difficult to see otherwise. Formerly, the patch was marked by a few timbers that remained after the schooner *Anne-Marie* sank there, but they had disappeared, leaving the reef again unmarked.

At the dock in Clifton, the crew began unloading the cement, but there was no dockside circus and it seemed doubtful if they could finish before dark. When the mail schooner came in, I felt that Providence had smiled. I said goodbye to Capt. Hazell, transferred my three gallons of copper paint (yes, I did go to Trinidad for paint after all) to the *Friendship Rose* and was in Bequia by dark.

fig. XXIII-1. *Trinidad pirogue, Port-of-Spain. February, 1975.*

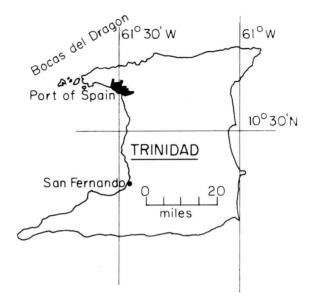

CHAPTER XXIII

TRINIDAD

Trinidad is an island of the West Indies for historical and political reasons only; in geography and natural history, it is a shoulder of the South American continent, separated from the mainland only by the Gulf of Paria, a part of the Orinoco River delta system. Owing to the discovery of oil on the island in the 1930's, Trinidad has become the wealthiest and most extensively developed island of the southern Caribbean, widely known for steel pan bands, calypso and the most elaborate carnival in the Caribbean. Although the islands to the north depend extensively on commerce carried to and from Trinidad in schooners, nothing I knew about the island itself inclined me to believe that there would be anything much there in the marine anthropology line. Then what to my wondering eyes should appear — even before the *Rosarene* had docked — but a new and exotic boat type (fig. XXIII-1).

A modest amount of inquiry disclosed that this was a pirogue and that all the pirogues in the north of Trinidad were built in a small shop on a side street

fig. XXIII-2. Builder L. Taitt in his shop on
Sackville Street, Port-of-Spain.
February, 1975.

in Port-of-Spain, where I discovered a neatly-lettered wooden sign stating: L. Taitt, Boatbuilder. Sackville St. Taitt (fig. XXIII-2), a quiet, unassuming individual, had been building pirogues for fifty years, the first twenty with his father, who had built them for forty years before that. Ninety years, he pointed out with quiet pride, that the same type had been built in that location, the only change being that the transom was now made broader to carry the weight of an outboard motor.

*fig. XXIII-3. Frames being added to pirogue.
Port-of-Spain. February, 1975.*

A pirogue was nearing completion at the front of the small covered yard (fig. XXIII-3) while construction was just beginning on another at the back. This rapid rate of work (a pirogue is completed in about two weeks!) gave me the opportunity to measure a hull one afternoon and return the following day to see the next one built. The operative word here is *built* — not *being built*, or *under construction*. It was no small part of the fascination of this unique boat-type that the hull took form in a single day.

fig. XXIII-4. *"Shell" of a pirogue awaits planks.*
Port-of-Spain. February, 1975.

Construction begins with the shaping of the "shell" (fig. XXIII-4) from a log of "red cedar" (probably *Guarea trichilioides*, a member of the mahogany family). The shaping is done in half a day by a man who comes in one day a week for this purpose only, working without molds or templates, by eye alone. Along the upper surface of this curious keel, a trough is cut. In the completed pirogue, this trough functions as a waterwav to keep the bilges dry, but provides, in addition, an important clue to the origins of this boat type. No need to be unnecessarily mysterious — the waiting keel has the appearance of a tiny dugout.

In the next step, the stem and transom are fastened to the shell. The long stem is shaped from a single piece of "cypre" (*Cordia alliodora*, called silver-balli in Bequia) and positioned by Taitt "according to taste." The transom is fabricated from wide planks of red cedar and held in palce by a long knee. With the bow and stern thus fixed, Taitt and his helpers immediately began to plank — with an ease and speed born of long practice.

The first plank, a 10" white pine board, was held along the shell, and the rake of the stem transferred to the end of the plank. Then the plank was allowed to pivot until nearly horizontal, and a line was scribed onto the lower side of the plank by running a pencil alongside the shell. The board was then placed on a workbench and cut away to the two lines using drawknives. Being used to the slower pace and solemn care with which cutting had been done in Bequia, I was surprised and, at first, dismayed by the reckless abandon of the two men who hacked, split and gouged their way down to the line. After the initial cut, the plank was again laid alongside the hull and high spots marked for additional hacking.

Without further ado, the plank was nailed in place, at first to the stem and afterward, to the "shell." The galvanized nails were driven downward through the plank and into the shell, the plank being twisted as it was fastened farther and farther aft. When in place, the upper edge of the plank was beveled, again with drawknives and again without finesse — the purpose being simply to knock the edge off so there would be no channel for water to lie in.

The next plank was treated in the same manner, with the scribed line following the upper edge of the first plank. Only this time the nailing was done without even the benefit of a second shaping. The trick was that the second plank was *lapped* on the outside of the first and the two nailed together surface to surface, instead of edge to edge. Nails were driven from outside to inside and clinched (fig. XXIII-5).

fig. XXIII-5. Lap-straking a pirogue. Port-of-Spain. February, 1975.

245

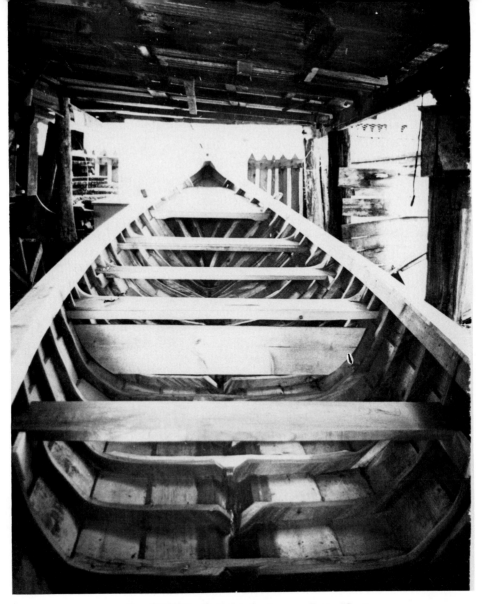

*fig. XXIII-6. Completed pirogue. Port-of-Spain.
February, 1975.*

The men worked without talking, and with such precision that the planking was finished well before the end of the day; and the hull, formed but wobbly, was carried to the front of the shop and set on horses. There, it would be finished in the next few days by the addition of frames, stringers, wales, thwarts and a small deck forward (fig. XXIII-6). The frames were sawed from natural crooks of saman (*Pithecellobium saman*) on a band saw (fig. XXIII-2), which was the only piece of power equipment used in the shop. The pirogues built by Taitt are so standardized that he had a pile of templates from which the frames are rough-shaped. Final fitting is done by hand. In addition to the two men in the shop, Taitt employs two others who work in the "bush," cutting the logs for the shells, frames and other members. The above labored description might, for the knowledgeable, be summarized by the terms "lap-straked" or "clinker-built," which I had read of but never before seen done.

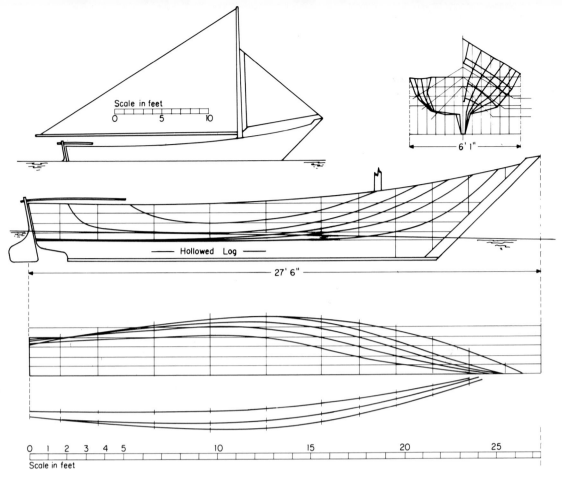

fig. XXIII-7. Lines of Trinidad pirogue. Built 1975 by L. Taitt in Port-of-Spain. Taken off February, 1975.

The lines (fig. XXIII-7) seem to confirm the hybrid ancestry of this type. The waterlines forward show much greater hollow than I found in any small craft other than the gommiers and yoles. And, of course, the use of the shell as a keel appears to a vestige of dugout construction. The odd thing is that raising strakes should be lapped instead of fastened on edge as is done elsewhere with dugouts. I questioned Taitt on these points, but he replied with bland disinterest that he had no idea about these matters. Nor could he give me any help with a rigging plan. For additional information, I was back to ringing doorbells.

Eventually, I met Frank Delmas who had been in his youth a pirogue-racing enthusiast, and who was happy to share with me his memories. He asserted without hesitation that the pirogue was of Amerindian origin, that raising strakes had been added as the logs available for dugouts had gotten smaller, and he surmised that lapping the strakes had been learned from the Royal Navy whose launches and tenders were always clinker-built.

From Delmas I got the sketches for the rigging plan in fig. XXIII-7. I was openly skeptical, but he insisted that the peculiar low aspect ratio of the mainsail was accurate. Still doubtful, I made a concerted effort to find a photo of a rigged pirogue, consulting museums, libraries and especially the photo archives of the *Trinidad Guardian* — all to no avail. Until further notice and better evidence, the Trinidad pirogue was rigged as shown.

Delmas' memories of pirogue racing were particularly interesting since the sailing vocabulary for these craft is in *patois* — beginning with the word pirogue itself which is the French version of the Spanish *piragua* derived in turn from the Carib word *piraguas*. When sailing close-hauled in a pirogue, the command *jambez* was given whereupon one of the crew wrapped the shroud around his waist and hiked to weather with his feet on the gunwale. Sailing in this attitude was called *contrapa*. To sheet in was *halez*; to make fast was *tenez*. The size of a pirogue was given as one *bordage*, two *bordáge*, etc., according to the number of planks (Fr. *bordé*) added to a shell. This conversation called to mind certain expletives used by the men in Taitt's shop such as *voilá*, *tenez*, *ça ça* and *oué*.

Here again I was encountering the curious association of a dugout with a French cultural heritage. The Trinidad pirogue has evolved a long way from the Carib dugout, and the French cultural heritage has dwindled to a few words of *patois* largely fallen into disuse since pirogues stopped sailing. Nevertheless the association was there, and it continued to intrigue me.

In the matter of larger vessels, I came to Trinidad with a certain amount of information already in hand. While copying the *Registers of Shipping* in Grenada and St. Vincent, I had found a few entries for vessels built in Trinidad in the late 1800's which had been transferred to St. Georges or Kingstown by a later owner. Thus I knew that there had been at least some boatbuilding in the past. When I presented myself at the Harbour Master's Office, I was told in a friendly but unequivocal manner that there were no older *Registers* and that there had never been any boatbuilding in Trinidad. I knew otherwise, but saw nothing to be gained by argument, choosing instead to make a pretty thorough sweep of all the persons (historians, archivists, sailing buffs, Coast Guard commandant) and institutions (libraries, museums, newspaper) that I could think of — here again to no avail. The general feeling seemed to be that sailing vessels were relics that were characteristic of the poorer islands to the north — that Trinidad looked inward toward her natural resources and had a continental rather than an insular destiny.

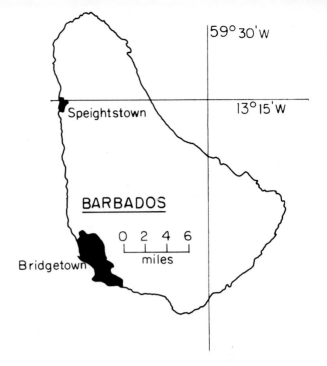

Speightstown

59° 30'W

13° 15'W

BARBADOS

0 2 4 6
miles

Bridgetown

CHAPTER XXIV

BARBADOS

It is a natural consequence of sailing geography that my final island as a marine anthropologist should have been my first as a cruising yachtsman. Barbados, 90 miles east of the main arc of the Antilles, must be reached by beating unless, of course, you are crossing the Atlantic, in which case it is the first possible landfall. This is how it happened that I first strolled the Bridgetown waterfront still riding the wave of well-being that comes from bringing your landfall up dead ahead after twenty-seven days at sea. And it was in this expansive mood that I paused beside the *Frances W. Smith* (fig. XIV-1, on the right with the topmast), one hundred and ten feet of decaying grandeur.

In the shade cast by an awning stretched over the stern, a white-haired man, seated in what if not a captain's chair, was supervising his sweating crew as they swayed up the bags of rice which filled the hold. From time to time when something didn't go to suit him, he leaned forward, spat tobacco juice over the rail and lashed out with his voice. I stood hypnotized by this scene until the sound of my own voice brought me back to reality.

"You surely have a lovely schooner there," I said.

"Thirty thousand and she's yours," came the instant response, a reflex from frequent repetition.

fig. XXIV-1. The Carenage, Bridgetown, Barbados. February, 1968. Photo by Willie Alleyne Associates.

"I'll be honest with you," he continued in the confiding tones of one who has other intentions entirely. "She needs new sails and rigging."

My eye swept involuntarily up the dark, oiled mainmast and back down the heavy iron rigging, sewn in sleeves of white-painted canvas and seized around wooden deadeyes as big as ham steaks.

"You will need top hamper as well. No engine," he explained, apologetically. "She draws nine feet loaded and bumps coming in on a low tide."

He held me with his glittering eye, and my imagination raced — green islands in the calm of early morning, the sounds and smells of strange ports, the romance of life under sail in the eternal springtime of the Tropics. Capt. Ben Hassel talked of this and that — of storms and calms, of freaks of weather and miraculous shoals of fish, of grounding and near catastrophe, of freight rates too low and canvas, wire and crew too high. The steeper he pitched it, the better it sounded to me. It was a consummate job of salesmanship.

Fortunately, the price was well beyond me, even with EC dollars at fifty cents against the US dollar. The *Frances W. Smith* was safe from me and I was saved from her, though it was with regrets, at least on my side. Curiously enough, she was not truly West Indian, having been built as a fishing schooner in Lunenburg, Nova Scotia, though she came to her end in the islands not long after I saw her. She was bought by Albert Lake, who took her to Anguilla and removed her foremast of Guyana greenheart to rig the *New London* (cf. Chapter VI). The stripped hull was anchored in Road Bay, finally sinking there in a winter gale. As I was leaving the islands, Anguilla was my last port of call, and I spent two hours diving over the sunken hull — my last official action in the Antilles — hoping to find a builder's plaque or other memento, for the vessel had a special significance for me.

fig. XXIV-2. The Carenage, Bridgetown, Barbados. January, 1975. Photo by Barbados Government Information Service.

Closer contacts with the realities of the schooner trade have dispelled many of my romantic notions about working sail, and the prudence of middle age has tempered the enthusiasms of youth; but the yearning felt that morning in Barbados has never entirely left me. If the world were a proper place, then wooden vessels built with skill and respect would sail seas unsullied by oil spills and cast-off plastic junk, yielding an honest return to the owners and a decent living for the crew.

When I returned to Barbados six years later with measuring tape and camera, many of the larger schooners were gone, their places taken by small coastal freighters brought from Europe (fig. XXIV-2). However, the warmth of the people and the easy charm of their manner had not altered with passing time. On my earlier visit to Barbados, I went one morning to the open market near the harbor with a friend, another recent alumnus of the Atlantic.

"How much are your mangoes, Mistress?" asked my friend.

The woman in the madras kerchief named her price. It wasn't much as I remember, but my friend offered her half because anyone who has read the guidebooks knows that any tourist who pays the asking price is regarded as a fool, no matter how low the price.

"No, please, sir," said the market lady, smilingly refusing to barter.

"How much are your limes, then?" countered my friend.

"White man," she replied sweetly, and completely without malicious intent, "you can't afford my limes."

We drifted on and got limes elsewhere. A few days later, I was walking alone near the market when a huddled figure intercepted me, hand extended in the wordless vocabulary of the beggar. It was the same woman.

"What happened?" I asked.

"Oh, sir," she answered, dejected but still without rancour, "some bad

251

boys shove me and hold me and steal my stock. Now I lost my capital and must go into the street."

I gave her twenty dollars, all that I had with me, hoping it would do something to replenish her capital. Even in the retelling, I still can't fully explain why this episode came to epitomize for me the flavor of Barbados — somehow different from all the other islands.

Although most of the schooners in the Carenage were transients from the smaller islands to the west or imported from Nova Scotia, there was at least one Barbados-built schooner (fig. XXIV-3) — enough to encourage me to seek out the *Register of Shipping* at the Harbour Master's Office. Older volumes could not be found, and the one in use began only in 1920. For this period at least, the *Register* confirmed my first impression gained from a quick look around the harbor:

Place of building	No. of entries
Barbados	9
Other W. I. Islands	5
U.S.A. esp. New England	12
Canada esp. Nova Scotia	55
England	3
Other European Countries	1
Total Entries for Sailing Vessels	85

While searching the *Register* for sailing vessels, I turned past a number of power vessels — at first with scarcely a glance, then, as the numbers grew, with quickening interest. Most of these vessels, built in Nova Scotia and registered *de novo* in Barbados, were under 100 feet in length — rather a small vessel to come all that distance to be registered. As my interest increased, I noted that, although most were transferred back to Nova Scotia ports after a few years, there were occasionally other reasons given for closing the registry: "Lost N. Atlantic, 1931;" "Lost 150 mi. E. of St. Pierre, 1932;" "Sold at Auction, Philadelphia, U.S.A., 1934;" "Forfeited to U.S. Gov't., 1937;" and then the clincher, "Rammed and sunk by the U. S. Coast Guard, 1932."

Between 1931 and 1933, 48 Nova Scotia-built vessels between 70 and 100 feet in length were registered in Barbados. All had a beam-to-length ratio of 1:5 or less, and none was deeper than 9 feet from deck to keel. Not much cargo capacity in such a trim hull, is there? And the owners' names had an odd, impersonal ring about them: Associated Traders, Blue Line Traders, Bear Cove Fisheries, etc. From the coincidence of dates and places, it would appear that these vessels were built for and engaged in a final flurry of rum-running before the repeal of prohibition made such activity unprofitable.

fig. XXIV-3. Schooner Confident I C *careened, Bridgetown, Barbados. February, 1968.*

Evidently it was expedient and possible to register these vessels in Barbados — vessels which had a sufficient reason not to wish to register nearer their sphere of action.

The activities of these enterprising Nova Scotians did make an interesting little interlude in the maritime affairs of the Caribbean, though they had no direct bearing on my primary line of inquiry — the building of trading vessels in Barbados. And here, the evidence of the *Register* was amply clear: for the period since 1920 at least, it was easier and more economical to import trading vessels from elsewhere than to build them on the island. This being the case, it was a little startling to discover that Barbados had a well-established tradition of boat-carpentry that has produced two interesting and unique types of local watercraft.

fig. XXIV-4. Barbados flying fish boats. Date uncertain. Photo by Barbados Government Indormation Service.

fig. XXIV-5. Barbados flying fish boats. Date uncertain. Photo by Barbados Government Information Service.

fig. XXIV-6.   Barbados flying fish boat, detail of
bow. Photo by Barbados Government
Information Service.

The flying fish boats (figs. XXIV-4, 5, 6 & 7) formed the basis, as the name suggests, for Barbados' only commercial fishery. I had been told of these craft by Stedman Wallace of Bequia who said admiringly, "they could really split the wind" (sail to weather). Strong praise from a Bequian; they are generally very grudging of kind words for any boats other than their own. Unfortunately, these boats went out of use as long ago as the 1930's, and were replaced by the small inboard launches seen in the background of fig. XIV-3.

After so long a time, not even a hulk remained from which measurements might be made. Only by luck did I happen to meet Carlton Hackett of the Government Information Office, who was (1) knowledgeable enough to remember that at some time photos had been made of these boats, (2) clever enough to find the negatives and (3) kind enough to print them for me. In lieu of lines drawings, these photos show an open boat around 20 feet in length belonging to the same general category as the beach boats of Anguilla, St. Martin, Nevis, St. Kitts, and Montserrat — islands where English cultural influences had predominated as they have in Barbados. Unique to the Barbados model are the recurved stem and the decurved bowsprit. Another

fig. XXIV-7. Barbados flying fish boats. Photo by Barbados Government Information Service.

fig. XXIV-8. Speightstown schooner bound for Bridgetown. Date unknown. Photo courtesty of Barbados Museum.

unusual feature can just be seen in fig. XXIV-7, where the boat in the background appears to have a very long gunter-staff fastened to the luff of the mainsail.

This was such an interesting type that I tried all the obvious places to find additional information. No dice. But in going through the Barbados Museum, I came upon a glass showcase containing a handsome model labelled, "Speightstown Schooner. Gift of the Hon. Errol Barrow, Prime Minister of Barbados."

Inquiry yielded two photographs (figs. XIV-8, 9) of these extraordinary vessels, two of which operated until 1955. They ran an all-sail packet service between Speightstown in the north and Bridgetown, carrying sugar, molasses and passengers down and returning with passengers and general cargo. Since these vessels operated only locally, they were never registered, explaining why I had found no trace of them earlier.

fig. XXIV-9. *Speightstown schooner* Challenor *beating up from Pelican Shoals. Prior to 1955. Photo courtesy of Barbados Museum.*

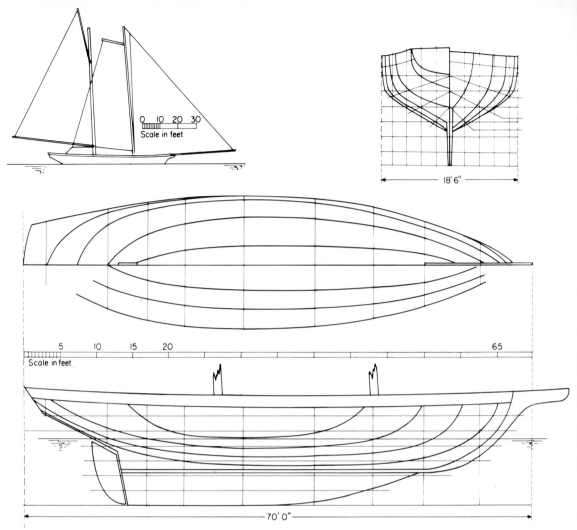

fig. XXIV-10. Lines of Speightstown schooner
model. Model built by R. Gibbon.
Taken off January, 1975.

The run between Speightstown and Bridgetown is a beam reach sailed in
the lee of a low-lying island — in short, ideal conditions which explains the
radical rig and the very high speeds attained. They commonly made the trip of
10 nautical miles in 45-50 minutes including the 2-mile beat from Pelican
Shoals into the Carenage — a calculated speed of 12-13 knots! On one occasion,
one of these schooners was blown off her moorings in a hurricane, was intercepted of St. Vincent, but had to be towed home when she was unable — with
such a long bowsprit — to sail in the open sea.

The high speeds are not difficult to believe if the proportions of the model
are accurate. The lines taken from the model (fig. XXIV-10) are very fine indeed and provide an almost classical example of a sharp-bottomed schooner.
Note particularly the sharp floors of the mid-section, the extreme deadrise of
the stern, the nearly symmetrical waterlines and diagonals, the fine entry and
the smooth run aft which begins well forward. The false keel and deadwood are
so unusual and the sail plan so radical that at first it seemed the model builder

must have been indulging some romantic streak in his nature. However, the photographs and the conversation that I had with the builder of the *Challenor* (fig. XXIV-9), last of the Speightstown schooners, confirmed that the model was, in reality, quite accurate.

Osbert Mascoll (fig. XXIV-11) was born in 1902 and learned ship carpentry from John Leacock, who was taught in his turn by Mascoll's grandfather, John Pickett. As we talked, Mascoll illustrated points about ship design with sketches and commented on my own sketches of the model in the museum, convincing me that the model was authentic, though not made by him. He explained several features of the model that had puzzled me: the Speightstown schooners carried an iron ballast keel bolted to the keel, enabling the vessel to stand up better to the large spread of sail. A deadwood was used in the stern on top of the keel, instead of a deep "tuck" in the after frames, making it simpler to give the vessel an "easy bottom".

The method of setting up a vessel outlined by Mascoll were the same as those I had encountered elsewhere in the islands. However, he had a clearer and more analytical understanding of the elements of design and how they shaped the finished vessel. For example, he volunteered the information that positioning frames farther forward on the keel gave a vessel more weather

fig. XXIV-11. Builder Osbert Mascoll and his wife. Six Mans Bay, Barados. January, 1975.

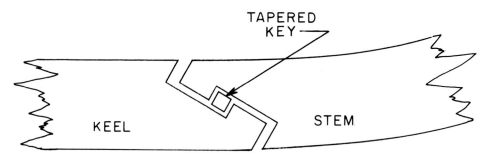

fig. XXIV-12. Detail of key splice described by Osbert Mascoll.

helm; that an easy bottom could be insured by starting the run at two-thirds of the keel and carrying it over transom frames which were modeled on the main frames; that a broad stern was necessary to carry a long boom, that a "tailboat" (vessel with counter stern) has a better turn of speed because the wake is smoother.

In designing a vessel, Mascoll told me that he used a scale half-model, which he took apart to get the "lofts" — the same type of lift half model which I had seen also in Carriacou and Bequia. When asked if he learned this technique from his master, he replied that he had worked it out for himself. He also described and sketched for me a "key splice" (fig. XXIV-12) which he used to join the forefoot to the keel. When the tapered key is driven into the keyway, the splice is forced tight and has a certain amount of strength both in flexion and tension.

Mascoll talked easily and with an air of suppressed mirth. He was proudest of having built the "Columbus boats" — replicas of the *Pinta, Nina* and *Santa Maria* used in a motion picture. For this project he had eighty men working under him, and the plans were drafted in England. In speaking of his past working life, the retired builder expressed himself well and without haste. He had built large vessels in his day; now other men built smaller vessels.

From our conversation and the other material that I had found, it was evident that the skills of boat carpentry have existed for a good while in Barbados and that boats and vessels of great merit have been built there. Yet there was never a maritime industry such as developed in Bequia, Carriacou or Anguilla, possibly because timber was scarce in Barbados and importing North American vessels was easy and economical.

And so, we come to the end of the chain of islands — wiser, I sincerely hope, without being sadder. Now all lines have been drawn and displayed, all photographs printed and pored over. However, there is one further aspect to boats and boatbuilding in the Lesser Antilles — the historical — which preoccupied me from the first but could not conveniently be dealt with until the end. My sources and informants were local and specific, but the resulting picture is vague in many details and deals more with the whole maritime culture of the islands than would a history. And that, Gentle Reader, is the stuff, as I later learned, of Culture History.

CHAPTER XXV

CULTURE HISTORY OF BOATBUILDING
IN THE LESSER ANTILLES

History celebrates the battlefields whereon we meet death, but scorns
to speak of the plowed fields whereby we thrive. It knows the names of kings'
bastards, but cannot tell us the origin of wheat. This is the way of human
folly.

J. H. Fabre

Ask a foolish question and get a foolish answer, as the old saw goes. That's
a quick way of saying that the answer you get depends on the question you
ask, and not only on the question, but also on when, where and or of whom it is
asked. Only small children ask completely spontaneous questions. By late
childhood most of us have learned to alloy our questions with judgement,
guile, humor, deceit, rhetoric, sympathy, calculation, compassion — and very
occasionally with an uncomplicated desire for information.

At the outset, my questions about the origins of boatbuilding belonged, I
thought, to this latter, uncomplicated category. But the answers I got or —
more commonly — didn't get, quickly made me aware that a question about
origins is never simple. And as time went on, I myself became confused about

the nature of the question. Did it even have an answer, and why was I asking it in the first place?

From the beginning, my interest in West Indian sailing craft had a historical bias — I wanted to know not only what boatbuilding was going on, but what had gone on before and where it had come from. And behind this bias there lay, I later came to realize, both an inspiration and a motive.

The inspiration arose out of a pleasant weekend passed with Earle Nelthropp, then the Administor for St. John, U.S.V.I. Nelthropp, a student of Virgin Islands history, had a manuscript, recently translated from Danish, of a report by Johan Lorentz Carstens to the Danish king concerning the state of the Danish colony at St. Thomas. In this 1742 account there were nuggets of information embedded in a magma of drivel and detail — largely self-serving — about how many guns were fired in salute when a vessel entered the harbor of Charlotte Amalie and how many flags were flown on the king's birthday. There were some observations of interest on social practices and usages among the creoles and the slaves, and a passing remark that immediately caught my eye — "In the harbor there are often seen sailing craft of a speed and grace which are unknown in Europe."(Carstens, 1742).

Now, the implications of such a brief remark are everything or nothing, depending on one's frame of mind. I chose to take the remark as evidence that fast sailing vessels were a West Indian innovation. This choice was, I now realize, simply an outgrowth of a rabidly pro-West Indian mood that had been developing in me for some while. From the moment of my arrival in St. Croix, I had heard West Indians and the West Indian character maligned more or less non-stop. Everyone, as is well known and widely accepted, has shortcomings, West Indians not excluded. But the complaints were often senseless, generally unsympathetic and always boring. I had had my fill and was in a revisionist mood. I was actively looking for something which could be pointed out as a unique production of the native creativity of the islanders. Carstens' remark seemed to suggest something along those lines, and I eagerly seized on it and made the corroboration of that suggestion one of the priorities of my study of present-day boatbuilding.

That is how it happened that my inquiries had such a strong bias toward the historical aspects of boatbuilding. Never mind that the fast sailing vessels seen by Carstens were probably "Bermudan" — sharp-bottomed, sloop-rigged vessels built in Bermuda, Jamaica, and the Chesapeake as early as 1707. And, never mind that this design was probably carried to the Lesser Antilles by the buccaneers when they were driven out of Hispaniola by the Spanish. Never mind, then, that the proportions and characteristics of fast sailing sloops and later schooners were already taking shape when the ancestors of the builders I knew were still slaves, given no opportunity to learn anything as potentially troublemaking as boatbuilding. Never mind all that — my mind was already made up, and all I needed were a few pliable facts to support my conclusion.

Just a few facts, but they proved more elusive than I had imagined. Take for instance the story of Capt. Bligh and the Tortola sloop, an early favorite in the historical sweepstakes. William Bligh, best known as the rigid disciplinarian who provoked/suffered (circle your choice) the mutiny on the *Bounty*, was also the ablest navigator of his day. After an abortive first attempt, Bligh returned to Tahiti in 1792 in the *Providence* and succeeded on this second attempt in transporting breadfruit seedlings to the West Indies. On this trip, so the story goes, the *Providence* called in Tortola, where local shipwrights came aboard and measured one of the ship's yawls (a yawl was an open boat carried on deck by the naval vessels of that day and used when filling water casks or bringing aboard stores). The form of the yawl was accordingly copied by laying a stick across the gunwales and carving a notch to mark the beam at each one foot interval on the keel. This, continues the story, is why in Tortola the boats are designated by the length of the keel instead of by the length overall.

How about that for some real fine culture history? It has just about all anyone could ask for, doesn't it? It ties the design of the Tortola sloop to one of the well-known nautical personalities of the day, as well as to the epoch-making arrival of the breadfruit in the West Indies. Very plausible, very circumstantial and not difficult to verify, since I was able to find a detailed biography of Bligh (Mackaness, 1951).

According to this account, Bligh and the *Providence* arrived the 23rd of January, 1793 in St. Vincent, their first port of call in the West Indies, where several breadfruit seedlings were delivered to the Royal Botanical Gardens in Kingstown (a scrawny specimen said to be the original transplant still grows there, while its descendants abound throughout the islands — a daily boon to thousands and, in retrospect, well worth the two attempts and a mutiny which its arrival required).

After a week's stay in St. Vincent, the *Providence* proceeded to Port Royal, Jamaica, arriving there on the 5th of February, a voyage of 940 nautical miles made in 6 days. There is no mention in the biography of an intermediate stop in Tortola or any other island, and furthermore there was simply not enough time. An average of 157 miles per day is already unusually good for a downwind passage in a ship that could not have been careened since Tahaiti, possibly even earlier. To detour *via* Tortola and stop even briefly would add 160 miles to the trip and subtract at least one day from the time, requiring an average of 220 miles per day — a figure so high that it would certainly have occasioned comment in the logbook.

Alas, another good theory aground on the hard rock of fact. But after all, it was only a hearsay account, and there were still the builders themselves to be consulted. Of course, it will come as no surprise to anyone less naive than myself to learn that the builders had no ideas about and no interest in the origins of boatbuilding, as I quickly discovered. By this time, however, I had found that all the sloops and schooners in the islands were built according to the same simple rules of proportioning — rules which accounted for the broad similarity of the vessels throughout the chain: Depth in the hold = ½ Beam; Beam = ¼ Length between Perpendiculars; Keel = ½ LBP.

Since it was ultimately these proportions which constituted the design of a vessel, I decided to concentrate my inquiries on this simple and concrete matter of proportions instead of the vaguer concept of "origins". Feeling very devious and infinitely subtle, I began to ask the builders where the rules of proportion had come from. Response was somewhat improved by my new approach — now there was a few second's pause before the shake of the head or shrug of the shoulders. And occasionally, a very patient in-dividual would take the time to explain that the rules of proportion had developed in order that boatbuilders could build "correct" boats. Then one hot afternoon while working on *Skywave*, Uncle Nappy seemed in a mood to explain things and I asked him. His response was immediate and triumphant.

"The *Bible*," he said. "It the *Bible*, Douggie. The Lord told Noah how to build the Ark and is the same way we building our own vessel."

By a masterful effort, I refrained from dancing on the deck, but at quitting time I hastened to find the operative passage in Genesis 6: 13-15 where, in the measured cadences of the King James Translation, the rules of proportion were laid down:

> And God said unto Noah, The end of all flesh is come before me; for the earth is filled with violence through them; and, behold, I will destroy them with the earth.
> Make thee an ark of gopher wood; rooms shalt thou make in the ark, and shalt pitch it within and without with pitch. And this is how thou shalt make it: the length of the ark three hundred cubits, the breadth of it fifty cubits, and the height of it thirty cubits.

The units were a little unfamiliar, but since it was proportions that mat-tered, it was easy to determine that the Ark was built on a 1:6 ratio, rather than the 1:4 which was pretty constant for the islands. My disappointment was keen, for another good story had fallen apart, and it meant discarding a certain amount of good copy that had been running through my head about how a reverence for Holy Scripture among these simple people had found its expression in their everyday lives and activities.

Frustration continued in the matter of origins until gradually I learned to distinguish between trading vessels on the one hand and small craft on the other. The reader is by now aware that the sloops and schooners of the Lesser Antilles are broadly similar in their general proportions and characteristics no matter where built. By contrast, small craft are highly variable in type and are often very specific to their location. As I turned my attention to the origins of small craft, the problem resolved itself into smaller components, and in several instances the origins were either self-evident or not difficult to infer.

The gommiers, yoles, canots, pirogues and sailing canoes make an obvious starting place, since they are the truly "original" small craft of the islands. For the reasons given earlier, there seemed to me to be little doubt that all were derived from the Carib dugout canoe, modifications occurring mostly in response to local scarcity of logs suitably large for hollowing. Dugouts, or some trace or derivative, occur on all the larger, higher islands from Guadeloupe south to Trinidad, the islands where the Caribs were established and held out longest against European colonization. The present users of these dugouts are Europeanized West Indians of African descent, who use or have recently used a French-creole dialect. It may be that the adoption on an aboriginal type of watercraft occurred more readily in French-speaking cultures because of some inherently greater flexibility of attitude on the part of French colonizers. After all, *laissez-faire* is a French expression.

The two-bow boats of Bequia are another example of a local type whose origins are essentially self-evident, particularly since two of these boats are still engaged in whaling. There is little need to belabor the obvious, but it was interesting to discover how closely I could pinpoint their antecedents using a combination of local lore and historical sources.

One afternoon while we were building *Skywave*, whaling was being discussed — a whale had been landed that morning — and Haakon commented, "It was Capt. Dunham what learned them boys whaling." Two years later, I made a trip through New England and Nova Scotia trying to establish a relationship between North American fishing schooners and West Indian trading vessels. At the Whaling Museum in New Bedford, Massachusetts, while looking in the photo collection for whaling vessels that might have been seen in the West Indies, I met C. F. Purrington, the archivist there.

Somewhat sheepishly, I mentioned the name Dunham, thinking the connection too remote to be any use. With an expressive sniff, Purrington turned to a card file that he had compiled of names and other information about any persons known to have gone whaling out of New Bedford. The name Dunham, John A. appeared as if by magic — master of the schooner *William A. Grozier*, which whaled out of New Bedford under Dunham's command from 1888 until 1903. In that year, George Dunham became master of the *Grozier*, continuing until 1911, when he became the owner and master of the schooner *Ellen A. Swift* until she went missing in 1919, possibly the victim of a U-boat.

Not content with one feat of legerdemain, Purrington then produced, from another file, crew lists for several of the voyages of the *Grozier* and the *Swift* which included several names familiar in Bequia — Olliverre, Sargent, Kydd and Hazell — entered as residents of St. Vincent, the administrative center for Bequia. The indication clearly was that the Dunhams, father and son, had been sailing from New Bedford with a skeleton crew and picking up Bequians for the heavy work of whaling.

These names and dates were still fresh in my mind one morning a few months later, as I waited on deck while the *Rosarene* made final preparations to sail to Trinidad. A light-eyed, brown-skinned woman who introduced herself as Lozina Kydd struck up a conversation by asking if I had seen the whale which was landed two days earlier.

"My father was Timothy Kydd, and he was Capt. Dunham's harpooner," she confided, proudly. "He was the onliest man ever to strike a right whale. If they did have a history book in them days, they would a put he in it because he was the onliest man ever to strike a right whale."

When I expressed my admiration and asked for further information, she smiled coyly and told the child at her side to "go 'long there." She then told me that when the whale ship came back to Bequia to discharge the crew, Capt. Dunham always stayed for a week or two the Kydd family.

"And my mother, you know, she make a little mistake with Capt. Dunham. Timothy Kydd is only my adopted father. And Capt. Dunham did love me more than all he other children, though we never see each other. He was coming for me the next time, but the ship get lost in the Gulf Stream. That must be 1921 on the way to Bequia. He was taking me to live with Frankie Brown, that is on Cape Code."

I listened quietly, without prompting or mentioning any of the names, though they were familiar to me. The pattern, even including the "little mistake" was not, I imagine, an uncommon one in the closing days of whaling. As petroleum replaced whale oil and whaling became less profitable, New Bedford whalers began to sail with skeleton crew to some island near a whaling ground and there to engage crew for whaling. From serving in a whale ship to whaling from a shore station was a small step once the islanders had acquired the skills and grown tired on the long voyages away from family and friends. There remains, however, the question of why the Dunhams chose Bequia for crew, and here another influence appears in the form of Old Bill Wallace.

In 1911, a young American named Frederic Fenger made a voyage in a sailing canoe from Trinidad to Puerto Rico, which he described in a fascinating book entitled *Alone in the Caribbean* (Fenger, 1958). On his trip northward, Fenger stopped off for nearly a month with some Bequia whalers who were operating from a small islet south of Carriacou (N.B. the head harpooner of this crew was named Jose Olliverre). Fenger next recounts calling in Bequia to deliver to Old Bill Wallace a letter from a shipmate informing Wallace of his son's death on a whaling voyage several years earlier. Old Bill was a Scot who went whaling as a youth, then invested his savings in a sea island cotton plantation on Bequia. When, after some years, cotton failed, Old Bill returned to what he knew best — he built whale boats, trained a crew and established a shore-based whale fishery in Bequia.

It was in the person of Old Bill Wallace then, that there existed the essential link between the skills of whaling and the skills of boatbuilding — the skills necessary for the establishment of a whale fishery, and growing out of that, a boatbuilding culture. And this, in turn, became the rootstock onto which a schooner-building industry would be grafted around the turn of the century.

More about that in due course; for the moment let us continue with the subject of small craft, turning next to the beach boats of the Leeward Islands and Barbados. When I asked Emile Gumbs, owner of the *Warspite* and widely knowledgeable in maritime matters, about the origins of the beach boat type, he shrugged and replied in a very commonsense vein, that he had always supposed that the early settlers knew how to build boats just as they knew how to build houses, or perform any other everyday operation.

A very plausible suggestion, though somewhat difficult to verify. The islands where the beach boats are presently found — Anguilla, St. Martin, St. Kitts, Nevis, Montserrat, Barbados, and with a modified sailing rig, St. Lucia — all share the English language and, with the exception of St. Lucia, have always been predominantly English in outlook. This being the case, then the archetype of the beach boat should be found somewhere on the shores of England, Scotland, or Wales. It would have been interesting to pursue this matter, but I was not able to find any catalogue of boat types for those areas with which to compare my lines.

The case for *le canot saintois* — used in the Iles des Saintes, St. Barts, and St. Thomas by white, French-speaking West Indians, and, as a recent transplant, in Guadeloupe — is rather similar to that of the beach boats. That is, the type seems to have come to the islands with the French settlers. I wrote to M. Bernard Cadoret, editor of *Le Petit Perroquet*, a French journal of maritime lore, sending photographs of *le saintois* and requesting information about possible antecendnets. He replied that French local boat types are not well catalogued, but suggested that my photos most closely resemble the small craft found along the Atlantic coast of France between Nantes and La Rochelle. This accords pretty well with the local tradition that the inhabitants of the Saintes came from the region around the mouth of the Loire. It is interesting to note in passing that *le saintois* was the most highly finished type of any I saw in the islands. And among American colonial shipbuilders "finished after the French manner" indicated a high standard of building.

We have now accounted for all the local small craft except the Tortola sloop. It was my hope that leaving it until last would somehow make the riddle easier to solve. Forlorn hope, I should say, because the Tortola sloop is a bit of an anomaly. To begin with, it is not truly a "sloop" in island terms, since it is not gaff-rigged. On the other hand, it is a little large to be a "boat" by island standards, which require that a "boat" he pulled ashore when not in use. And there is nothing about the Tortola sloop which indicates any relationship at all vith types found on nearby islands, except, of course, with the Antigua fishing sloop, which is avowedly patterned after the Tortola model. There is great irony in this setback because it was the difficulty of assessing kinship of the Tortola boat that caused Prof. Doran to wish that someone would make a survey of all the sailing craft of the Lesser Antilles. Well, someone has now done said survey, and the origins of the Tortola boat are still obscure.

Aside from this one frustration, plausible origins can be established for the various small craft of the islands, and this provides the background for a more fruitful approach to the origins of the sloops and schooners. The first step is to consider the related but simpler question of design influence. For this essential understanding, I am indebted to Nils Jannesch, director of the Nova Scotia Provincial Museum in Halifax, who pointed out that design and construction of sailing vessels are conceptually quite different, even though in the West Indies the two aspects are merged in practice.

Construction requires a detailed knowledge of tools, materials, methods, procedures and priorities which is difficult to acquire by any method other than apprenticeship, formal or informal. The techniques of construction are essentially conservative and change very little over long periods of time. Furthermore, there is little difference in technique between a row boat and a schooner, as I had occasion to observe: Haakon, with only his experience as a builder of two-bow boats, managed to do a very creditable job on a sloop.

Design, on the other hand, is essentially abstract and only indirectly affected by the details of construction techniques. And, far from being conservative, design is flexible, innovative and easily influenced — within limits. These two aspect of boatbuilding might be aphoristically contrasted by asserting that a skilled builder may very well achieve a workable, even pleasing, vessel without benefit of a designer (this is sometimes called "vernacular" design or unself-conscious design), but a skilled designer can produce nothing without the services of a builder.

Now, I am certainly aware that all master builders are to some degree designers, and that all good design requires intimate knowledge of material and technique. And furthermore, I am fully aware that design and construction did not become separate functions in shipbuilding (or in any other field) until comparatively recently. In fact, the separation has not occurred in the traditional culture of the West Indies, which is why I floundered around for so long and had to go all the way to Nova Scotia to receive enlightenment.

Design and construction in the islands are merged into the single activity of building, and my failure to distinguish between the two had me looking for some sort of bolt-of-lightning origin for schooner-building. I was, in essence, wandering around looking for a builder who would, under the glare of strong lights, finally confess that he had sent for and received, in a plain brown wrapper, a schooner kit with clear, concise instructions and all parts pre-cut to be assembled in a few hours of spare time using only simple hand tools.

After my conversation with Jannesch, the light of day began to break all around, quickly dispersing the gray mists of confusion that had engulfed me: the techniques of construction employed on the schooner-building islands were not new, and had no "origins" in the sense I searched for. They were simply borrowed from an older tradition of boat-carpentry, which was itself a part of the everyday skills of an earlier period. My problem, then, reduced itself to establishing patterns of design influence which had shaped the construction of the inter-island trading vessels. And in the matter of design influence, information had been accumulating all along.

There was, after all, the *Frances W. Smith* and others of her breed, retired from the hard life of a fishing schooner in northern waters to serve out their remaining years among the sunny Caribees, a ready source of inspiration to island builders. If there were any doubt of this, it completely disappeared one afternoon when I was asking Haakon why his center frames were wider at the turn of the bilge than at the heads.

"Well, Douggie," he replied, "that is call tumblehome. When I was a boy, I going in my father schooner to Barbados, and we see plenty Nova Scotiamen. They all having tumblehome and they be plenty fast. So I trying it, too."

Emile Gumbs could recall Canadian fishing schooners calling in Anguilla to load salt as recently as 1948. In the *Register of Shipping* in Barbados, the majority of sailing vessel entries since 1929 were transfers from Nova Scotia. In the Dalhousie University Archives in Halifax, Nova Scotia, there were clearance papers and other port records indicating that fishing schooners had been sailing to the West Indies in the winter months since around the turn of the century — carrying flour, lumber and, especially, salt fish to the islands and returning with rum, molasses and salt for the next season's fishing. (Some Gloucester schooners appeared in the Barbados register, but in the off-season they more frequently cleared for the Azores and Portugal).

All in all, there was ample evidence that North American fishing schooners, especially those from Lunenburg, Nova Scotia, were frequently seen in the West Indies. But did they influence local builders? The clearest way to answer this is with Figures XXV-1 thru 6 and the following explanation.

According to Nils Jannesch, the Lunenburgers were farmers until the 1860's, when they began to fish on the banks in vessels copied after Gloucester fishing schooners. Innovations in design which were developed in Boston and Gloucester by designers such as Dennis Lawlor, Thomas McManus and Edward Burgess were reproduced, after a certain lag, in Nova Scotia. By means of the contacts already documented, these innovations and design characteristics finally appeared in West Indian vessel after about 25-30 years, as I believe the juxtapositions in Figs. XXVI-1 thru 6 show.

The foregoing establishes, to my satisfaction at least, that West Indian schooner-building in this century was primarily influenced in design by Canadian fishing schooners. However, even in New England, fishing schooners of a recognizable modern type were not developed before the 1850's (Chapelle, 1935). The question then arises, "What were West Indian builders doing before there was an opportunity to be influenced?"

fig. XXV-1. Schooner Hattie A. Heckman, *105 Tons. Built 1895 at Essex, Massachusetts. Photo courtesy of Peabody Museum, Salem, Mass.*

fig. XXV-2. Schooner Warspite, *71 Tons. Built 1918 at Sandy Ground, Anguilla.*

fig. XXV-3. Schooner Richard, *134 Tons. Built 1907 at Essex, Massachusetts. Photo courtesy of Peabody Museum.*

fig. XXV-4. Schooner Gloria Colita, *178 Tons. Built 1939 at Port Elizabeth, Bequia.*

fig. XXV-5. Schooner Leo, 37 Tons. Built 1908 at
Essex, Massachusetts. Photo
courtesy of Peabody Museum.

fig. XXV-6. Schooner Emeralda, 51 Tons. Built
1940 at Friendship Bay, Bequia.

The answer to this question, and others not yet asked, may be deduced from a bar graph (fig. XXV-4) that I prepared from pages and pages of scrawled copies of scrawled entries in dusty volumes residing in hot harbor offices sprawled the whole length of the Lesser Antilles. And if I may for the moment sweep aside the curtain of narrative prose and address the reader directly, I have this to say: "Don't you *dare* turn the page without studying that graph carefully!"

It may not look like much, but it took me all one winter, making lists, checking lists, puzzling over my own handwriting, adding, subtracting, drawing and erasing, trying to get it all on one page. And for what, you ask? Well, for this: it shows that sloops were built before schooners; that the aggregate tonnage of sloops is greater than that of schooners on all islands except Bequia; that the building of trading vessels began in the Lesser Antilles in the 1840's; that boatbuilding is an economic activity which shows in this century two peaks corresponding to World Wars I & II, separated by the valley of the Great Depression; that the building of larger vessels has all but stopped at the present time; and that Carriacou and Bequia deserve additional attention to see if there be some special reason(s) for their markedly greater output.

In the case of Carriacou, there is, to begin with, a very good historical source: John Davy, a military surgeon who traveled extensively in the islands during the first half of the nineteenth century and wrote *The West Indies, Before and Since Emancipation.* Davy makes several interesting references to Carriacou: that smuggling by the inhabitants was a problem as early as 1765; that slaves on the island grew poultry and were selling their produce in Grenada as early as 1833 by means of small boats they built themselves; that Scottish shipwrights were brought to Carriacou to build trading vessels for landowners who wanted to sell produce in Grenada.

In consequence of the last remark, a roll call of the family names in the little boatbuilding community of Windward, Carriacou is especially interesting: McFarlane, McLawrence, McKensie, MacLaren, McQuilkin, McIntosh and Roberts with a sprinkling of others: Bethel, Martineau, Mitchell, Patrice and Fleary.

Don Hill at the American Museum of Natural History did research for his doctoral dissertation in Carriacou and mentions in his dessertation a folk hero named John Rock who came to Carriacou from Barbados in 1888 and, according to local tradition, brought a new style in boatbuilding — the overhanging (counter) stern. Here, in brief outline, we have all the traditional attributes of a folk hero: a stranger arriving from the east (Barbados is almost due east of Carriacou) bearing gifts (a new method of building vessels). Even the name is perfect — John Rock. The only thing missing is a tragic and mysterious departure accompanied by promises to return at some future time.

In fact, John Rock lived in Carriacou until his death in 1942, being

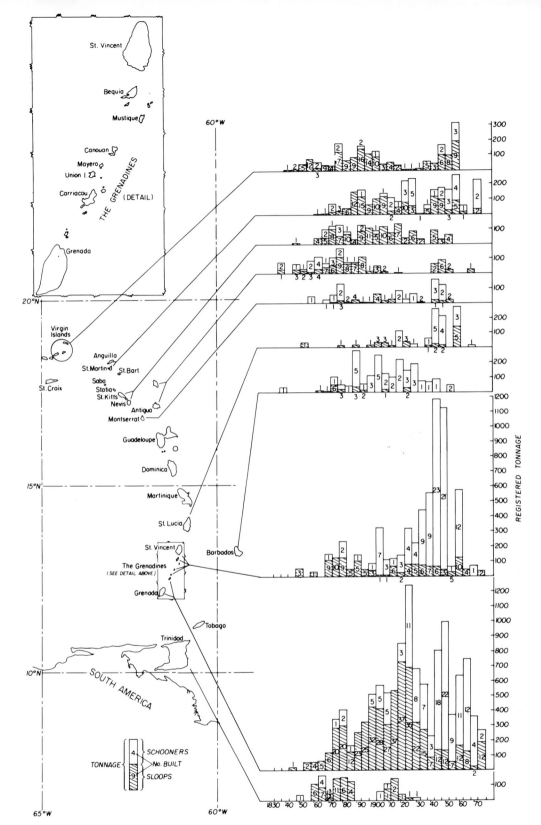

fig. XXV-7. Graph of sloop and schooner building activity in the Lesser Antilles, 1830-1970. Taken from the Registers of Shipping.

eminently real, as I ascertained by checking the Grenda *Register of Shipping.* The name John Rock first appeared in 1902 (builders' names were not given before 1899) as the builder of a 21 Ton sloop *Island Gem.* From that time until the last entry in 1941, John Rock built 11 sloops and 11 schooners — 816 Tons of shipping — including the first vessel described as having a "counter" stern. Thus, it appears that the unusually large output of vessels in Carriacou may have resulted from purely human (as opposed to economic, geographic, or historical) factors — first, in the form of the unnamed Scottish shipwrights and later, in the person of John Rock.

The case in Bequia was similar, and the story was even more detailed and circumstantial. It began to unfold in St. Lucia when I asked Malings Compton where the people of the islands had learned shipbuilding.

"I can answer that question for you," he replied, little knowing what waves of incredulity were sweeping over me. "In 1838 at the time of Emancipation, Sir William Snagg came out to take charge of the island of Canouan [in the Grenadines]. With him, he brought Benjamin George Compton, a shipwright and native of Hampshire. Compton married a native woman named Albertha and had two children — a son named Benjamin in 1840 and in 1842, a daughter named Mary Frances. Benjamin was my father (Malings Compton was born in 1898). He learned boatbuilding from his father and taught it to me. He died in 1914, the year that I came to St. Lucia. Mary Frances married a man named William A. Mitchell who came to Canouan from St. Vincent to learn boatbuilding from her father."

During this recitation, my skepticism melted away. Compton's account was too circumstantial to have been fabricated, and it fitted closely with several other pieces of information of which he could not have been aware — for example, that the *Mercantile Navy List* for 1878 contained an entry for the 18 Ton sloop *Sir Wm. Snagg,* built in Canouan in 1870.

Compton's account also dovetailed nicely with what I knew of the Mitchell family of Bequia. The founder of the family was a shadowy figure simply called Old Mitch who came to Bequia from elsewhere, was a boatbuilder and had three sons. The eldest son went to Panama and was never heard from again. The next, James Fitzallan, called Uncle Harry, lived in Bequia, built 5 schooners and left numerous offspring. The youngest son, Romulus St. Clair, called Jack, went to Dominica and built 5 sloops and 9 schooners. Altogether, the descendants of Benjamin Compton and Mary Frances Compton Mitchell have produced to date 41 vessels (known to me) and 2 Prime Ministers. An impressive contribution which, added to that of others such as Old Bill Wallace and the whalers, accounts in large measure for the unusual output of vessels, especially schooners, on the island of Bequia.

Although presented in the manner of spaghetti thrown at a wall, I believe that all the elements necessary for an outline of the culture history of boatbuilding in the Lesser Antilles have been assembled in this chapter. Perhaps at least some of the tangle can now be eliminated by starting with a fairly early period, however shadowy, and working forward. In the paragraphs that follow it is essential to distinguish canoes, which are made of hollowed trees, from boats, which are small and made of ribs and planks, and from vessels, which are sloops and schooners.

I postulate — with no evidence whatsoever, other than unvarnished commonsense — that slave-owners neither permitted slaves to learn ship carpentry nor encouraged the building of any watercraft that had the ability to sail out of sight. From this arises my conviction that the building of interisland trading vessels (which require registration) began only in the 1840's (Emancipation occurred in 1838). During this period, the indigenous watercraft of the islands would all have been small craft — boats or canoes according to local traditions and influences — though the skills of boat capentry did exist in conjunction with these small craft.

During this period the principal design influence — in the form of vessels seen in the islands and suitable for island construction and use — was the sharp-bottomed "Bermuda" type used by buccaneers and free traders (with no regrets whatever, I consign the origins of the "Bermuda" type — whose influence was felt all through colonial America, and ultimately, Europe — to someone else, since Bermuda is not even on my chart).

At this time the islands of the Lesser Antilles were either unsettled, settled by slave-owners seeking to establish a plantation economy, or settled by smallholders with few or no slaves and no prospects of a plantation economy. A further distinction also cuts across the chain: islands from Guadeloupe south where a Carib influence is manifested by the persistance of dugout canoes, and a French influence is evidenced by the use of *patois*.

Now, if the reader will project onto the heretofore blank inner wall of his imagination a mosaic map of the Antilles formed by the two sets of constraints just mentioned, the following categories appear:

1) Plantation islands with French, Carib and African cultural influences, where some form of canoe is still used and larger vessels are built not at all or only when someone comes from one of the islands in category 4.

2) Small, non-plantation islands of French cultural heritage where the small craft are boats derived from some traditional French type and where vessels are built only sporadically.

3) Plantation islands with an English cultural heritage, where the small craft are of English origin and larger vessels were built intermittently as economic conditions dicatated.

4) Small, non-plantation islands with predominantly English influence, where the small craft are boats, not canoes, and trading vessels are produced in such quantity that a true maritime industry could be said to exist. In at least two cases, there were purely human and contingent factors in the form of skilled individuals who shaped and influenced this industry.

Thus far and no farther. I leave to the interested reader all additional analysis of why these categories exist. If there are any questions before the quiz, I suggest that you send a self-addressed, stamped envelope with your question(s), neatly typed or written in a clear, legible hand, along with 25¢ to cover time and typewriter ribbon, to the author, who will make every effort to evade, equivocate and embarrass the eager student.

CHAPTER XXVI

THE LAST SCHOONER

The big tamarind tree cast a welcome shadow in the glare of the afternoon sun, strong even in February, and I was glad to stop. The road that wound upward from the harbor was still steep, and the view from the top still spectacular. I drank in the panorama of sea and islands, and marveled again at the sequence of events that had brought me back to Bequia after seven years. The view of the Grenadines was spectacular and unaltered, but elsewhere there was evidence of change.

Admiralty Bay was jammed as never before with yachts and yachtspersons (political pressures and increasing hostility in Grenada and St. Lucia have displaced much yacht traffic to Bequia). And the little town of Port Elizabeth had a prosperous glow that merely enhanced its original charm. I, by contrast, was aglow from the sun and sweating freely. The seven intervening years of living in temperate latitudes had bleached me white, and raising hogs had made me fat.

When my involvement with island boats first began, I thought it a temporary association, begun on the assumption that the day of the island schooner was passing, if not already past, and that sail-powered watercraft whose form and substance were not soon recorded would go unrecorded forever. As I sailed the islands and measured boats in the early 70's, everything I saw confirmed this assumption. Fishing boats and small craft were replacing sails with outboards, and even the builders agreed that the day of the schooner was over.

There were too many headaches in the schooner trade. Crew were harder and harder to find to work for the wages and under the conditions that the trade demanded. Insurance on wooden vessels or even on cargo was no longer available, with the result that schooners mostly got the dangerous or low-paying consignments that no one else wanted. And finally, poor facilities and poor organization meant that there were many profit-consuming delays in port — while schooners waited for cargo that was simultaneously waiting for transportation.

After my trip to Trinidad in the *Rosarene*, I worked up a balance sheet for the voyage — based on estimated data, since schooner owners are no more prone to discuss personal finances than anyone else. For lading I used the quantities that I saw loaded and unloaded; for freight rates I used those published by the St. Vincent government. From conversation I learned what the crew earned; for the captain and mate, I made an educated guess.

SCHOONER *ROSARENE*

Balance sheet for one voyage to Trinidad in Eastern Caribbean dollars

Income
Outbound

Passengers (2)	50.00
Livestock (9 sheep, 6 hogs)	38.10
Sweet potatoes (1150 bags)	2300.00
Carrots (460 bags)	460.00

Homeward

Passengers (1)	25.00
Cement (500 sacks)	500.00
M-T drums (200)	800.00
Clay tiles (1500)	110.00
Biscuits (850 cartons)	190.00
Total Income	$4473.10

Operating Expenses

Crew (½ of monthly wage)	450.00	
Captain and mate	400.00	
Fuel (100 gals. diesel @ $.80/gal.	80.00	
Food ($1.00/man/day)	120.00	
Commissions and Wharfage (10%)	447.31	
Total Operating Expenses	$1497.31	

Net Income for the voyage	$2975.79

The *Rosarene*, being under charter to the St. Vincent Marketing Board, was fairly steadily employed, making two trips a month throughout the year. Under these circumstances then, I projected an annual operating revenue of $71,418.96 EC. From this are subtracted the annual maintenance costs, which I again estimated, allowing two careenings and one new sail a year, and an engine overhaul every three years.

Bequia schooners are careened in Port Elizabeth using a heavily ballasted barge (cf. fig. V-11, on extreme left) which rents for $25 a day. The crew do the cleaning and painting; if caulking or repairs are required, a shipwright could at that time be had for $12 a day. Estimating four days of barge time, two days of carpentry and ten gallons of paint at $40 per gallon gives the figure $525 each time the vessel is careened, or $1050 annually.

For the new sail I allowed 200 yards of canvas at $8 a yard and $800 labor, totaling $2400, and to be on the safe side I added another $600 for rigging and miscellaneous repairs. For the engine I estimated $3000 for an overhaul, an annual cost of $1000 for a reserve fund. The total annual maintenance cost would then amount to $5050, which, subtracted from operating revenues, gives a net annual profit of $66,368.96.

Taking the analysis one step further, I cast around for some way to estimate the capital investment represented by the *Rosarene*. A year earlier, the owner of the *Yankee Girl R* (cf. Chapter IV) had been willing to sell for $70,000 EC (the deal fell through, but it seems fair to use the figure for estimating). The *Rosarene* was somewhat larger than the *Yankee Girl,* so we could be generous and put the replacement cost of the *Rosarene* as high as $100,000. The annual return on invested capital would then be 66%.

This figure agrees pretty well with the Anguilla owner who told me that with luck a vessel might return her cost in her first year. Naturally, allowances must be made for the hazards of the high seas and the usual vagaries of economic life, but on the paper at least, the schooner trade looks attractive. However, the same thing might be said of the steel-hulled coastal freighters that began to appear in the islands in the early 70's as the ports of northern Europe were converted to containerized cargo-handling. Small freighters, some as little as ten years old, could be bought for as little as $80,000 EC; moreover, they had a number of important advantages over the traditional schooners.

First, there was the matter of size: the steel freighters were shallow enough in draft to enter the same ports and use the same wharves as the schooners while carrying two or three times the tonnage. Secondly, the freighters with their machinery could handle cargo and be manned by no more than a captain, an engineer and two deck hands — who lived in better quarters and did lighter work than on a schooner. And finally, cargo insurance was more easily obtained by these more conventional carriers. All of this added up to pretty stiff competition for the schooners. Former schooner owners and captains were acquiring the capital and the navigational skills to purchase such freighters and bring them to the West Indies, and that more than any other thing was hastening the end of the schooner trade.

As I saw schooners at work, a number of improvements in the system suggested themselves to me — improvements whereby all aspects of the commercial life of the islands might benefit. The first improvement would be a simple increase in interisland trade. All European colonial empires pursued the policy, called mercantilism, of channeling all commerce through the mother country and prohibiting intercolonial trade (it was in part these restrictions placed on the vigorous commercial interests of New England that led to the American War of Independence). Whether from habit or from policy, this pattern still persists in the Lesser Antilles, though there are efforts by some of the more far-sighted island governments to develop intra-Caribbean trading partners.

A logical extension of such a policy would be to provide adequate navigational aids for these inter-island routes.

Another great bottleneck and obstacle to Caribbean commerce were the poor facilities for handling cargo and the equally cumbersome methods whereby cargo was procured and consigned. The latter bottleneck — a system of ship's agents charging too much for doing too little — could be eliminated by instituting a system that I saw in the inland waterways of France called the *bourse d'affrètement* (consignment market). Each of the inland ports in France had a small office to which the bargemen reported whenever seeking cargo. There they placed their names on a list in the order of arrival. Shippers with cargo to move contacted the office, stating the nature of their cargo, its destination and the rate they proposed to pay for shipping. This consignment was offered to the barge at the head of the list, who took the consignment if the terms suited. Otherwise the offer was made to the second on the list, and so on until someone was found whose position on the list made the proposition desirable. In this way each consignment quickly and fairly found a carrier, thereby eliminating both commissions and long waits in port. A recent arrival in port had only to look at the length of the list to make an intelligent decision about waiting or deadheading to another port.

The schooner fleet navigates entirely by dead reckoning, and most of that is pretty informal. Under the generally fair conditions prevailing in the Antilles, this is usually sufficient. However, it never hurts to know where you are, and the better you know your position, the better you are able respond in emergencies. Navigation might be taught in West Indian schools, where it might to advantage replace the geography of northern Europe.

With my final proposal, I pass from the merely improbable into the realm of the wildly fanciful: I propose, in short, a change in the form of marine insurance. Insurance of all types is generally subject to any number of distortions of its sole genuine purpose — that of sharing risks too great to be borne individually. Marine insurance seems particularly afflicted with these distortions — undoubtedly the result of its curious origins in the gambling mania that beset early 18th century London. This mania was extended even to betting on ship losses, a bizarre diversion which centered in Lloyd's Coffee House, the forerunner of Lloyd's of London, a clearinghouse for insurance underwriters.

From a merely ghoulish interest in disaster, this activity was transformed into something downright sinister by shipowners who discovered that they could overload and underequip their vessels, then bet *against* themselves as a hedge. A system so conceived invites — even demands — abuse. From these humble origins developed the time-honored tradition — still in use — of retiring an unprofitable vessel by insuring well and sinking her.

This activity has produced in the West Indies schooner trade, though not elsewhere, uninsurable risks, with the result that cargos as well as vessels must sail uninsured. And as noted earlier, this increases the difficulties that schooners have in locating cargo. To overcome this obstacle I suggest a mutual insurance fund formed by a schooner owners' association.

"How," the alert reader will ask, "could a small local fund accept risks which Lloyd's of London finds unacceptable?" My proposal is that insurance be written on cargo *only*, with strict upper limits of valuation and with the consignor made directly the beneficiary of any loss payment. The effect of this would be to impose a very hefty deductible on the insured parties (even in the case of collusion between owners and shippers) and eliminate the profits of barratry (fraud under Maritime Law).

Any or all of the foregoing suggestions might improve interisland commerce and make it more profitable, but by themselves would not preferentially aid the schooner trade. Nor should they. More often than not it is a mistake to created artificial conditions for the preservation of a selected activity (though it is frequently difficult to say at what point reasonable encouragement becomes artificial respiration — witness the continuing debate over whether the government in the United States has artificially aided the trucking industry by building highways). If working sail is to persist in the islands, it is preferable that it be the result of some "natural" market force.

It would not be easy to be so rigidly conservative in my views had not the forces of geopolitics dealt a hand in which the schooner trade has received what I believe may prove an ace-in-the-hole. I speak, of course, of the rapidly rising price of petroleum, which is causing changes in the way many things are done.

When the notes for this chapter were first made, there was no OPEC, and there had been no oil embargo. When I made a balance sheet for the *Rosarene*, diesel oil in the islands was $.80 EC/gal. (now it is over $3.00). When I saw outboard motors replacing sails on fishing boats, gasoline was $1.00/gal., and fresh fish was $1.00/lb. (now gasoline is $4.00/gal. and fish is still $1.00). When I made my study, the age of sail was closing in the Antilles, and the original notes for my concluding chapter were valedictory in tone. Now the demise of sailing craft seems less certain, and the long delay in writing this final chapter

fig. XXVI-1.   Sloop Skywave *arriving in Carriacou
for the Regatta. August, 1972.*

may have saved me considerable embarassment. Personal knowledge of what I
hope is a new trend comes — as did much of my earlier experience — from contact with the Mitchell family.

   After *Skywave* was launched in 1971, I left Bequia and returned to a
teaching job in St. Croix which provided the means to stay in the islands. And
the following August found me already anchored off Hillsborough when
Skywave arrived to make her debut in the Carriacou Regatta (fig. XXVI-1).
The competition was exciting, but in spite of our best efforts, the results were
disappointing. Although *Skywave* invariably led on the downwind leg, she
was no match on the wind for the bigger, deeper Carriacou sloops.

fig. XXVI-2. *Horris Martineau at the helm of*
Vaeta *during the Carriacou Regatta.*
August, 1971.

First prize for the series went to Horris Martineau, owner of *Vaeta* (fig.
XXVI-2), and *Skywave* "brought" only third. After the prize sharing, Martineau (with whom I had sailed in two previous regattas) asked me to in-
troduce him to Haakon. They talked for some time, and Haakon told me afterward:

"They all saying she is sail good, Douggie. Is only better sails she wanting
to beat all."

The following year *Mermaid* came out of retirement to race a new
challenger built at Petit Martinique, and in this field *Skywave* with new sails
came in fourth. After this Haakon did not race again, but *Skywave* had
already begun to bring in substantial returns as a trading vessel.

In 1974 I visited Bequia, this time after two years' absence, making again
the familiar climb up from the harbor, then down toward the bay. I was part
way along the beach before I noticed a new house that had joined the others in
the little colony of vacation homes which had been growing up in this quiet
corner. It appeared that Haakon had sold some of his land in spite of my advice, since the new house was lying up the hill from the little blue house and
well inside his boundary line.

When I came into view, the younger Mitchell children, no longer small,
stopped their play and came running.

"This way, Douggie, this way. Mommie been up the new house."

They led me up the hill to where Winnie waited on the verandah of a house
so spaciously built that I had mistaken it for the island retreat of some

fig. XXVI-3. Schooner Wave Dancer *awaits launching, Friendship, Bay, Bequia. February, 1981.*

wealthy North American. Winnie showed me proudly around her house, timbered in greenheart and floored and sided with purpleheart — an extravagance of solid hardwood.

We sat on the gallery, enjoying the view over the bay and exchanging news while we waited for Haakon. Uncle Nappy had died that spring, a new daughter had been born to Haakon and Winnie, Orbin was planning to marry soon and would live in the small blue house, and Granny had a new post at the railing of the verandah. No one was around but the children, which puzzled me since there was a tan Land Rover parked just below the house. Finally curiosity overcame me, and I asked whose it was.

"That Haakie's," Winnie laughed proudly, "and he done already forget how to walk."

I marveled quietly at the dramatic changes that *Skywave* had wrought in the fortunes of this family. After I left the islands for the mainland, the Mitchells and I stayed in touch — as much as the erratic postal service and my writing habits permitted. At first our correspondance dealt with the progress and problems of children and grandchildren, but then Haakon wrote that he was planning to build a schooner.

The new schooner was completed as I was completing this book, and once again I returned to Bequia — this time for the launching of *Wave Dancer* (fig. XXVI-3). Granny was still at her post on the verandah, two of the older boys were now married and had established households on the hillside, making four houses now in the compound. Roderick, Osrick and Carlos — who had been building gumboats when *Skywave* was built — were now putting the finishing touches on an 80 ft. schooner, while Orbin was building a vessel of his own (fig. XXVI-4), and Osrick was working on the principles of celestial navigation.

One schooner does not make a fleet, and it is early yet to say that a new era is opening for working sail in the Lesser Antilles. But it still pleases me to think that while the skills of boatbuilding are practiced and transmitted, the last schooner may be only the one most recently launched (fig. XXVI-5).

fig. XXVI-4. Builder Orbin Olliverre works on his sloop, Friendship Bay, Bequia. February, 1981. Photo by Earlin Olliverre.

*fig. XXVI-5. The last schooner, Wave Dancer,
anchored just ahead of Skywave,
Friendship Bay, Bequia. March, 1981.*

BIBLIOGRAPHY

Carstens, Johan Lorentz. *Account of Life among the Negro Slaves of the Danish West Indies.* Unpublished translation of unpublished manuscript, 1742.

Chapelle, Howard I. *The Search for Speed under Sail.* New York: W. W. Norton & Co., 1967.

Davy, John. *The West Indies, Before and Since Emancipation.* London: W. & F. G. Cash, 1854.

Doran, Edwin M., Jr. "The Tortola Boat: Characteristics, Origin, Demise." Suppl. to *The Mariner's Mirror*, Vol. 56, No. 1, 1970.

Edwards, Clinton R. "Aboriginal Sail in the New World." *Southwest Journal of Anthropology* 21: 351–358, 1965.

Fenger, Frederic A. *Alone in the Caribbean.* Belmont, Mass: Wellington Books, 1958.

Hall, J. Clark. *The Mercantile Navy List and Maritime Directory.* London: Spootiswoode & Co., 1853, 1857, 1863, 1898.

Hernandez de Oviedo y Valdés, Gonzalo. *Dela natural hystoria delas indias.* Toledo: Remo de Petras, 1526.

Highfield, Arnold R. *The French Dialect of St. Thomas, U. S. Virgin Islands.* Ann Arbor: Karoma Publishers, 1979.

Labat, Père Jean-Baptiste. *Nouveau Voyage aux Isles de l'Amérique.* La Haye, 1724.

Little, Elbert L. & Frank H. Wadsworth. *Common Trees of Puerto Rico and the Virgin Islands.* Washington, D. C.: U. S. Department of Agriculture Handbook No. 249, 1964.

Mattioni, Mario. *Qui Etait le Caraïbe?* Fort-de-France: Bulletin de la Société d'Histoire de la Martinique, 1972.

Mackaness, George. *The Life of Vice-Admiral William Bligh.* Sydney: Angus and Robertson, 1951.

McKusick, Marshall. *Aboriginal Canoes in the West Indies.* Yale University Publications in Anthropology 63, 1960.

Oviedo, see Hernandez de Oviedo.

Raspail, Jean. *Secouons le cocotier.* Paris: R. Laffont, 1966.

Rigg, J. Linton. *The Alluring Antilles.* Princeton, N. J.: Van Nostrand, 1963.

Stoddard, Charles Augustus. *Cruising among the Caribees.* New York: Chas. Scribner's Sons, 1895.

Stoneman, John. "The Voyage of M. Henry Challons . . .," in *Hakluytus Posthumus or Purchas His Pilgrimes* 19. Glasgow: J. MacLehose and sons, 1906.

Treves, Sir Frederick. *The Cradle of the Deep.* New York: E. P. Dutton, 1908.

Westlake, Donald E. *Under an English Heaven.* New York: Simon and Schuster, 1972.

INDEX OF ILLUSTRATIONS

Boatbuilders, owners, captains 68, 69, 79, 99, 103, 117, 189, 197, 204, 218, 221, 242, 259

Boatbuilding and design—tools & techniques
  boatmeasuring
    basic 14
    body plan 10
    buttock lines 10
    key to structural members 13
    semi-automated 191
    waterlines 10
  half-model 11, 57
  keel rabbet 184
  key splice 260
  lap-straking 245
  rabbetting guide 94
  setting up 13
  shaping a timber 127
  "shell" of pirogue 244
  ship-lap joint 91
  stepping a mast 113

Landscape views, misc.
  hillside above Tyrrell Bay, Carriacou 30
  Saba 144-6

Launchings 42-4, 109-112

Models and toys
  gumboats 99
  half-models 11, 57
  models 190, 191

Ports and harbors
  Bridgetown, Barbados: Carenage 250, 251
  Charlestown, Nevis 155
  Gustavia, St. Barts, after hurricane 169
  Hillsborough, Carriacou 28
  Kingstown, St. Vincent 2, 223
  Oranjestad, St. Eustatius 150
  Port Elizabeth, Bequia ii-iii, 55
  Port-of-Spain, Trinidad 235, 236, 239
  Road Bay, Anguilla 7
  St. Georges, Grenada 18
  Windward, Carriacou 36

Races & regattas
  Bequia, Easter Monday regatta 95; Whitsun regatta 50, 53
  Carriacou Workboat Regatta 30, 31, 34, 35, 45, 214, 284
  Martinique, municipal regattas 201, 206, 209
  St. Martin, Bastille Day regatta 74, 140, 162

Sloop and schooner building activity, graph 274

Sloops & schooners, see Vessels

Vessels
  Schooners
    at anchor or afloat 68, 167, 168, 287
    awash 60
    careened or ashore 56, 69, 198, 253, 271 285; New England schooner 271
    launching 57, 271
    life aboard 77, 229, 230, 231, 232, 240
    lines 23, 58, 67, 70, 82, 192, 258 (Speightstown schooner model)
    under construction or repair 8, 21, 65, 66, 67
    under sail 39, 55, 75, 78, 228, 270, 278; Speightstown schooners 256, 257; New England schooners 270, 272
  Sloops
    at anchor or afloat 38, 44, 166, 287

    from aboard 284
    launching 42, 43, 110-113
    lines 33 (from model), 37, 49, 106
    under construction or repair 46, 85, 90, 91, 92, 103, 286
    under sail 31, 35, 45, 115, 199, 283, 284
  Sailing lighters
    at anchor 155, 157
    ashore 157
    lines 159
    under sail 156
  Other vessels
    at anchor 152
    under construction or repair 13, 151, 224, 225, 226

West Indian boats
  canoe and dugout types
    canoes (Grenada)
      beached 24
      under construction 25
    canots (St. Lucia)
      beached 214, 218
      lines 215
    gommiers and yoles (Martinique)
      compared 202
      lines 203, 205
      under construction 196, 204
      under power 202
      under sail 201, 203, 209
    pirogues (Trinidad)
      lines 247
      under construction 242-6
      under power 240
  framed boats
    Antigua fishing sloop (see also Tortola sloops)
      under construction 181, 182, 184
      lines 183
    beach boats
      at anchor or afloat 27, 71
      beached 71, 72, 161, 162, 164, 177, 224
      lines 27, 73, 138, 163, 219
      under construction 26, 177
      under sail 50, 74, 140, 161, 162, 216, 217
    canot saintois
      afloat 172
      lines 171, 173, 188
      under sail 174, 175
    fishing boats, see beach boats
    flying fish boats
      beached 254-6
      under sail 256
    seine boats, see two-bow boats
    Tortola sloops
      beached 132
      lines 130, 131
      under sail 133
    two-bow boats
      beached 48, 53
      from aboard 117, 123
      lines 52, 54
      under sail 50, 95, 119
    whaleboats, see two-bow boats

Whaling 117, 119, 123, 124

SUBJECT INDEX

Boatbuilders, owners, captains
  Bocage, François 185-6
  Cassin, Georges 185
  Chance, Bertil 144
  Compton family 275; *see also* Mitchell family
    Compton, Benjamin 275
    Compton, Benjamin George (English boat-
      builder) 275
    Compton, Malings 218, 219, 275
  Connor, Arthur 77, 81
  Connor, Egbert 63, 70
  Connor, Mack 69
  Evans, Joseph 217
  Gumbs, Emile 61, 78, 266
  Hughes, John Thomas 78
  Justlyn, George 23
  Lake, Albert 68
  MacLaren, Zepharin 30–31, 34
  Mascoll, Osbert 259–60
  Mitchell family 275; *see also* Compton family
    Mitchell, Haakon 84-113 *passim*
    Mitchell, James Fitzallen ("Uncle Harry")
      275
    Mitchell, Reginald 57
    Mitchell, Romulus St. Clair ("Jack") 195,
      197, 275
    Mitchell, William A. ("Old Mitch") 275
  Oliverre, Athneal 52, 97, 114–125 *passim*
  Oliverre, Napoleon III ("Uncle Nappy") 88 *ff*
  Oliverre, Orbin 286
  Palmier, Bernardin 171
  Roberts, Hobin 36
  Rock, John 273-4
  Richardson, MacDuff 9
  Samson, Theodore 189
  Simon, Vincent 179–80
  Smith, Leo/Leopold 125-6
  Steill, Henry 21
  Taitt, L. 242
Boatbuilding and design terminology (West In-
    dian dialect in " ", *patois* in italics)
  Ballast keel 257
  bends 83
  "bolt" 87
  bordage 248
  caulking 107
  center frames 84
  clinker-built 246
  counter stern 38, 92, 99, 274
  covering boards 98
  "cutting down" 42, 111, 144
  cypre (Cordia alliodora) 244
  deadwood 259
  gabarits 185
  garboard 102
  "garboard streak" 93
  "gum tree" *(Bursera simaruba)* 98
  "gumboats" 98
  horn timbers 93
  keel rabbet 93-4
  key splice 260
  knees 87
  lap-straked 246
  "ledges" 38, 92, 99

lisses 185
lofting 12
Maho pine *(Thespesia populnea)* 100
"moon shear" 180
"navel piece" 36, 92-3
outer sternpost 92
"pointer" 93
pricking 104
"purpleheart" *(Peltogyne pubescens)* 98
"red cedar" *(Guarea trichilioides)* 244
"ribbands" 13, 84
"scarlin" 86
"screw bolt" 87
"setting up" 13, 21, 84
"shell" of a pirogue 244
ship-lap joint 91
"silverballi" *(Cordia alliodora)*
"spiling" 103-5
"stretching" 78
"tailboat" 260
taking off lines 15
transom stern 36
"tuck" 36, 70
tumblehome 105, 269
"white cedar" *(Tabebuia pallida)* 85
Chantier de Coquelotte 187 *ff*
Dialect and patois terms, general *(see also* Boat-
    building & design terminology, Sailing
    terms)
  bobol 167-8
  boucan 192
  cocoa tea 233
  colouring 105
  cou-cou 96
  droguing 227
  farine 116
  fungee 96
  Irish hurricane 5
  jack iron 41
  mutton pot 105
  Norwegian steam 41
  spree 96-8
  strong rum 96
  trafficker 228, 230
Influences on design and construction of West
    Indian watercraft
  "Bermudan" sailing vessels 262, 276
  Bligh, Capt. William 263
  Caribs 192 *ff*, 208, 226, 276
  Emancipation 275, 276
  FAO fisheries project 179-80
  Napoleonic Wars 167
  OPEC 282
  patois 248, 276
  Prohibition
  Rigg, J. Linton 29 *ff*
  Scottish shipwrights 273
  Snagg, Sir William 219, 275
  Wars, European and world 151, 167, 272
Interisland commerce
  hindrances 281
  suggested improvements 281-2
Knights of Malta 168
Launching 39, 40, 109-113

Lloyd's of London 282
Marine insurance 281-2
Models, toys, replicas
  "Columbus boats" 260
  gumboats 286
  half-models 16, 55
  model *L'Etoile des Marins* 189
Nelson, Horatio 153
Nisbet, Mrs. Frances 153
Photography 16
Proportions of West Indian vessels 264
Races and regattas
  Anguilla: Whitsun and New Year's regattas 69
  Bequia: Easter Monday and Whitsun regattas
    95-6
  Carriacou Workboat Regatta, August Bank
    Holiday 30–31, 283-4
  Martinique: municipal regattas 206
  Out Island Regatta (Bahamas) 31
  pirogue racing 247-8
  St. Martin: Bastille Day regatta 137-9
Schooner trade
  balance sheet 279
  economics 279-80
Sailing performance data
  Alma Gloria 138
  Big Stuff 51
  Dart 112
  Mermaid of Carriacou 34
  Vini Oué Ça 207
  Warspite 76
Sailing terms (W. I. dialect in " ", French &
    patois in italics)
  contrapa 248
  cranky 70
  grande voile 203
  halez 248
  jambez 248
  mizaine 201
  "snotter" 116
  speed coefficient 34
  "sprite" 116
  tenez 248
Vessels
  defined 15
  sailing lighters 153 *ff*; *Victoria* 154-7
  schooners
    A L Sea Author M 39
    Arthur V. S. Woodruff (New Bedford) 150
    Challenor (Speightstown schooner) 257, 259

Ellen A. Swift (Provincetown) 265
Emeralda 89
Frances W. Smith (Lunenburg, N. S.) 146,
    249–50, 269
Friendship Rose 220
Gloria Colita 57 *ff*
Lady Angela 84
Lady Mack 67, 68
New London 63, 65
Rosarene 277-40, 279-80
Ruby 165
Ruth 165
Speightstown schooners 256-9
Warspite 72 *ff*, 81
Wave Dancer 285
sloops (for Antigua and Tortola sloops, *see*
    West Indian boats)
  Mermaid of Carriacou 32 *ff*, 284
  Sir Wm. Snagg 275
  Skywave 104–111, 283-4
  Vaeta 284
  Yankee Girl R 41 *ff*
  Yolanda 127
West Indian boats
  dugout and canoe types 199, 226, 244, 247-8,
    265, 276
  canoes (Grenada) 22, 265
  canots (St. Lucia) 212-3, 223, 225, 265
  gommiers 191, 192 *ff*, 200–212 *passim*, 247,
    265
  pirogues 241-8 *passim*, 265
  yoles 199, 200–212 *passim*, 265
framed boats
  Antigua fishing sloops 180 *ff*; *see also* Tortola
    sloops
  beach boats 26, 46, 70, 135-7, 159, 214-7
  canot saintois 184 *ff*, 267
  fishing boats, *see* beach boats
  flying fish boats 255-7
  seine boats 52-3; *see also* two-bow boats
  Tortola sloops 1-4, 126-35 *passim*, 178, 263,
    265; *see also* Antigua fishing sloops
  two-bow boats 22, 51-53, 225, 265-6
  whaleboats 51, 114-125 *passim*; *see also*
    two-bow boats
Whaling 114–125, 265-6; *see also* whaleboats
  Dunham, Capt. George and Capt. John A.,
    New Bedford whaling captains 265-6
  Kydd, Lozina 228, 230
  Wallace, "Old Bill" (Scottish whaler) 266